The citations from reviews will perhaps stimulate
the reader to form his own opinion. We do not wish
to form it for him.

T. S. Eliot, 'Ezra Pound: his Metric and Poetry'
(1917); *To Criticize the Critic* (1965) 163.

Topics in Criticism

An ordered set of positions in literary theory

Arranged by Christopher Butler
and Alastair Fowler

Longman

LONGMAN GROUP LIMITED
London
Associated companies, branches and
representatives throughout the world

This collection © Christopher Butler and
Alastair Fowler 1971

First published 1971

ISBN 0 582 48420 0 Cased
     0 582 48421 9 Paper

Printed in Great Britain by
Northumberland Press Limited,
Gateshead

Contents

Acknowledgements

We are grateful to the following for permission to reproduce copyright material:
Edward Arnold (Publishers) Ltd., for extracts from *The Waning of the Middle Ages* by J. Huizinga translated by F. Hopman, *An Introduction to English Studies* by R. L. Brett, *Shakespeare Survey* iX (1956) by Fredson Bowers; The Athlone Press for extracts from *The Language Poets Use* by W. Nowottny; F. W. Bateson for an extract from *Essays in Criticism* ii by W. W. Robson; G. Bell & Sons Ltd., for an extract from *English Prose Style* by Sir Herbert Read; Basil Blackwell and Mott Ltd., for extracts from 'Intention' by T. M. Gang from *Essays in Criticism* vii, 1957, extracts by John Wain from *Essays in Criticism* ii, 1952, an extract by Terence Hawkes from *Essays in Criticism* xii, 1962, an extract from *Style in the French Novel* by Stephen Ullmann, extracts from 'Does Traditional Aesthetics Rest on a Mistake' by W. E. Kennick from *Collected Papers in Aesthetics* edited by C. Barrett, an extract by W. W. Greg in *The Works of Thomas Nashe* ed. R. B. McKerrow, rev. F. P. Wilson, v. 1958 supplement 33, the author for extracts from *Philosophy of Literary Form, Counterstatement* and *Aristotle Poetics and English Literature* edited by Elder Olson, by Kenneth Burke; Calder & Boyars Ltd., for an extract from 'The Playwright's Role' from *Notes and Counter-Notes* by Eugene Ionesco; University of California Press for extracts from *Eras and Modes in English Poetry* by Josephine Miles, 1964, an extract by Franklin R. Rogers—Introduction to *Mark Twain's Satires and Burlesques*, p.l., 1967, extracts from *Elements of Critical Theory* by Wayne Shumaker, 1952; Cambridge University Press for extracts from *Textual and Literary Criticism* by F. Bowers, *Plagiarism* by W. A. Edwards, *Aspects of the Novel* by E. M. Forster, *Spenser's Images of Life* by C. S. Lewis, *Shakespeare's Imagery and What it Tells Us* by C. F. E. Spurgeon, *The Decline and Fall of the Romantic Ideal* by F. L. Lucas, *Hamlet* and *The Manuscript of Shakespeare's 'Hamlet'* edited by J. Dover Wilson, *Aristotle* translated by L. J. Potts; Jonathan Cape Ltd., and Harcourt Brace and World for an extract from *Messages* by Ramon Fernandez translated by M. Belgion; Jonathan Cape Ltd., for an extract

from *Critique of Poetry* by Michael Roberts; Chatto and Windus Ltd., for extracts from *Revaluation* and *The Common Pursuit* by F. R. Leavis, *The Structure of Complex Words* and *Some Versions of Pastoral* by William Empson, *Culture and Society* by Raymond Williams, *Art* by Clive Bell reprinted by permission of Quentin Bell, *The Rise of the Novel* by Ian Watt, *Character and the Novel* by W. J. Harvey reprinted by permission of Mrs. M. A. Harvey, *Point Counter Point* and *Chrome Yellow* by Aldous Huxley reprinted by permission of Mrs. Laura Huxley, *Seven Types of Ambiguity* by William Empson; University of Chicago Press for extracts from *Samuel Johnson's Literary Criticism* by Jean H. Hagstrum, 'An Outline of Poetic Theory' by Elder Olson from *Criticis and Criticism* edited by R. S. Crane, *The Structure of Literature* by Paul Goodman, *Criticis and Criticism* by R. S. Crane, *Elizabethan and Metaphysical Imagery* by Rosemond Tuve, *The Rhetoric of Fiction* by Wayne C. Booth; Clarendon Press for extracts from *Prolegomena for the Oxford Shakespeare* by R. B. McKerrow, *The Business of Criticism* by Helen Gardner, *The Editorial Problems in Shakespeare* by Sir W. W. Greg, *W. W. Greg: Collected Papers* edited by J. C. Maxwell, *The Concept of Criticism* by F. E. Sparshott, *The Allegory of Love* by C. S. Lewis, *The Ballad of Tradition* by G. H. Gerould *Augustan Satire* by I. R. J. Jack; Columbia University Press for an extract by N. H. Pearson from *Literary Forms and Types* edited by R. Kirk, English Institute Essays (1940); author's agents for an extract from *Conversation Between Ivy Compton-Burnett and M. Jourdain* and *Conversation* by Ivy Compton-Burnett; Cornell University Press for extracts from *Allegory: The Theory of a Symbolic Mode* by Angus Fletcher © 1964 by Cornell University, *Models and Metaphors: Studies in Language and Philosophy* by Max Black © 1962 by Cornell University; Thomas Y. Crowell Co., for an extract from *Aesthetic Analysis* by D. W. Prall. Copyright renewed © 1964 by Elizabeth Prall Anderson with permission of Thomas Y. Crowell Co. Inc.; Dickenson Publishing Co. Inc., and The American Society for Aesthetics for extracts from 'The Domain of Criticism' by W. K. Wimsatt and 'The Interpretation of Poetry' by Isabel C. Hungerland from *Aesthetic Inquiry* edited by Monroe C. Beardsley; Dennis Dobson and Harcourt Brace and World for extracts from *The Well Wrought Urn* by Cleanth Brooks; Gerald Duckworth & Co. Ltd., for extracts from *An Essay in Criticism, Image and Experience* and *The Dream and the Task* by Graham Hough; Duke University Press for an extract from American Literature (1949) by F. O. Matthiesen; Encyclopaedia Britannica International Ltd., for an extract from 'Textual Criticism' by John Percival Postgate from *Encyclopaedia Britannica* (1911); English Association for an extract from *Hamlet the Man* by Elmer Stoll; Eyre & Spottiswoode Ltd., Farrar, Straus & Giroux Inc., and author's agents for an extract from *Against Interpretation* by Susan Sontag; Faber and Faber Ltd., and University of Chicago Press for an extract from A *Reading of George Herbert* by Rosamond Tuve; Faber and Faber Ltd., and Alfred A. Knopf for extracts from 'Adagia' from *Opus Posthumous* and *The Necessary Angel* by Wallace Stevens; Faber and Faber Ltd., for extracts from *Poetic Diction* by Owen Barfield and *Here Comes Everybody* by Anthony Burgess; Faber and Faber Ltd., and New Directions Publishing Corp. for extracts from 'Vers Libre and Arnold Dolmetsch' and 'A Retrospect' by Ezra Pound from *Literary Essays of Ezra Pound* edited by T. S. Eliot; Faber and Faber Ltd., for extracts from 'Vorticism' by Ezra Pound from *The Fortnightly Review* xcvi (1914), 'Johnson as Critic and Poet', 'Milton', British Academy Lecture, 'The Music of Poetry', from *On Poetry and Poets* by T. S. Eliot, extracts from 'Philip Massinger', 'The Function of Criticism', 'The Metaphysical Poets', 'Tradition and the Individual Talent' from *Selected Essays* by T. S. Eliot, an extract from *The Use of Poetry and the Use of Criticism* by T. S. Eliot, an extract from 'Note' from the *The Waste Land* and title only from *The Waste Land* by T. S. Eliot, extracts from *Collected Essays in Literary Criticism, Phases of English Poetry* and *Wordsworth* by Sir Herbert Read; the author for an extract from *Reflections on the Word 'Image'* by P. N. Furbank; Victor Gollancz Ltd., for an extract from *Hamlet and Oedipus* by Ernest Jones; author and author's agents for an extract from *The Common Asphodel* by Robert Graves; Dr. G. M. Grieve for the Poem 'perfect' and a passage from a letter to the Times Literary Supplement 28th January, 1965 by Hugh MacDiarmid; Hamish Hamilton Ltd. and Editions Gallimard for an extract from *Nausea* by Jean-Paul Sartre translated by R. Baldick; Harcourt Brace Jovanovich Inc., for an extract from *Theory of Literature* by Rene Wellek and Austin Warren, and for an extract from *Aesthetics* by Monroe C. Beardsley; Harper & Row, Publishers and author's agents for an extract from *Art and Its Objects* by Richard Wollheim; Harvard University Press for an extract from *Philosophy in a New Key* by Susanne K. Langer; The Hogarth Press Ltd., and Mrs. Elna Lucas for an extract from *Tragedy* by F. L. Lucas; Hogarth Press Ltd., for extracts from 'Modern Fiction', and 'The Novels of E. M. Forster' from *Collected Essays* and an extract from *Orlando* by Virginia Woolf; Holt, Rinehart and Winston Inc., for an extract from 'Five Types of Lycidas' by M. H. Abrams, from *Milton's 'Lycidas': The Tradition and the Poem*, edited by C. A. Patrides; Houghton Mifflin Co., for an extract from *The Road to Xanadu* by J. L. Lowes; author's agents for an extract from *The Struggle of the Modern* by Stephen Spender; Macmillan & Co. Ltd., Mr. M. B. Yeats and author's agents for an extract from Plays and Controversies by W. B. Yeats; Macmillan & Co. Ltd. for an extract from *Oxford Lectures on Poetry* by A. C. Bradley, and *Illusion and Reality* by Christopher Caudwell; Manchester University Press for an extract from *Dryden's 'Aeneid' and its 17th Century Predecessors* by L. Proudfoot;

Massachusetts Institute of Technology for extracts by Sol Saporta, Edward Stankievica, Rulon Wells and John Hollander from *Style in Language* edited by T. A. Sebeok, an extract from 'On Free Rhythms in Modern Poetry' by Benjamin Hrushovski from *Style in Language* edited by T. A. Sebeok and an extract from *Aspects of the Theory of Syntax* by Noam Chomsky; Methuen & Co. Ltd., for extracts from *The Harvest of Tragedy* by T. R. Henn, *The Fire and the Fountain* by John Press; Methuen & Co. Ltd., and Oxford University Press, New York and the author for an extract from *The Kipling that Nobody Read* by E. Wilson, The University of Michigan Press for an extract from *Language, Thought and Culture* edited by Paul Henle, The Proprietors for The Modern Language Review and Professor Pascal for an extract by Roy Pascal from *Modern Language Review* lvii (1962); author's agents and Mr. Peter Newbolt for an extract from 'Le Byron de Nos Jours' from *Poems Old and New* by Henry Newbolt; Thomas Nelson & Sons Ltd., for an extract from *Saturn and Melancholy* by Raymond Klibansky et al; The Proprietors of the *New Statesman* for an extract by Charles Tomlinson from the *New Statesman* 28.4.61., and an extract by T. S. Eliot from the *New Statesman*; The New York Review of Books for an extract from *The Fruits of the M.L.A.* by Edmund Wilson; W. W. Norton & Co. Ltd., for an extract from *The Nature of Poetry* by D. A. Staufer; University of Notre Dame Press for an extract from *The Human Metaphor* by Elizabeth Sewell; Oxford University Press for extracts from a letter dated 14th August, 1879 by Gerard Manley Hopkins from *Letters of Gerard Manley Hopkins to Robert Bridges* ed. C. C. Abbot, *The Personal Heresy* by E. M. W. Tillyard and C. S. Lewis, 'On Stories' from *Essays Presented to Charles Williams* by C. S. Lewis, *Anna Karenina* and *What Is Art?* by Leo Tolstoy translated by A. Maude, *The Dickens World* by H. House, *The Problem of Style* by J. M. Murry, *The Chequer'd Shade* by John Press, *Archetypal Patterns in Poetry* by Maud Bodkin; Oxford University Press Inc., New York, for extracts from *The Philosophy of Rhetoric* by I. A. Richards, copyright 1936 by Oxford University Press Inc., renewed 1964 by I. A. Richards, *The Dynamics of Literary Response* by Norman N. Holland copyright © 1968 by Norman N. Holland, *Gates of Horn* by Harry Levin; *The Study of Literature* by George Watson; Prentice-Hall Inc., for an extract from *Philosophy of Language* by William P. Alston © 1964; Princeton University Press for extracts from *Mimesis* by Erich Auerbach, *A Preface to Chaucer: Studies in Medieval Perspectives* by D. W. Robertson copyright © 1962 by Princeton University Press, *The Intent of the Critic* by Donald A. Stauffer, copyright 1941 by Princeton University Press, extracts by Norman Friedman and Paul Fussell from *Encyclopedia of Poetry and Poetics* ed. Alex Preminger copyright © 1965 by Princeton University Press, *The Idea of a Theater: A Study of Ten Plays*, *The Art of Drama in Changing Perspective* by

Francis Fergusson copyright 1949 by Princeton University Press, 'Allegory' by Northrop Frye from *Encyclopedia of Poetry and Poetics* ed. Alex Preminger, *Anatomy of Criticism* by Northrop Frye; the author for extracts from *The Twentieth Century* by W. W. Robson, 1955; Routledge & Kegan Paul Ltd., for extracts from *Essays on Style and Language* ed. Roger Fowler, *Speculations* by T. E. Hulme, *Puzzles and Epiphanies* and *Romantic Image* by Frank Kermode, *Aesthetics and Criticism* and *The Theory of Beauty* by Harold Osborne, *The Art of Drama* by Ronald Peacock, *Practical Criticism* and *Principles of Literary Criticism* by I. A. Richards; Routledge & Kegan Paul Ltd., and Harcourt Brace Jovanovich Inc., for extracts from *Speculative Instruments* by I. A. Richards; Routledge & Kegan Paul Ltd., and W. W. Norton & Co. Inc., for extracts from *Poetries and Sciences* (1970) by I. A. Richards; Routledge & Kegan Paul Ltd., and Charles Scribner's Sons for an extract from *Feeling and Form* by Susanne K. Langer; Routledge & Kegan Paul Ltd., and the Swallow Press Inc., for an extract from *In Defense of Reason* and *The Functions of Criticism : Problems and Exercises* by Yvor Winters; Routledge & Kegan Paul Ltd., and University of Toronto Press for an extract from *The Structure of Aesthetics* by F. E. Sparshott; Routledge & Kegan Paul Ltd., and McGraw-Hill Inc., for an extract from *Understanding Media* by Marshall McLuhan; Rowohlt Verlag for an extract from *The Necessity of Art* by Ernst Fischer; Martin Secker & Warburg Ltd., and The Viking Press Inc., for an extract from *Beyond Culture* and *The Liberal Imagination* by Lionel Trilling; Martin Secker & Warburg Ltd., and Alfred A. Knopf Inc., for an extract from 'Freud and the Future' from *Essays of Three Decades* by Thomas Mann translated by H. T. Lower-Porter, and Doctor Faustus by Thomas Mann; Martin Secker & Warburg Ltd., for an extract from Principles of English Prosody by Lascelles Abercrombie; the author for an extract from 'On the Reasons that can be given for the interpretation of a Poem' by Charles L. Stevenson from *Philosophy Looks at the Arts* edited by J. Margolis; Sidgwick & Jackson Ltd., for an extract from *Letters to a Young Poet* by Rainer Maria Rilke translated by R. Snell; The Proprietors of *The Times Newspapers Ltd.*, for an extract from *The Critical Moment* reproduced from *The Times Literary Supplement*; The University of Toronto Press for an extract from *The Languages of Criticism and the Structure of Poetry* by R. S. Crane; C. A. Watts & Co. Ltd., for an extract from *Modern English and American Poetry* by M. Schlauch; Van Nostrand Reinhold Co., for an extract from *Essays* II x by Montaigne translated by D. M. Frame, 'L'Arte poetica' iv by Minturno, 'Discorsi del poema Eroico' iii by Tasso, 'The Poetics of Aristotle' by Lodovico Castelvetro, Letter to Can Grande vii-viii by Dante, 'Life of Dante xxii' by Boccaccio from *Literary Criticism: Plato to Dryden* edited by A. H. Gilbert; George Weidenfeld & Nicolson Ltd., for an extract from *Other Victorians* by Stephen Marcus; Yale University

Preface

We hope that this book may be useful in two main ways. First, the reader will find in it *loci critici* of modern interest, some familiar, others out of the way, grouped under topics in the theory of literature. Taken with their contexts, these offer a guide to the state of the subject, and may also provide a convenient store of specific instances on which to focus discussion.

The second possible way of using the book is more experimental. We are interested to know how far a reader will participate in developing a line of thought when presented simply with a structure of theoretical positions and examples from literature. In other words, we challenge him to insert his own logical connectives between the items. The sequences are designed to invite this; but they are not puzzles with single correct solutions: we doubt whether any two participants, including ourselves, would synthesize quite the same theses from them.

At the same time when he treats the extracts anachronistically as contributions to a continuing series of debates, we hope that the reader will also get a sense of the ways in which our thinking about literature has changed over the centuries. For, though he will notice many fluctuations in levels of abstraction, terminology, extra-literary concerns and even degrees of descriptive adequacy, he may yet discern, as we have, a genuine development within literary criticism as a self-critical discipline.

Although we have tried to give a conspectus of critical opinion, ancient and modern, we do not mean every extract to represent its source's main contention, nor our book to pretend to exhaust all points of view, even on the topics selected. It is indeed with a hope of encouraging exploration far beyond these confines that we have supplied finding references wherever appropriate. We generally give the title and date of first appearance of each extract, followed by a reference, if necessary, to an accessible modern edition. In a number of instances we have tacitly modernized orthography, retranslated, or omitted parts of a sentence at the beginning or end of an item.

A grateful debt is owed to pupils who contributed passages or ideas and to colleagues, particularly T. J. Reed, who helped to track down elusive sources.

I.C.B.

A.D.S.F.

What is Literature?

1

BOSWELL 'Then, Sir, what is poetry?'
JOHNSON 'Why, Sir, it is much easier
to say what it is not. We all *know*
what light is; but it is not easy to
tell what it is.'

James Boswell, *Life of Samuel Johnson*, 12
April 1776; ed. G. B. Hill and L. F. Powell iii
(Oxford 1934) 38.

2

Definition is indeed, not the province of
man : everything is set above or below
our faculties. The works and operations
of nature are too great in their extent,
or too much diffused in their relations,
and the performances of art too
inconsistent and uncertain, to be reduced
to any determinate idea.... Definitions
have been no less difficult or uncertain
in criticisms than in law. Imagination ...
has always endeavoured to baffle the
logician, to perplex the confines of
distinction, and burst the inclosures of
regularity.

Samuel Johnson, *Rambler* No. 125 (28 May
1751); *Works*, Yale edn. iv (New Haven and
London 1969) 300.

3

Literature begins with the telling of a tale.
The tale represents certain events by the
means of auditory and visual signs. The
events thus represented are mental events
in the narrator's mind. His motive is
the urge to communicate these events
to others, to make them relive his
thoughts and emotions; the urge to *share*.
The audience may be physically present,
or an imagined one; the narrator may
address himself to a single person or
to his god alone, but his basic need
remains the same : he must share his
experiences, make others participate in
them, and thus overcome the isolation
of the self.

To achieve this aim, the narrator must
provide patterns of stimuli as substitutes
for the original stimuli which caused
the experience to occur. This obviously
is not an easy task, for he is asking his
audience to react to things which are
not there, such as the smell of grass on
a summer morning. Since the dawn of
civilisation, bards and story-tellers
have produced bags of tricks to provide
such *ersatz* stimuli. The sum of these
tricks is called the art of literature.

Arthur Koestler, *The Act of Creation* (1964)
301.

4

So I should propose an initial working
distinction between 'strategies' and
'situations', whereby we think of
poetry (I here use the term to include any
work of critical or imaginative cast)
as the adopting of various strategies

for the encompassing of situations.
These strategies size up the situations,
name their structure and outstanding
ingredients, and name them in a way
that contains an attitude towards them.

This point of view does not, by any
means, vow us to personal or historical
subjectivism. The situations are real;
the strategies for handling them have
public content; and in so far as
situations overlap from individual to
individual, or from historical period
to another, the strategies possess
universal relevance.

Kenneth Burke, The Philosophy of Literary
Form (Baton Rouge, La. 1941) 1.

5

I write poems to preserve things I have
seen/thought/felt (if I may so indicate
a composite and complex experience)
both for myself and for others, though I
feel that my prime responsibility is to
the experience itself, which I am trying
to keep from oblivion for its own
sake. Why I should do this I have no
idea, but I think that the impulse to
preserve lies at the bottom of all art.

Philip Larken, in Poets of the 1950's ed. D. J.
Enright (Tokyo 1955) 77.

6

A poem is the very image of life
expressed in its eternal truth. There is
this difference between a story and a
poem, that a story is a catalogue of
detached facts, which have no other
connection than time, place, circumstance,
cause and effect; the other is the
creation of actions according to the
unchangeable forms of human nature,
as existing in the mind of the Creator,
which is itself the image of all other
minds. ... A story of particular facts
is as a mirror which obscures and distorts
that which should be beautiful; poetry
is a mirror which makes beautiful
that which is distorted.

P. B. Shelley, A Defence of Poetry (1821);
Complete Works ed. R. Ingpen and W. E. Peck
vii (1930) 115.

7

All good poetry is the spontaneous
overflow of powerful feelings; but though
this be true, poems to which any value
can be attached, were never produced on
any variety of subjects but by a man
who being possessed of more than usual
organic sensibility had also thought
long and deeply. For our continued
influxes of feeling are modified and
directed by our thoughts, which are
indeed the representatives of all our past
feelings; and as by contemplating the
relation of these general representatives
to each other, we discover what is
really important to men, so by the
repetition and continuance of this act
feelings connected with important
subjects will be nourished, till at length,
if we be originally possessed of much
organic sensibility, such habits of mind
will be produced that by obeying
blindly and mechanically the impulses
of those habits we shall describe objects
and utter sentiments of such a nature
and in such connection with each other,
that the understanding of the being to
whom we address ourselves, if he be in

a healthful state of association, must necessarily be in some degree enlightened, and his affections ameliorated.

William Wordsworth, Preface to *Lyrical Ballads* (1800); ed. R. L. Brett and A. R. Jones (1963) 240f.

memory from one generation to another, and in many such communities certain individuals are charged with its preservation and its transmission to other similarly charged persons as their successors.

R. H. Robins, *An Introduction to General Linguistics* (1964) 369.

8

The best general notion which I can give of poetry is, that it is the natural impression of any object or event, by its vividness exciting an involuntary movement of imagination and passion, and producing, by sympathy, a certain modulation of the voice, or sounds, expressing it.

William Hazlitt, 'On Poetry in General' (1818); *Complete Works* ed. P. P. Howe v (1930) 1.

10

Poetry can be recognized by this property, that it tends to get itself reproduced in its own form; it stimulates us to reconstruct it identically. That is an admirably and uniquely characteristic property.

Paul Valéry, 'Poetry and Abstract Thought' (1939); *Oeuvres complètes* ed. J. Hytier i (Paris 1957) 1314.

9

Literature comprises a number of particular uses and styles, and forms an important and valuable part of the linguistic material in the study of a particular language and in the study of mankind's use of the faculty of language. Moreover, once the bias towards written language is overcome, it may be seen that literature, considered as utterances that are regarded for one reason or another as worthy in their own right of preservation and as aesthetically valuable, is a form of language use present, so far as is known, in all cultures, literate and preliterate. *Oral literature* is as much a distinct component of cultures as *written literature*; and in the absence of writing, it may be preserved by

11

In literature, questions of fact or truth are subordinated to the primary literary aim of producing a structure of words for its own sake, and the sign values of the symbols are subordinated to their importance as a structure of inter-connected motives. Wherever we have autonomous verbal structure of this kind, we have literature.

Northrop Frye, *Anatomy of Criticism* (Princeton, N.J. 1957) 74.

12

The Yale Formalist Fallacy reduces itself, for me, to a single key word, the word *structure*: literature as a verbal structure, even an organic structure. . . .

What I deplore in the structural metaphor is that it ignores or denies by implication the primacy of time in the literary artifact. We go to the Shakespeare Memorial Theatre at Stratford just before 7.30 p.m. and we come out at 10.30. Our mental experience during those three hours excluding the intervals, *was* (for us) *Hamlet*. Or we start reading *Lycidas* at twelve noon and we finish it at 12.15. What occurred to the reader psychologically in that quarter of an hour *was Lycidas* for him. A 'structure', on the other hand, exists in space—and so does a Well Wrought Urn or a Verbal Ikon. The suggestion of solidity and immobility such words convey makes them misleading metaphors for a psychic activity that is essentially mobile.

F. W. Bateson, *English Studies Today* ii (Bern 1961) 73.

13

... letting the look of the poem on the page prompt and regulate *through the eye* the precise tone of voice. Most of us have yet to find out about this aesthetic experience, the secret of which is bound up with the speed at which, word by word and cadence by cadence, the elements of the poem are permitted to come into view.

Charles Tomlinson, in *The New Statesman* (28 April 1961) 674.

14

Two statements are made as if they are connected, and the reader is forced to

consider their relations for himself. The reasons why these facts should have been selected for a poem is left for him to invent; he will invent a variety of reasons and order them in his mind. This, I think, is the essential fact about the poetical use of language.

William Empson, *Seven Types of Ambiguity* (1930); (Harmondsworth 1961) 25.

15

Discourses may be arranged, roughly, in an order with respect to their reliance on secondary meaning, that is, the proportion of meaning represented *implicitly*, by suggestion and connotation. Toward one end we put discourse that is highly charged with meaning, that condenses, so to speak, a great deal of meaning into a small space. Of course this spectrum is fairly continuous, but we can choose some standard discourses to mark off certain points along it, if we want to take the trouble. Moreover, we can draw a line, even if a somewhat vague one, between discourse that has a good deal of secondary meaning and discourse that has not. We may now try out a definition: a literary work is discourse in which an important part of the meaning is implicit. This is a Semantic Definition of 'literature', since it defines 'literature' in terms of meaning.

Monroe C. Beardsley, *Aesthetics* (New York 1958) 126.

16

A poem seemed to him [Johnson] to possess no independent, autonomous existence. It was in no sense a Neoplatonic thing, a particular that occupied a place in an ever ascending hierarchy of spiritual reality. Nor was it an Aristotelian thing with a genus and an assortment of differentiae. It was for Johnson a moral and psychological instrument of communication that pointed outside itself to the empirical reality which it 'imitated', to the mind that has created it, or to the mind that was to enjoy it and be instructed by it. It is perhaps for this reason (and not for the reason that he was following in the Horatian tradition of the *dulce* and the *utile*) that most of Johnson's definitions of poetry are couched in the language of psychology, of education, and of communication: the business of the poet is to 'move ... with delight or terror'; 'the end of writing is to instruct; the end of poetry is to instruct by pleasing'; every author undertakes either 'to instruct or please, or to mingle pleasure with instruction'; 'poetry is the art of uniting pleasure with truth, by calling imagination to the help of reason.'

Jean H. Hagstrum, *Samuel Johnson's Literary Criticism* (Chicago 1967) 37.

17

Literature can never be aesthetically 'pure' or abstractly contemplative. There can be no such thing as 'abstract literature' as there is such a thing as abstract painting. By its nature—

because its medium, language, is used by almost everybody in all sorts of everyday situations; and because it tries both to *say* and to *be*—literature is an art which invites impurities.

We might call it the most creaturely of the arts. Perhaps this is also a source of its strength. No other art, no way of exploring human experience, bodies out so wholly and many dimensionally 'the felt sense of life', makes us feel first of all that the experience must have been just like that, that desire and will and thought would all have been caught up with those gestures, those smells, those sounds. It's not reality; it's a mirroring: but it mirrors more nearly than any other imaginative or intellectual activity the *whole* sense of an experience.

Literature is both in time and outside time. It is in time because it works best when it creates a sense of a certain time and place and of particular persons, when it works through (and re-creates) identifiable life and manners ... Tom Jones hiding in a particular copse with Molly Seagrim, Marvell lying in a certain garden, Dimitri Karamazov in *that* prison cell, Tess baptizing her baby in *that* cottage bedroom.

It is outside time in two ways. First, in a sense we are all used to: that, if it is rooted in time and place and is imaginatively penetrating, it will go beyond particular time and place and speak about our common humanity, will become—as we used to say more readily—universal.

Richard Hoggart, in *The Critical Moment* (1964) 34.

Poetry and Prose

18

The expression or embodiment of beautiful or elevated thought, imagination, or feeling in language adapted to stir the imagination and the emotions.

OED s.v. *Poetry* II 3 c.

19

Sweepings from butchers' stalls, dung, guts, and blood,
Drowned puppies, stinking sprats, all drenched in mud,
Dead cats, and turnip-tops, come tumbling down the flood.

Jonathan Swift, 'A Description of a City Shower' (1710); *Swift's Poems* ed. H. Williams i (Oxford 1958) 139.

20

Composition in verse or metrical language, or in some equivalent patterned arrangement of language.

OED s.v. *Poetry* II 3 a.

21

Consider, for example, Pound's 'Papyrus' (a translation of part of a Sappho fragment that is generally recognized today to be a good English poem in its own right):

   Spring ...
   Too long ...
   Gongula ...

The dots at the end of each of Pound's lines invite us as grammarians to read the poem as three separate uncompleted sentences. For the reader of poetry, however, the dots act rather as a kind of visual rhyme, which is reinforced both by the actual half-rhymes (-*ing*, -*ong*, *Gong*-) and by the syllabic crescendo (one syllable line followed by two-syllable line followed by three-syllable line).

F. W. Bateson, in *Essays in Criticism* xvii (1967) 341.

If in a poem there should be found a series of lines, or even a single line, in which the language, though naturally arranged, and according to the strict laws of metre, does not differ from that of prose, there is a numerous class of critics, who, when they stumble upon these prosaisms, as they call them, imagine that they have made a notable discovery, and exult over the poet as over a man ignorant of his own profession.... It would be a most easy task to prove ... that not only the language of a large portion of every good poem, even of the most elevated character, must necessarily, except with reference to the metre, in no respect differ from that of good prose, but likewise that some of the most interesting parts of the best poems will be found to be strictly the language of prose when prose is well written.... It may be safely affirmed, that there neither is, nor can be, any essential difference between the language of prose and metrical composition.... Where shall we find bonds of connection sufficiently strict to typify the affinity betwixt metrical and prose composition? They both speak by and to the same organs; the bodies in which both of them are clothed may be said to be of the same substance, their affections are kindred, and almost identical, not necessarily differing even in degree; poetry sheds no tears 'such as angels weep', but natural and human tears; she can boast of no celestial ichor that distinguishes her vital juices from those of prose; the same human blood circulates through the veins of them both....

Much confusion has been introduced into criticism by this contradistinction of poetry and prose, instead of the more philosophical one of poetry and matter of fact, or science. The only strict antithesis to prose is metre; nor is this in truth, a *strict* antithesis, because lines and passages of metre so naturally occur in writing prose, that it would be scarcely possible to avoid them, even were it desirable.

William Wordsworth, Preface to *Lyrical Ballads* (1802); ed. R. L. Brett and A. R. Jones (1963) 245-8.

23

There is no force, however great, can stretch a cord, however fine, into a horizontal line, which is accurately straight.

William Whewell, *Elementary Treatise on Mechanics* (1819) 44. Omitted from a later edn, after Adam Sedgwick had recited the lines in an afterdinner speech.

24
London: John Lane, The Bodley Head
New York: Charles Scribner's Sons

Imprint of *The Works of Max Beerbohm.*

London: John Lane, The Bodley Head
New York: Charles Scribner's Sons
This plain announcement, nicely read,
Iambically runs.

Max Beerbohm, *Max in Verse*, ed. J. G. Riewald
(1964): discussed John Updike, *Assorted Prose*
(1968) 150.

25

In easy state upon this couch, there sat/
a jolly Giant, glorious to see;/ who bore
a glowing torch, in shape not unlike/
Plenty's horn, and held it up, high
up,/ on Scrooge, as he came peeping
round the door.

Charles Dickens, *A Christmas Carol* (1843) iii;
ed. E. Farjeon (1954) 39.

26

Such is the inherently rhythmical strain
of the English language, that the bad
writer ... the inexperienced writer, as
Dickens in his earlier attempts to be
impressive, and the jaded writer, as any
one may see for himself, all tend to fall
at once into the production of bad
blank verse. And here it may be
pertinently asked, Why bad? And I
suppose it might be enough to answer
that no man ever made good verse by
accident, and that no verse can ever
sound otherwise than trivial when
uttered with the delivery of prose. But
we can go beyond such answers. The
weak side of verse is the regularity of
the beat, which in itself is decidedly less
impressive than the movement of the
nobler prose; and it is just into this weak
side, and this alone, that our careless
writer falls.

Robert Louis Stevenson, 'On Some Technical
Elements of Style in Literature' (1885); *Works*,
Vailima edn. iv (1922-3) 440.

27

Among the possible effects of practical
adherence to a theory that aims to
identify the style of prose and verse (if
it does not indeed claim for the latter a
yet nearer resemblance to the average
style of men in the viva voce intercourse
of real life), we might anticipate the
following as not the least likely to
occur. It will happen, as I have indeed
before observed, that the metre itself,
the sole acknowledged difference, will
occasionally become metre to the eye
only. The existence of *prosaisms*, and
that they detract from the merit of a
poem, *must* at length be conceded, when
a number of successive lines can be
rendered, even to the most delicate ear,
unrecognizable as verse, or as having
been intended for verse, by simply
transcribing them as prose; when, if the
poem be in blank verse, this can be
effected without any alteration, or at most
by merely restoring one or two words to
their proper places, from which they

have been transplanted for no assignable cause or reason but that of the author's convenience; but, if it be in rhyme, by the mere exchange of the final word of each line for some other of the same meaning, equally appropriate, dignified and euphonic.

Coleridge, *Biographia Literaria* (1817) ch. xviii; ed. J. Shawcross ii (Oxford 1907) 62.

28

James, pointing to its summit, over which they had all purposed to return together, informed them that he would wait for them there. They parted, and his comrades passed that way some two hours after, but they did not find him at the appointed place, *a circumstance of which they took no heed*: but one of them, going by chance into the house, which at this time was James's house, learnt *there*, that nobody had seen him all that day.

William Wordsworth, from *The Brothers*, rewritten as prose by Coleridge, *Biographia Literaria* (1817) ch. xviii; *ibid*. Coleridge's itals. indicate the sole departure from 'the phraseology of common conversation'.

29

In printed prose a new line is started at the beginning of a new paragraph to secure a momentary pause before beginning a new train of thought. In strictly scientific prose we take care of the sense and trust that the sounds will take care of themselves. In verse a new line may be started to indicate a pause not grammatically necessary. Some use of

devices such as rhyme and rhythm, including the slight pauses at the end of a line, which contribute to the emotional effect and not to the plain sense, is necessary in verse but not in prose.... Where the acoustical properties of words (rhyme, rhythm, assonance, pitch, etc.) are deliberately used to contribute to the general effect we may call the writing poetic. Poetic verse is poetry.... The merit of good prosaic writing depends solely upon the ease with which the totality can be grasped and mentally manipulated.... Poetry you must read word by word, and preferably aloud.

Michael Roberts, *Critique of Poetry* (1934) 65, 72f.

30

One doesn't 'listen' when reading standard prose; it is only in poetry that one looks out for metre and rhythmic variations on it. The writers of *vers libre* rely on their printers to call your attention to what is called 'cadence' or 'rhythmic relation' (not easy to follow) which might have escaped you if printed as prose; *this* sentence you'll find, has its thumb to its nose.

Robert Graves, 'Observations on Poetry' (1922-5); *The Common Asphodel* (1949) 8.

31

I wish our clever young poets would remember my homely definitions of prose and poetry; that is, prose = words in their best order;—poetry = the *best* words in the best order.

S. T. Coleridge, *Table-Talk* i (1835) 84.

32

The definition of good prose is—proper words in their proper places;—of good verse—the most proper words in their proper places. The propriety is in either case relative. The words in prose ought to express the intended meaning, and no more; if they attract attention to themselves, it is, in general, a fault. In the very best styles, as Southey's, you read page after page, understanding the author perfectly, without once taking notice of the medium of communication; —it is as if he had been speaking to you all the while. But in verse you must do more;—there the words, the *media,* must be beautiful, and ought to attract your notice—yet not so much and so perpetually as to destroy the unity which ought to result from the whole poem.

S. T. Coleridge, *Table-Talk* ii (1835) 214.

33

Poetry is not like reasoning, a power to be exerted according to the determination of the will. A man cannot say 'I will compose poetry'.

P. B. Shelley, A *Defence of Poetry* (1821); *Complete Works* ed. R. Ingpen and W. E. Peck vii (1930) 135.

34

Anything can be poetry, from a letter to the editor or a recipe to an epic.

Ted Berrigan, reported in *The Guardian* (23 July 1969) 9.

35

Poetry is properly speaking a transcendental quality—a sudden transformation which words assume under a particular influence—and we can no more define this quality than we can define a state of grace.... I believe the difference between poetry and prose to be, not one of surface qualities, not of form in any sense, nor even of *mode* of expression, but absolutely of essence. It is not a case of the mind, in need of expression, choosing between two ways— one poetry, the other prose. There is no choice for the particular state of mind in which poetry originates. It must either seek poetic expression, or it must simply not be expressed; for an altogether lower tension, involving a different kind of mentality, must be substituted before the activity of prose expression can intervene.

Sir Herbert Read, *Collected Essays in Literary Criticism* (1951) 41f.

36

That he wrote all his first in prose, for so his master Cambden had learned him. That verses stood by sense without either colours or accent, which yet other times he denied.

Ben Jonson's 'opinion of verses' in *Conversations with Drummond* (1619); *Ben Jonson* ed. C. H. Herford and others i (Oxford 1925) 143.

37

Tudor held her wrist, wet, and cold as iron, and drew her to the window, and

on her palm lay the small frail skull of a
seagull, white, and complete as a pebble. It
was lovely, all the bones pure white and
dry, and chalky, but perfect without a
crack or a flaw anywhere. At the back,
rising out of the beak were twin domes
like bubbles of thin bone, almost
transparent, where the brain had been
that fixed the tilt of the wings, with the
contour of the delicate sutures inked in
a crinkled line across the skull....

Glyn Jones, *The Blue Bed* (1937) 241f.

38

I found a pigeon's skull upon the machair,
All the bones pure and white and dry, and chalky,
But perfect,
Without a crack or a flaw anywhere.

At the back, rising out of the beak,
Were domes like bubbles of thin bone,
Almost transparent, where the brain had been
That fixed the tilt of the wings.

'Perfect' (on authorship, see following item).

39

I either automatically memorized it and
subsequently thought it my own, or
wrote it into one of my notebooks with
the same result. Any plagiarism was
certainly unconscious.... The poem will
of course not appear again over my name.

Hugh MacDiarmid, in *The Times Literary
Supplement* (28 January 1965) 67 [Item 39 was
first ascribed to Hugh MacDiarmid in
Selected Poems ed. R. C. Saunders (Glasgow
1944)].

40

Can prose become poetry through
typographical rearrangement? I rather
think it can.

Edwin Morgan, *The Times Literary Supplement* (28 January 1965) 67.

41

If words are the *media* of poetry, what
are the *media* of prose? ... the answer
would seem to be, Ideas. 'In prose', as
Whately once pointed out, 'the language
is the vehicle for the matter; in poetry,
the matter is the vehicle for the language.'
In prose, that is, the words tend to be
submerged in the ideas or things they
represent. One synonym is as good as

another. In poetry, on the other hand, the words are always liable to interfere with, and even in extreme cases to contradict, the theme or argument. 'Pure' prose is entirely a matter of ideas; 'pure' poetry is entirely a matter of phrases. It is for this reason that prose is more easily translated than poetry.... Why does poetry employ both the connotations and the denotations of words when prose is restricted to their denotations? The explanation, I believe, lies in the difference between the nature of the prosaic and the poetic statement.

Prose is essentially, as the etymology of the word suggests, a mode of progression. A novel and a treatise both take you from one point to another.... A poem, on the other hand, stands still....

The structure of prose is, in the widest sense of the word, logical.... The structure of poetry, on the other hand, is ultimately determined by its technique. The part, that is, that is played by logic in prose falls in poetry to the metre, the rhymes, the alliterations, and the associative values of the words.

F. W. Bateson, *English Poetry and the English Language* (Oxford 1934) 16-21.

gentle alteration in the prose language which turned it solemn and pious, or meddled with it and turned it quaint for readers who could not quite find the tone. The alteration interfered with the functions of language unless it was really a deference to some unspecified authority. Modern readers of the old measured verse can still, I am sure, recognize the tone, and by some strange and awkward vocal work get it into the reading.

There is also the question of how to read those modern poets who have abandoned the metres altogether, and write free verse. If the authority of the measured rhythms has played out for them, I suggest that their prose-poetry is Delphic in character, or Sibylline, it is cryptic, metaphorical, portentous, prophetic; for against those prose norms which have been so carefully worked out it is demonstrably elliptic, distorted, over-emphatic, and sometimes not easily intelligible.

John Crowe Ransom, 'The Strange Music of English Verse', *Kenyon Review* xviii (1956) 476f.

42

Must it not be said that the age tends to prose, at least in the sense that the strict old prosodical code has pretty well lost its mysterious authority? I hope it may also be said that the old 'measure' seems to have been 'ritualistic' in the way it made a massive and persistent though

43

Poetry is a composition of words set to music. Most other definitions of it are indefensible, or metaphysical. The proportion or quality of the music may, and does, vary; but poetry withers and 'dries out' when it leaves music, or at least an imagined music, too far behind it.

Ezra Pound, 'Vers Libre and Arnold Dolmetsch' (1918); *Literary Essays of Ezra Pound* ed. T. S. Eliot (1960) 437.

Genre and Mode

44

Let us talk of the art of poetry as a whole, and its different species with the particular force of each of them; how the fables must be put together if the poetry is to be well formed; also what are its elements and their different qualities; and all other matters pertaining to the subject.

To begin in the proper order, at the beginning. The making of epics and tragedies, and also comedy, and the art of the dithyramb, and most flute and lyre art, all have this in common, that they are imitations. But they differ from one another in three respects: the different kinds of medium in which they imitate, the different objects they imitate, and the different manner in which they imitate (when it does differ).

Aristotle, *Poetics* i; tr. L. J. Potts (Cambridge 1959) 17.

45

As philosophers have divided the universe, their subject, into three regions, celestial, aerial, and terrestrial, so the poets (whose work it is, by imitating human life in delightful and measured lines, to avert men from vice and incline them to virtuous and honourable actions) have lodged themselves in the three regions of mankind, court, city, and country, correspondent in some proportion to those three regions of the world. For there is in princes and men of conspicuous power, anciently called heroes, a lustre and influence upon the rest of men resembling that of the heavens; and an insincereness, inconstancy, and troublesome humour of those that dwell in populous cities, like the mobility, blustering, and impurity of the air; and a plainness, and though dull, yet a nutritive faculty in rural people, that endures a comparison with the earth they labour.

From hence have proceeded three sorts of poesy, Heroic, Scommatic [satiric], and Pastoral. Every one of these is distinguished again in the manner of representation, which sometimes is narrative, wherein the poet himself relateth, and sometimes dramatic, as when the persons are every one adorned and brought upon the theatre to speak and act their own parts. There is therefore neither more nor less than six sorts of poesy. For the heroic poem narrative ... is called an epic poem. The heroic poem dramatic is tragedy. The scommatic narrative is satire, dramatic is comedy. The pastoral narrative is called simply pastoral, anciently bucolic; the same dramatic, pastoral comedy. The figure therefore of an epic poem and of a tragedy ought to be the same, for they differ no more but in that they are pronounced by one or many persons. Which I insert to justify the figure of yours [Davenant's *Gondibert*], consisting of five books divided into songs, or cantos, as five acts divided into scenes has ever been the approved figure of a tragedy.

They that take for poesy whatsoever is writ in verse will think this division imperfect, and call in sonnets, epigrams, eclogues, and the like pieces, which are but essays and parts of an entire poem, and reckon Empedocles and Lucretius (natural philosophers) for poets, and the moral precepts of Phocylides, Theognis, and the quatrains of Pybrach and the *History* of Lucan, and others of that kind amongst poems, bestowing on such writers for honour the name of poets rather than of historians or philosophers. But the subject of a poem is the manners of men, not natural causes; manners presented, not dictated; and manners feigned, as the name of poesy imports, not found in men.

Thomas Hobbes, *The Answer to Davenant's Preface Before 'Gondibert'* (1650); *Critical Essays of the Seventeenth Century* ed. J. E. Spingarn ii (Bloomington, Ind. 1957) 54-6.

46

A heroic poem, truly such, is undoubtedly the greatest work which the soul of man is capable to perform.... The action of it is always one, entire, and great.... Even the least portions of them must be of the epic kind; all things must be grave, majestical, and sublime: nothing of a foreign nature, like the trifling novels, which Ariosto and others have inserted in their poems. By which the reader is misled into another sort of pleasure, opposite to that which is designed in an epic poem. One raises the soul and hardens it to virtue, the other softens it again and unbends it into vice. One

conduces to the poet's aim, the completing of his work; which he is driving on, labouring and hastening in every line: the other slackens his pace, diverts him from his way, and locks him up like a knight errant in an enchanted castle, when he should be pursuing his first adventure.

John Dryden, Dedication of the *Aeneis* (1697); *Poems*, ed. J. Kinsley iii (Oxford 1958) 1003.

47

VESPASIANO   Since we have gone on so far in our reasoning, just what is the romance?

MINTURNO   I shall not deny that it is an imitation of great and illustrious actions that are worthy of epic poetry. ... Our writers began to imitate the romantic and classical compositions of the barbarians. And since our authors, as Cicero teaches us, always improve what they find in others, they make also the poetry of the romances more graceful and beautiful, if in truth it is to be called poetry.

VESPASIANO   Why is it not worthy of this name? Is not M. Ludovico Ariosto a most excellent poet, as he is a most noble writer of romances?

MINTURNO   Yes, indeed, nor do I judge that a lower estimate should be made of him. But I cannot affirm that his romances and those of the others contain the kind of poetry that Aristotle and Horace taught us.... I cannot but be greatly astonished that there are some learned men, well versed in good literature and of excellent abilities, who (as I understand) acknowledge that there is not in the romances the form and the rule that Homer and Virgil follow, and that Aristotle and Horace command as appropriate, and who nevertheless labour to defend this error. Nay more, since that sort of composition gives the deeds of errant knights, they obstinately affirm not merely that it is not fitting to write poetry in the manner of Virgil and Homer, but even that it is desirable that poetry also should be errant, passing from one manner to another, and binding together various things in one bundle.

VESPASIANO Will you teach us in what the romance differs from the heroic poem?

MINTURNO The heroic poem ... sets out to imitate a memorable action carried to its conclusion by one illustrious person. The romance, they say, has as its object a crowd of knights and ladies and of affairs of war and peace, though in this group one knight is especially taken whom the author is to make glorious above all the others; he is to treat as many deeds by him and by the others as he thinks sufficient for the glory of those he is disposed to praise ... and he takes for description diverse and contrasted lands and the things that happened in them during all the time occupied by the fabulous story of the matter he sets out to sing.

VESPASIANO Does not the father of poetry do the same, since he deals with many very illustrious deeds of Odysseus, Diomedes, the two Ajaxes, Menelaus, King Agamemnon, Nestor, and the other demigods, though he intends to praise Achilles above all the others?

MINTURNO Yes, that is true; but he makes all spring from one beginning, and directs all to one end. This is not done in the romance.

Antonio Sebastiano Minturno, L'Arte poetica (Venice 1564) i; Literary Criticism: Plato to Dryden ed. A. H. Gilbert (New York &c. 1940) 277f.

48

If then the romance and the epic are of the same species, they should be confined by the same bonds of law, especially when these laws are absolutely necessary not merely to the heroic poem, but to every poem. Such a law is unity of plot, which Aristotle prescribes for every species of poem, for the tragic and the comic no less than for the heroic. ... The Orlando Furioso, which contains several plots, is more delightful than any other Tuscan poem, or even than the poems of Homer. ... In the Furioso one can read of amours, chivalry, adventure, and magic, in short, inventions very delightful and well suited to our ears. ... In the propriety of action and in the decorum of persons Ariosto is more excellent than any of the others. ... Perhaps the variety was less necessary in the times of Virgil and Homer, since the ancients were less sated in their tastes; at any rate they did not attain so much, though more is found in Virgil than in Homer. Variety is especially pleasing to our times, and therefore our poets have to season their poems with this spice of variety if they wish not to be rejected by our delicate palates. ... I too think it very pleasant in a heroic poem and possible of introduction there. ... The great poet ... is able to form a poem in which as in a little world can be read

in one passage how armies are drawn
up, and in various others there are
battles by land and sea, attacks on cities,
skirmishes, duels, jousts, descriptions of
hunger and thirst, tempests,
conflagrations, prodigies; there are a
variety of celestial and infernal councils,
and the reader encounters seditions,
discords, wanderings, adventures, incan-
tations, works of cruelty, audacity, court-
esy, and generosity and actions of love,
now unhappy, now happy, now pleasing,
now causing compassion. Yet in spite
of all, the poem that contains so great
a variety of matter is one, one is its
form and its soul; and all these things
are put together in such a way that
one has relation to the other.

Torquato Tasso, *Discorsi del Poema Eroico*
(Naples n.d.) iii; *Literary Criticism: Plato to
Dryden* ed. A. H. Gilbert (New York &c. 1940)
499f.

49

The error begins when we try to deduce
the expression from the concept, and to
find in the thing substituting, the
laws of the thing substituted for....
This error is known as *the theory of
artistic and literary kinds.*

What is the aesthetic form of
domestic life, of knighthood, of the idyll,
of cruelty, and so forth? How should
these contents be *represented*? Such is
the absurd problem implied in the
theory of artistic and literary kinds. It
is in this that consists all search after
laws or rules of genres. Domestic life,
knighthood, idyll, cruelty, and the like, are
not impressions, but concepts. They are
not contents, but logico-aesthetic forms.
You cannot express the form, for it is
already itself expression....

From the theory of the artistic and
literary kinds derive those erroneous
modes of judgement and of criticism,
thanks to which, instead of asking before
a work of art if it be expressive, and
what it expresses, whether it speak or
stammer, or be silent altogether, it is
asked if it be obedient to the *laws* of the
epic poem, or to those of tragedy, to those
of historical portraiture, or to those
of landscape painting. Artists, however,
while making a verbal pretence of
agreeing, or yielding a feigned
obedience to them, have really always
disregarded these *laws of kinds.* Every
true work of art has violated some
established genre and upset the ideas
of the critics, who have thus been
obliged to enlarge the number of genres,
until finally even this enlargement has
proved too narrow, owing to the
appearance of new works of art, which
are naturally followed by new scandals,
new upsettings, and—new enlargements.

Benedetto Croce, *Aesthetic* (1907) ch. iv; tr. D.
Ainslie (1909) 59-61.

50

By mere accident, I opened the next book
that lay by me, which was an Ariosto
in Italian; and the very first two lines
of that poem gave me light to all I
could desire: 'Le donne, i cavalier,
l'arme, gli amori,/Le cortesie, l'audaci
imprese io canto, etc.' For the very next
reflection which I made was this, that
an heroic play ought to be an imitation,
in little, of an heroic poem; and,
consequently, that love and valour ought
to be the subject of it.

John Dryden, *Of Heroic Plays* (1672); *Of
Dramatic Poesy and Other Critical Essays* ed.
G. Watson i (1962) 158.

Their clothes were tolerably well suited to the furniture of their heads, the apparel of the upper bench being decent and clean, while that of the second class was thread-bare and soiled; and at the lower end of the room, he perceived divers efforts to conceal rent breeches and dirty linen: nay, he could distinguish by their countenances, the different kinds of poetry in which they exercised the muse; he saw tragedy conspicuous in a grave solemnity of regard, Satire louring in a frown of envy and discontent, elegy whining in a funereal aspect, pastoral dozing in a most insipid languor of face, ode-writing delineated in a distracted stare, and epigram squinting with a pert sneer.

Tobias Smollett, *Peregrine Pickle* (1751) ch. ci; ed. J. L. Clifford (1964) 640.

52

Imagination, a licentious and vagrant faculty, unsusceptible of limitations, and impatient of restraint, has always endeavoured to baffle the logician, to perplex the confines of distinction, and burst the inclosures of regularity. There is therefore scarcely any species of writing, of which we can tell what is its essence, and what are its constituents; every new genius produces some innovation, which, when invented and approved, subverts the rules which the practice of foregoing authors had established.... Any man's reflections will inform him, that every dramatic composition which raises mirth is comic; and that, to raise mirth, it is by no means universally necessary, that the personages

should be either mean or corrupt, nor always requisite, that the action should be trivial, nor ever, that it should be fictitious.

If the two kinds of dramatic poetry had been defined only by their effects upon the mind, some absurdities might have been prevented, with which the compositions of our greatest poets are disgraced.

Samuel Johnson, *Rambler* No. 125 (28 May 1751); *Works*, Yale edn. iv (New Haven and London 1969) 300f.

53

The poem [*Winter*], which, being of a new kind, few would venture at first to like, by degrees gained upon the public. ... As a writer he is entitled to one praise of the highest kind: his mode of thinking, and of expressing his thoughts, is original.

Samuel Johnson, Life of Thomson, in *Lives of the Poets* (1781); ed. G. B. Hill iii (Oxford 1905) 285.

54

Cooper's Hill is the work that confers upon him the rank and dignity of an original author. He seems to have been, at least among us, the author of a species of composition that may be denominated *local poetry*, of which the fundamental subject is some particular landscape, to be poetically described, with the addition of such embellishments as may be supplied by historical retrospection, or incidental meditation.

To trace a new scheme of poetry
has in itself a very high claim to praise,
and its praise is yet more when it is
apparently copied by Garth and Pope.

Samuel Johnson, Life of Denham, in *Lives of
the Poets* (1781); ed. G. B. Hill i (Oxford 1905)
77.

55

Concerning a literate age we may ask not
only what are its established forms (that
is, patterns), but how the writer responds
to them. Thus, forms may be regarded
as institutional imperatives which both
coerce and are in turn coerced by the
writer.

N. H. Pearson, in *Literary Forms and Types*
ed. R. Kirk, English Institute Annual (New
York 1940) 70.

56

What is the role of language in literature?
The problem resolves itself immediately
... if Saussure's seminal distinction
between *langue* and *parole* is extended
from linguistic to literary theory.
Langue ... is the speech-system, the
vocabulary, accidence and syntax that a
speech-group learns, adjusts and stores
away in its individual memories for
use when required.... *Parole*, on the
other hand, is the particular speech-act,
the words exchanged between A and B
in a particular place on a particular
occasion.... The literary artifact, then,
is *parole* extended and elaborated. Its
only essential difference from conversation
is that it is much more memorable.

One may say that it 'wants' to get itself
repeated. The extension I am proposing
of *parole* necessarily implies a similar
elaboration of *langue* into linguistic
memorability-devices—metre, for
example, poetic diction, all the figures
of speech, all the conventional literary
subject-matter that Curtius has taught
us to call 'topoi', and (last but not least)
the traditional literary *genres* or 'kinds'.

F. W. Bateson, *English Studies Today* ii (Bern
1961) 74f.

57

As it is possible the mere English reader
may have a different idea of romance with
the author of these little volumes; and
may consequently expect a kind of
entertainment, not to be found, nor
which was even intended, in the following
pages; it may not be improper to
premise a few words concerning this
kind of writing, which I do not
remember to have seen hitherto
attempted in our language.

Henry Fielding, Preface to *Joseph Andrews*
(1742); ed. M. C. Battestin (Oxford 1967) 3.

58

The interpreter's aim is to posit the
author's horizon and carefully to exclude
his own accidental associations.... That
is the reason that the genre concept is
so important to textual study. By
classifying the text as belonging to a
particular genre, the interpreter
automatically posits a general horizon
for its meaning. The genre provides a

sense of the whole, a notion of the
typical meaning-components. But these
generic classifications ... give only a
rough notion of the horizon of a
particular meaning.

E. D. Hirsch, Jr., 'Objective Interpretation',
*Publications of the Modern Language Associa-
tion* lxxv (1960) 469.

59

Again, epic poetry inevitably has the
same kinds as there are in tragedy—
either Simple, or Complex, or Moral, or
Emotional; and the same elements, except
Melody and *mise en scène*—for it needs
Irony of events, and Disclosure, and
Crises of Feeling; and the thoughts and
language must also be well formed....

But epic poetry differs in the size
of the plot, and in metre. As for size,
the definition I have given is sufficient:
we must be able to survey it from
beginning to end. That would be so if
the plots were smaller in bulk than those
of the old epics but about the equal
of all the tragedies produced at one
hearing. Epic poetry has a property that
tends to increase its amplitude
considerably. In tragedy it is not
possible to imitate several parts of a
story as happening at the same time,
but only the part played by the actors
on the stage; in the epic, because it is a
narrative, many simultaneous transactions can be depicted, by which, if
they are related to one another, the
weight of the poem will be increased.
So that it has the merit of richness,
diverting the audience by the interpolation
of dissimilar scenes; for monotony soon
surfeits, and this can make a tragedy
fail.

As for metre, the heroic metre has
established itself by experience. If any
one wrote narrative imitation in any
other metre, or in several metres, it
would be obviously improper; for
heroic verse is more deliberate and
weightier than any other, which
enables it to absorb loan-words and
metaphors better, and makes narrative
imitation the most uncommon of the
arts.... Accordingly, no one has ever
written a poem with an extended plot
in any other metre than the heroic; as I
have said, the very nature of the thing
teaches us to choose what is appropriate
to it.

Aristotle, *Poetics* xxiv; tr. L. J. Potts (Cambridge 1959) 52f.

60

We should not try to get all sorts of
pleasure from tragedy, but the particular
tragic pleasure.

Aristotle, *Poetics* xiv; tr. L. J. Potts (Cambridge 1959) 35.

61

POLONIUS   The best actors in the world,
either for tragedy, comedy, history,
pastoral, pastoral-comical, historical-
pastoral, tragical-historical, tragical-
comical-historical-pastoral, scene
individable, or poem unlimited....

William Shakespeare, *Hamlet* II ii 424ff.

62

The ground of all this Bedlam-buffoonery
we saw in the case of the French

strollers; the company for acting Christ's passion or the Old Testament were carpenters, cobblers, and illiterate fellows, who found that the drolls and fooleries interlarded by them brought in the rabble and lengthened their tune, so they got money by the bargain.

Our Shakespeare, doubtless, was a great master in this craft. These carpenters and cobblers were the guides he followed. And it is then no wonder that we find so much farce and apocryphal matter in his tragedies: thereby un-hallowing the theatre, profaning the name of tragedy; and instead of representing men and manners, turning all morality, good sense, and humanity into mockery and derision.

Thomas Rymer, A *Short View of Tragedy* (1693) vii; *Critical Essays of the Seventeenth Century* ed. J. E. Spingarn, ii (Bloomington, Ind. 1957) 234.

63

Reduce all tragedy by rules of art
Back to its antique theatre, a cart,
And make 'em henceforth keep the beaten roads
Of reverend choruses and episodes;
Reform and regulate a puppet-play,
According to the true and ancient way,
That not an actor shall presume to squeek
Unless he have a licence for 't in Greek.

. . . . .

Now pudding [clown] shall be suffered to be witty,
Unless it be to terrify or pity.

. . . . .

And only those held proper to deter
Wh' have had th'ill luck against their wills to err;
Whence only such as are of middling sizes,
Between mortality and venial vices,
Are qualified to be destroyed by fate,
For other mortals to take warning at;
As if the antique laws of tragedy
Did with our own municipal agree.

Samuel Butler, 'Upon Critics Who Judge of Modern Plays Precisely by the Rules of the Ancients' (1678?); *Critical Essays of the Seventeenth Century* ed. J. E. Spingarn, ii (Bloomington, Ind. 1957) 278f.

The tragi-comedy, which is the product of the English theatre, is one of the most monstrous inventions that ever entered into a poet's thoughts. An author might as well think of weaving the adventures of Aeneas and Hudibras into one poem, as of writing such a motly piece of mirth and sorrow. But the absurdity of these performances is so very visible, that I shall not insist upon it.

Joseph Addison, *Spectator* No. 40 (16 April 1711); ed. D. F. Bond i (Oxford 1965) 170.

instruction of tragedy or comedy cannot be denied, because it includes both in its alternations of exhibition and approaches nearer than either to the appearance of life, by showing how great machinations and slender designs may promote or obviate one another, and the high and the low co-operate in the general system by unavoidable concatenation.

Samuel Johnson, *Preface to Shakespeare* (1765); Works, Yale edn. vii (New Haven and London 1968) 66f.

65

Shakespeare's plays are not in the rigorous and critical sense either tragedies or comedies, but compositions of a distinct kind; exhibiting the real state of sublunary nature, which partakes of good and evil, joy and sorrow, mingled with endless variety of proportion and innumerable modes of combination; and expressing the course of the world, in which the loss of one is the gain of another; in which, at the same time, the reveller is hasting to his wine, and the mourner burying his friend; in which the malignity of one is sometimes defeated by the frolic of another; and many mischiefs and many benefits are done and hindered without design. . . .

That this is a practice contrary to the rules of criticism will be readily allowed; but there is always an appeal open from criticism to nature. The end of writing is to instruct; the end of poetry is to instruct by pleasing. That the mingled drama may convey all the

66

Literary compositions run into each other, precisely like colours: in their strong tints they are easily distinguished; but are susceptible of so much variety, and of so many different forms, that we never can say where one species ends and another begins. As to the general taste, there is little reason to doubt, that a work where heroic actions are related in an elevated style, will, without further requisite be deemed an epic poem.

Henry Home, Lord Kames, *Elements of Criticism* (1762).

67

Although *Absalom and Achitophel* has always been known as a satire, the style in which it is written is by no means a characteristically satiric idiom. The object of Dryden's first official production as Laureate is not merely to attack the men who plotted against the King, but to present the whole constitutional position to the reader in a certain way. While the King's enemies are represented in an unfavourable light, the Royal party is eulogistically portrayed. It is appropriate, therefore, that the idiom is not the middle or low style of lampoon or the commonest sorts of denigrating satire, but a basically heroic style with occasional base details in the portraits of Shaftesbury's followers. . . .

Dryden called *Absalom and Achitopel* a satire . . . and it is as a satire that it has always been considered. Yet it has practically nothing in common with classical *satura*, and has marked similarities to a heroic poem. In what sense is it a satire? . . . It is the prominence of the element of attack in *Absalom and Achitophel* that makes it a satire in the English sense of the word?

I. R. J. Jack, *Augustan Satire* (Oxford 1952) 59f., 76.

68

As Boileau saw it, or came to see it, the mock-epic included as many of these epic ingredients as possible.

G. Tillotson, Introduction to Pope's *The Rape of the Lock* (1962) 109.

69

Though it wants one particular, which the critic enumerates in the constituent parts of an epic poem, namely metre; yet, when any kind of writing contains all its other parts, such as fable, action, characters, sentiments, and diction, and is deficient in metre only; it seems, I think, reasonable to refer it to the epic;

at least, no critic hath thought proper to range it under any other head, nor to assign it a particular name to itself.

Henry Fielding, Preface to *Joseph Andrews* (1742); ed. M. C. Battestin (Oxford 1967) 3.

70

Genre should be conceived, we think, as a grouping of literary works based, theoretically, upon both an outer form (specific metre or structure) and also upon an inner form (attitude, tone, purpose—more crudely, subject and audience).

René Wellek and Austin Warren, *Theory of Literature* (rev. edn., Harmondsworth 1963) 231.

71

To treat lyrics as a class, one must examine individual lyrics from the standpoint of their generic attributes. And to do this, one must have terminological prepossessions, prior to the analysis, even before one can select a poem that he considers representative of the lyric.

Kenneth Burke, *Aristotle's Poetics and English Literature*, ed. E. Olson (Chicago 1965) 135.

72

It might be objected that nothing is gained in clearness of insight and precision of method by thus treating criticism from an evolutionary point of view, while dangerous analogies are suggested when we fall into the habit of regarding products of the human mind as subordinate to the same laws of development as living organisms.... But ... a type of art, once started, must, according to my view, fulfil itself, and bring to light the structure which its germ contained potentially. As this structure is progressively evolved, it becomes impossible to return upon the past.... Originality has to be displayed by eliciting what is still left latent in the partially exhausted type. To create a new type, while the old one is existent, baffles human ingenuity, because the type is an expression of the people's mind.... The novel could be analysed on evolutionary principles. But the novel is one of the most 'hybridisable genera' known to us in literature.

John A. Symonds, *Essays Speculative and Suggestive* i (1890) 75f., 80.

73

Art develops further until a form is achieved and valued for its own sake.... The achievement of form is signalized by a revolution in the ordering and constitution of the parts: once the specifically pleasurable effect has luckily been produced, the part which is primarily effective becomes principle, develops its proper extension and qualities, and all other parts readjust to it, in their proper artistic order. A distinctive synthesis—a species of art—has now formed, and its poetics may begin, for the formulation of the distinctive means, object, manner, and effect of the synthesis gives all four of the causes which

are collectively, but not singly, peculiar to it, and a definition results.

Elder Olson, 'An Outline of Poetic Theory' in *Critics and Criticism*, ed. R. S. Crane (Chicago 1952) 558.

74

Although the criticism of qualities and the investigation of historical origins and significances may achieve important results independently of the criticism of forms ... both of these modes of judging literary productions would gain considerably in rigour and scope if they were founded on, and hence controlled by, a prior analysis of works from the point of view of their particular principles of construction and the special artistic problems which these presented to their writers.

R. S. Crane, *Critics and Criticism* (Chicago 1952) 647.

75

The attempt to criticize poetry by 'species' goes along with the Chicago interest in objects or things. And so far as the Chicago philosophy is a reaction against positivism, process philosophy, and mere semantics ... I am far from having any quarrel with it. But one does the philosophy of 'things' no great service by attempting to revive anything like what has always been a 'perversion' of that philosophy, the Hellenistic-Roman and neoclassic criticism by rules of genre.

W. K. Wimsatt and M. C. Beardsley, *The Verbal Icon* (New York 1958) 53.

76

The narrative method whereby the novel embodies this circumstantial view of life may be called its formal realism; formal, because the term realism does not here refer to any special literary doctrine or purpose, but only to a set of narrative procedures which are so commonly found together in the novel, and so rarely in other literary genres, that they may be regarded as typical of the form itself. Formal realism, in fact, is the narrative embodiment of a premise that Defoe and Richardson accepted very literally, but which is implicit in the novel form in general: the premise, or primary convention, that the novel is a full and authentic report of human experience, and is therefore under an obligation to satisfy its reader with such details of the story as the individuality of the actors concerned, the particulars of the times and places of their actions, details which are presented through a more largely referential use of language than is common in other literary forms.

Ian Watt, *The Rise of the Novel* (1957) 32.

inspection if we look at the ordinary meanings of these terms. Tragedy and comedy may have been originally names for two species of drama, but we also employ the terms to describe general characteristics of literary fictions, without regard to genre. It would be silly to insist that comedy can refer only to a certain type of stage play, and must never be employed in connection with Chaucer or Jane Austen. Chaucer himself would certainly have defined comedy, as his monk defines tragedy, much more broadly than that. If we are told that what we are about to read is tragic or comic, we expect a certain kind of structure and mood, but not necessarily a certain genre. The same is true of the words romance, and also of the words irony and satire, which are, as generally employed, elements of the literature of experience, and which we shall here adopt in place of 'realism'. We thus have four narrative pregeneric elements of literature which I shall call *mythoi* or generic plots.

Northrop Frye, *Anatomy of Criticism* (Princeton, N.J. 1957) 162.

77

We have thus answered the question: are there narrative categories of literature broader than, or logically prior to, the ordinary literary genres? There are four such categories: the romantic, the tragic, the comic, and the ironic or satiric. We get the same answer by

78

IRONIC: A mode of literature in which the characters exhibit a power of action inferior to the one assumed to be normal in the reader or audience, or in which the poet's attitude is one of detached objectivity.

Ibid. 366.

Originality

79

Thy sire no pick-purse is of others' wit,
Those jewels be his own which thee adorn;

William Drummond, Sonnet to the Author before
Patrick Gordon, *History of Penardo and Laissa*
(Dort 1615); ed. L. E. Kastner ii (Edinburgh and
London 1913) 162.

80

Yet these mine own, I wrong not other men,
　　Nor traffic further than this happy clime,
Nor filch from Portes nor from Petrarch's pen,
　　A fault too common in this latter time.
Divine Sir Philip, I avouch thy writ,
I am no pickpurse of another's wit.

Michael Drayton, Sonnet to Cooke, before *Idea's
Mirror* (1594); *Works* ed. J. W. Hebel i (Oxford
1961) 96.

81

And this I swear by blackest brook of hell,
I am no pick-purse of another's wit.

Sir Philip Sidney, *Astrophil and Stella*, (1598)
lxxiv; ed. W. A. Ringler (Oxford 1962) 204.

82

Sidney kept his oath and never merely copied from others. . . .

William A. Ringler, ed., *The Poems of Sir Philip Sidney* (Oxford 1962) 480.

83

Stella think not that I by verse seek fame,
  Who seek, who hope, who love, who live but thee;
  Thine eyes my pride, thy lips my history:
If thou praise not, all other praise is shame.
Nor so ambitious am I, as to frame
  A nest for my young praise in laurel tree:
  In truth I swear, I wish not there should be
Graved in mine epitaph a poet's name:
  Ne if I would, could I just title make,
That any laud to me thereof should grow,
Without my plumes from others' wings I take.
For nothing from my wit or will doth flow,
  Since all my words thy beauty doth endite,
  And love doth hold my hand, and makes me write.

Sir Philip Sidney, *Astrophil and Stella* (1598) xc; *ibid.* 224.

84

E certo ogni mio studio in quel tempo era
    Pur di sfogare il doloroso core
In qualche modo, non d'acquistar fama.

                    Petrarch, *Rime* ccxciii.

Et puis je n' escry pas pour gloire en acquérir

                    Desportes, *Diane* i.

E voglio anzi un sepolcro bello e bianco,
Che 'l vostro nome a mio danno si scriva
In alcun marmo

                    Petrarch, Rime lxxxii.

I will not yet in my grave be buried;
Nor on my tomb your name yfixed fast,
As cruel cause that did the spirit soon haste.

      Sir Thomas Wyatt, 'Was I Never Yet of your Love Grieved'.

Ch' a parte a parte entro a' begli occhi leggo
Quant' io parlo d'Amore e quant' io scrivo.

                    Petrarch, *Rime* cli.

Amour guide ma plume

                    Desportes, *Diane*, 'Chant d' amour'.

85

You that poor Petrarch's long deceased woes,
With new-born sighs and denizened wit do sing;
You take wrong ways, those far-fet helps be such,
As do bewray a want of inward touch:
And sure at length stolen goods do come to light.

Sir Philip Sidney, *Astrophil and Stella* (1598) xv; ed.
W. A. Ringler (Oxford 1962) 172.

86

Nothing is said now that has not been said before.

Terence, *Eunuchus* Prol. 41.

consists. But if we consider it as a whole, it is not true that everything has already been said.

Lodovico Castelvetro, *The Poetics of Aristotle* (Basel 1576) ix; *Literary Criticism: Plato to Dryden* ed. A. H. Gilbert (New York &c. 1940) 216f.

87

Some of these thieves, who wish to be thought poets, are found to be so shameless that they dare to affirm it is permissible to steal things found by other poets, because the theft is committed without any damage to those from whom something is taken, and mockingly they say: If you do not believe it, go to see if in their books anything is lacking because of our theft.... They have even greater presumption and affirm that they do not steal nor take anything from anyone when they write what others have already written in earlier poems, since the others do not find or are unable to find anything that has not been said before.... It is true that nothing is said which has not been said before, if we consider the fundamental parts of which each thing is composed and

88

Come then, all you young men! and careless of censure, give yourselves up to steal and drive the spoil from every source! Unhappy is he (for such have often been found) who, rashly trusting to his own strength and art, as though in need of no external help, in his audacity refuses to follow the trustworthy footsteps of the ancients, abstaining, alas unwisely, from plunder, and thinking to spare others. O vain superstition! O care unhallowed by Phoebus! Not long do such men prosper—often they outlive their own works, and, unpraised, lament their short-lived offspring before their own death, and living see the funeral of their fame. How they could wish to have spared their idle labour and learnt other arts from their parents! Often I love to play on ancient phrase, and utter some far other thought in the same words. Nor will any wise man care to blame my self-confessing thefts—thefts open and to be praised and approved by our children's children. So far be it from me to wish to hide my stolen goods, and conceal my plunder, from any fear of the penalty of infamy!

Marco Girolamo Vida, *De arte poetica* (Rome 1527) iii 243-63; tr. G. Saintsbury, *Loci critici* (Boston &c. 1903) 85f.

89

I will conclude my reflections on it [his own imitation of Euripides] with a passage of Longinus [*On the sublime* xiii 4] concerning Plato's imitation of Homer: 'We ought not to regard a good imitation as a theft, but as a beautiful idea of him who undertakes to imitate, by forming himself on the invention and work of another man; for he enters into the lists like a new wrestler, to dispute the prize with the former champion. This sort of emulation, says Hesiod, is honourable, "this strife is wholesome to men", when we combat for victory with a hero, and are not without glory even in our overthrow. Those great men whom we propose to ourselves as patterns of our imitation serve us as a torch, which is lifted up before us to enlighten our passage; and often elevate our thoughts

as high as the conception we have of our author's genius.'

John Dryden, Preface to *Troilus and Cressida* (1679); *Of Dramatic Poesy and Other Critical Essays* ed. G. Watson i (1962) 242f.

90

Be influenced by as many great artists as you can, but have the decency either to acknowledge the debt outright, or to try to conceal it.

Don't allow 'influence' to mean merely that you mop up the particular decorative vocabulary of some one or two poets whom you happen to admire. A Turkish war correspondent was recently caught red-handed babbling in his despatches of 'dove-grey' hills, or else it was 'pearl-pale', I can not remember.

Ezra Pound, 'A Retrospect' (1918); *Literary Essays of Ezra Pound* ed. T. S. Eliot (1960) 5.

91

All languages, both learned and mother tongues, be gotten, and gotten only by Imitation. For as ye use to hear, so ye learn to speak: if ye hear no other, ye speak not your self: and whom ye only hear, of them ye only learn.

And therefore, if ye would speak as the best and wisest do, ye must be conversant, where the best and wisest are.

Roger Ascham, *The Schoolmaster* (1570) ii; ed. E. B. Mayor (1863) 135.

92

In tenui labor; at tenuis non gloria, si quem
Numina laeva sinunt, auditque vocatus Apollo.

> Virgil, *Georgics* iv 6f.

The subject's humble, but not so the praise,
If any Muse assist the poet's lays.

> *Ibid.*, tr. Sir Charles Sedley; *Works* ed. V. de S. Pinto
> i (1928) 74.

Slight is the subject, but the praise not small,
If Heaven assist, and Phoebus hear my call.

> *Ibid.*, tr. Dryden, *Virgil's Georgics* (1697) iv 8f; ed.
> Kinsley ii (Oxford 1958) 980.

Slight is the subject, but not so the praise,
If she inspire, and he approve my lays.

> Alexander Pope, *The Rape of the Lock* (1714) i 5f.

93

Only to point out and nakedly to join together their sentences, with no further declaring the manner and way, how the one doth follow the other, were but a cold help to the increase of learning.

But if a man would take this pain also, when he hath laid two places, of Homer and Virgil, or of Demosthenes and Tully together, to teach plainly withal, after this sort. 1. Tully retaineth thus much of the matter, these sentences, these words: 2. This and that he leaveth out, which he doth wittily to this end and purpose. 3. This he addeth here. 4. This he diminisheth there. 5. This he ordereth thus, with placing that here, not there. 6. This he altereth and changeth, either in property of words, in form of sentence [thought], in substance of the matter, or in one or other convenient circumstance of the author's present purpose. In these few rude English words, are wrapped up all the necessary tools and instruments, wherewith true Imitation is rightly wrought withal in any tongue.

> Roger Ascham, *The Schoolmaster* (1570) ii; ed.
> E. B. Mayor (1863) 140f.

94

Those ancients have been faithful imitators and wise observers of that nature which is so torn and ill represented in our plays; they have handed down to us a perfect resemblance of her; which we, like ill copiers, neglecting to look on, have rendered monstrous and disfigured.

> John Dryden, *Of Dramatic Poesy* (1668); *Of Dramatic Poesy and Other Critical Essays* ed.
> G. Watson i (1962) 27.

Suppose ... that in considering Dryden alone, a critic unwittingly chose for particular commendation lines which had been taken over verbatim from earlier men. I think, to put it mildly, that this unnoticed fact would detract from the value of his statement. Indeed, it would be difficult for a man with a natural taste for irony to avoid indulging it in commenting on several passages in Book IV [of the Aeneis], which can only be called Dryden's by the same figure of speech which we use when we call cow's milk by the name of the milkman who distributes it.... I would very cheerfully undertake to translate into verse any text that I know reasonably well faster and with less labour than any man alive, if he were tied to following Dryden's method. I conclude that Dryden's procedure is intelligible only if we presume that he was seeking a definitive version, constantly embodying in his own work what he thought had been well done, and constantly measuring himself against the best version he could find of any given passage.

L. Proudfoot, *Dryden's Aeneid and its Seventeenth Century Predecessors* (Manchester 1960) 7, 267.

96

The greatest man of the last age (Ben Jonson) was willing to give place to them [the ancients] in all things: he was not only a professed imitator of Horace, but a learned plagiary of all the others; you track him every where in their snow: if Horace, Lucan, Petronius Arbiter, Seneca, and Juvenal had their own from him, there are few serious thoughts which are new in him.

John Dryden, *Of Dramatic Poesy* (1668); *Of Dramatic Poesy and Other Critical Essays* ed. G. Watson i (1962) 31.

97

Let people see in what I borrow whether I have known how to choose what would enhance my theme. For I make others say what I cannot say so well, now through the weakness of my language, now through the weakness of my understanding. I do not count my borrowings, I weigh them. And if I had wanted to have them valued by their number, I should have loaded myself with twice as many. They are all, or very nearly all, from such famous and ancient names that they seem to identify themselves enough without me. In the reasonings and inventions that I transplant into my soil and confound with my own, I have sometimes deliberately not indicated the author, in order to hold in check the temerity of those hasty condemnations that are tossed at all sorts of writings, notably recent writings of men still living, and in the vulgar tongue, which invites everyone to talk about them and seems to convict the conception and design of being likewise vulgar. I want them to give Plutarch a fillip on my nose and get burned insulting Seneca in me. I have to hide my weakness under these great authorities. I will love anyone that can unplume me, I mean by clearness of judgment and by the sole distinction of the force and beauty of the remarks.

For I who, for lack of memory, fall short at every turn in picking them out by knowledge of their origin, can very well realize, by measuring my capacity, that my soil is not at all capable of producing certain too rich flowers that I find sown there, and that all the fruits of my own growing could not match them.

Michel Eyquem de Montaigne, *Essays* II x, tr. D. M. Frame (1958) 296f.

98

The third requisite in our poet or maker is imitation, *imitatio*, to be able to convert the substance or riches of another poet to his own use. To make choice of one excellent man above the rest, and so to follow him till he grow very he, or so like him as the copy may be mistaken for the principal. Not as a creature that swallows what it takes in, crude, raw, or undigested; but that feeds with an appetite, and hath a stomach to concoct, divide, and turn all into nourishment. Not to imitate servilely, as Horace saith, and catch at vices for virtue, but to draw forth out of the best and choicest flowers, with the bee, and turn all into honey, work it into one relish and savour; make our imitation sweet; observe how the best writers have imitated, and follow them : how Virgil and Statius have imitated Homer; how Horace, Archilochus; how Alcaeus, and the other lyrics, and so of the rest.

Ben Jonson, *Timber; or Discoveries* (1640); *Ben Jonson* ed. C. H. Herford and others viii (Oxford 1947) 638f.

99

One of the surest of tests is the way in which a poet borrows. Immature poets imitate; mature poets steal; bad poets deface what they take, and good poets make it into something better, or at least something different. The good poet welds his theft into a whole of feeling which is unique, utterly different from that from which it was torn; the bad poet throws it into something which has no cohesion. A good poet will usually borrow from authors remote in time, or alien in language, or diverse in interest. Chapman borrowed from Seneca; Shakespeare and Webster from Montaigne. The two great followers of Shakespeare, Webster and Tourneur, in their mature work do not borrow from him; he is too close to them to be of use to them in this way.... An echo, rather than an imitation or a plagiarism —the basest, because least conscious form of borrowing.

T. S. Eliot, 'Philip Massinger' (1920); *Selected Essays* (1951) 206f.

100

We look for innovations, we expect revelations, we stress whatever is unique in the experience of a writer, and minimize whatever he shares in common with other men; and by sincerity we come to mean the truthful unveiling of private worlds.

Now plagiarism is so often understood to be the opposite of original and sincere that it is well to remind ourselves that these are not the only forms of originality and sincerity....

There is a vast difference between

imaginative and unimaginative borrowing; between the borrower who makes poetry of the first order from his borrowings and the derivative artist; and between the derivative artist and the plain thief. And this difference between the successful and the unsuccessful borrowers, is the difference between the artist and the plagiarist. The plagiarist is simply the bad borrower.

W. A. Edwards, *Plagiarism* (Cambridge 1933) 2, 115.

101

There is another road, besides those we have mentioned, which leads to sublimity. What and what manner of road is this? Zealous imitation of the great historians and poets of the past. That is the aim, dear friend, and we must hold to it with all our might. For many are carried away by the inspiration of another.... From the natural genius of those old writers there flows into the hearts of their admirers as it were an emanation from the mouth of holiness. Inspired by this, even those who are not easily moved by the divine afflatus share the enthusiasm of these others' grandeurs. Was Herodotus alone 'Homeric in the highest'? No, there was Stesichorus at a still earlier date and Archilochus too, and above all others Plato, who has irrigated his style with ten thousand runnels from the great Homeric spring.

Longinus, *On the Sublime* xiii 2f; tr. T. S. Dorsch (Harmondsworth 1965) 119.

102

If we take as our examples poets of little merit, we shall fall to such a depth that we shall deserve no praise. If we use as our models those of greater merit, when we fall we shall nevertheless remain among the number of those who are much praised.... Nor does that imitation please me that takes over some passage in similar words, or rather in the same words, unless it is from a writer of foreign speech.... Who will ever praise imitating the moderns, if you do not make what is taken yours to such an extent that it will not any more appear to belong to others? In such borrowing your activity is properly to be praised not merely in that it is like that of the bees, who sometimes change the softness of the flowers into the sweetness of honey, in such a way that in the honey nothing of the flowers can be recognized, but also because it knows so well how to make another's work its own that what is borrowed seems to have sprung up in your own garden and not to have been transplanted from that of another.... Since the model himself has taken many things from others, and yet has changed many words, our author permits himself to do only what the model thought was permitted.... And since it has been demonstrated from what logical places are taken those ornaments which make speech splendid, our imitative author will take changes in words and ornaments of speech to be used in describing ... a similar thing from no other place than that whence the one set up for imitation took them.

Antonio Sebastiano Minturno, *L'Arte Poetica* (Venice 1564) iv; *Literary Criticism: Plato to Dryden* ed. A. H. Gilbert (New York &c. 1940) 301f.

Illustrious examples engross, prejudice, and intimidate. They engross our attention, and so prevent a due inspection of ourselves; they prejudice our judgement in favour of their abilities, and so lessen the sense of our own; and they intimidate us with the splendour of their renown, and thus under diffidence bury our strength.... He that imitates the divine *Iliad* does not imitate Homer; but he who takes the same method, which Homer took, for arriving at a capacity of accomplishing a work so great. Tread in his steps to the sole fountain of immortality; drink where he drank, at the true Helicon, that is, at the breast of Nature: imitate; but imitate not the composition, but the man.... The less we copy the renowned ancients, we shall resemble them the more.

Edward Young, *Conjectures on Original Composition* (1759); *English Critical Essays* ed. E. D. Jones (1922) 276f.

Young insinuates ... that one is aided in becoming a genius by being brainless and ignorant.

Irving Babbitt, 'Romantic Genius', *Rousseau and Romanticism* (1947) 43.

The mind of a man of genius is a fertile and pleasant field, pleasant as Elysium, and fertile as Tempe; it enjoys a perpetual spring. Of that spring, originals are the fairest flowers: imitations are of quicker growth, but fainter bloom.... I shall not enter into the curious inquiry of what is, or is not, strictly speaking, original, content with what all must allow, that some compositions are more so than others; and the more they are so, I say, the better. Originals are, and ought to be, great favourites, for they are great benefactors; they extend the republic of letters, and add a new province to its dominion. Imitators only give us a sort of duplicates of what we had, possibly much better, before; increasing the mere drug of books, while all that makes them valuable, knowledge and genius, are at a stand. The pen of an original writer, like Armida's wand, out of a barren waste calls a blooming spring. Out of that blooming spring an imitator is a transplanter of laurels, which sometimes die on removal, always languish in a foreign soil.... An original may be said to be of a vegetable nature; it rises spontaneously from the vital root of genius; it grows, it is not made. Imitations are often a sort of manufacture wrought up by those mechanics, art and labour, out of pre-existent materials not their own.

Again: we read imitation with somewhat of his languor, who listens to a twice-told tale. Our spirits rouse at an original; that is a perfect stranger, and all throng to learn what news from a foreign land: and though it comes, like an Indian prince, adorned with feathers only, having little of weight; yet of our attention it will rob the more solid, if not equally new.

Edward Young, *Conjectures on Original Composition* (1759); *English Critical Essays* ed. E. D. Jones, (1922) 273f.

When Time, like him of Gaza in his wrath,
Plucking the pillars that support the world,
In nature's ample ruins lies intombed;
And midnight, universal midnight! reigns.

Edward Young, *Night Thoughts* (1745) conclusion.

Lo! thy dread empire, Chaos! is restored;
Light dies before thy uncreating word:
Thy hand, great anarch! lets the curtain fall;
And universal darkness buries all.

Alexander Pope, *The Dunciad* (1743) conclusion.

107

Originality is found, here [in *The Seasons*], in a 'mode of thinking and of expression'. But the thought itself does not have to be novel or difficult of apprehension and acceptance; it may be, and for Johnson most often is, the commonplace, or a thought which, when grasped, is so quickly admitted that the reader wonders that he never thought of it for himself. Originality does not require the rejection of convention. We have grown accustomed, during the last century and more, to such a riot of individual styles that we may forget that originality is as significant in a settled period as it is in one of constant change; we have become so accustomed to differences of poetic style recognizable by anybody, that we may be less sensitive to the finer variations within a form, which the mind and ear habituated to that form may perceive. But originality, when it becomes the only, or the most prized virtue of poetry, may cease to be a virtue at all; and when several poets, and their respective groups of admirers, cease to have in common any standards of versification, any identity of taste or of tenets of belief, criticism may decline to an advertisement of preference. The originality which Johnson approves, is an originality limited by the other qualities which he demands.

T. S. Eliot, 'Johnson as Critic and Poet' (1944);
On Poetry and Poets (1957) 182.

108

Originality in art is commonly regarded as a good thing; the question is why. Now, first of all, we must note that it is Genetic, in the strict sense: to say was known by its creator to exist at that when it was created it differed in some notable way from anything else that was known by its creator to exist at that time. In this strict sense, it is clear that originality has no bearing upon worth: it might be original and fine, or original and terrible. Caravaggio was one of the most original painters who ever lived— but that does not make him one of the greatest. But suppose we confine ourselves

to good works of art—including Caravaggio's—and ask whether originality is
not a ground for admiring them more
than we would on other grounds. Even
here, we can easily set up test cases to
divorce originality from value. Suppose
there are two of Haydn's symphonies
very much alike, and we do not know
which he wrote first; are we going to say
that A becomes better when we decide
that it was the earlier, but reverse our
judgment when newly discovered band
parts give priority to B?

M. C. Beardsley, *Aesthetics* (New York 1958)
460.

No analysis could possibly reduce to
order, I believe, the mass of inconsistent
detail that appears about the central
theme, or disentangle what is accretion
from what is the original story [of *Two
Sisters*]. Yet the fact remains that a
large number of the versions are excellent,
each in its way, and impress us almost
equally by the pathos with which they
invest the tale. In other words, a single
ballad—since we must assume that
somewhere and sometime it had a
beginning—has become diversified by the
processes of variation into a number of
virtually independent ballads, which
treat the same theme in different ways,
but with approximately equal success.

G. H. Gerould, *The Ballad of Tradition* (1932)
176.

Mimesis

110

There seem to be two causes that give rise to poetry in general, and they are both natural. The impulse to imitate is inherent in man from his childhood; he is distinguished among the animals by being the most imitative of them, and he takes the first steps of his education by imitating. Every one's enjoyment of imitation is also inborn. What happens with works of art demonstrates this.

Aristotle, *Poetics* iv; tr. L. J. Potts (Cambridge 1959) 20.

111

Poesy therefore, is an art of imitation : for so Aristotle termeth it in the word *mimesis*, that is to say a representing, counterfeiting, or figuring forth so to speak metaphorically. A speaking picture, with this end, to teach and delight.

Sir Philip Sidney, *The Defence of Poesy* (1595); *Works* ed. A. Feuillerat iii (Cambridge 1912) 9.

112

All poetry, to speak with Aristotle and the Greek critics (if for so plain a point authorities be thought wanting) is, properly, imitation. It is, indeed, the noblest and most extensive of the mimetic arts; having all creation for its object, and ranging the entire circuit of universal being.

Bishop Richard Hurd, 'Discourse on Poetical Imitation' (1751); *Works* ii (1811) 111f.

113

An 'imitation' is brought about ... on the assumption that the poet, in making it, was intent on using certain possibilities of language in order to create in us, by certain devices of technique, the illusion of human beings more or less like ourselves doing or undergoing something, for the sake of the emotional effects naturally evoked by such characters, passions or actions in real life when we view them as disinterested yet sympathetic spectators.

R. S. Crane, *The Languages of Criticism and the Structure of Poetry* (Toronto 1953) 48.

114

While these categories [Time, Identity, Casuality and Freedom] as they operate in art and life, are not sharply discontinuous, they are sufficiently distinct to provide us with a standard beyond the work of art, a frame of reference located in life itself. By this means we may judge any work more or less adequate as an imitation of reality and we may compare different works in these terms. These categories control and regulate experience, so that if a novelist convinces us that his handling of them is truthful, then there is a good chance that the particular experience he portrays as an end-product of these categories will also strike us as true to life. The texture of the created fictional world—the society portrayed, the values assumed, the emotions rendered,—may be alien, but the shape of the world will be familiar.

W. J. Harvey, *Character and the Novel* (1965) 22.

115

[The poet's] imitation in language is much more devious. He often prefers to enact his meaning; to make a pattern which, when it plays itself through to the reader's mind, enacts the quality of the experience or the movement of consciousness that he is writing about.

W. Nowottny, *The Language Poets Use* (1965) 112.

116

When poetry—or literary art generally —wishes ... to convey affective attitudes in an organised way, it is still compelled to make some statement about reality. The emotions are only found in real life adhering to bits of reality; therefore bits of reality—and moreover *organised* bits—must always be presented to achieve the emotional attitude.

Christopher Caudwell, *Illusion and Reality* (1946) 153.

117

We renounce that erroneous aesthetic (even though it has been responsible for certain masterpieces) which would have the poet fill the delicate pages of his book with the actual and palpable wood of trees, rather than with the poet's shuddering or the silent scattering of thunder through the foliage....

It is not *description* which can unveil the efficacy and beauty of monuments, seas, or the human face in all their maturity and native state, but rather evocation, *allusion, suggestion*. These somewhat arbitrary terms reveal what may well be a very decisive tendency in modern literature, a tendency which limits literature and yet sets it free. For what is the magic charm of art, if not this: that, beyond the confines of the fistful of dust or of all other reality, beyond the book itself, beyond the very text, it delivers up that volatile scattering which we call ... the Spirit, who cares for nothing except universal musicality.

Speech is no more than a commercial approach to reality. In literature, allusion is sufficient: essences are distilled and then embodied in Idea.

Out of a number of words, poetry fashions a single new world which is total in itself and foreign to the language —a kind of incantation. Thus the desired isolation of language is effected.

Stéphane Mallarmé, 'The Crisis in Poetry' (1886-1896); *Oeuvres complètes* (Paris 1945) 365f.

118

In a sense, every poem is a microcosmos, a discrete and independent universe with its laws provided by the poet; his decision is absolute; he can make things good or bad, great or small, powerful or weak, just as he wills; he may make men taller than mountains or smaller than atoms, he may suspend whole cities in the air, he may destroy creation or reform it; within his universe the impossible becomes the possible, the necessary the contingent—if he but says they do.

Elder Olson, 'Sailing to Byzantium': Prolegomena to a poetics of the lyric', *The University of Kansas City Review* viii (1942) 216f.

out of the material supplied to it by actual nature. It affords us entertainment where experience proves too commonplace, and we even use it to remodel experience, always following, no doubt, laws that are based on analogy, but still also following principles which have a higher seat in the reason.... By this means we get a sense of our freedom from the laws of association.

Immanuel Kant, *Critique of Judgment* (Liebau and Berlin 1790) II xlix; tr. J. C. Meredith (Oxford 1952) 176.

119

The Imagination (as a productive faculty of cognition) is a powerful agent for creating, as it were, a second nature

120

To imagine a language means to imagine a form of life.

J. J. Wittgenstein, *Philosophical Investigations* (Oxford 1958) 19.

Story

121

Is it a story, that our first parents fell
from a paradisiacal state?

Richard Watson, An Apology for the Bible
(1796) 74.

122

JAQUES   And so, from hour to hour we ripe and ripe,
　　　　And then from hour to hour we rot and rot,
　　　　And thereby hangs a tale.

William Shakespeare, As You Like It II vii 26-8.

123

Old fabulous and fantastical books,
of the table round ... whose ... vain
fabulosity, the light of God has abolished
utterly.

A Declaration of the Faith (1539), reprinted
Jeremy Collier, An Ecclesiastical History of
Great Britain ii (1714) 36.

124

He [the poet] doth as if your journey
should lie through a fair vineyard, at
the very first, give you a cluster of
grapes, that full of that taste, you may
long to pass further. He beginneth not
with obscure definitions, which must blur
the margent with interpretations, and
load the memory with doubtfulness: but
he cometh to you with words set in
delightful proportion ... and with a tale
forsooth he cometh unto you, with a
tale, which holdeth children from play,
and old men from the chimney corner;
and pretending no more, doth intend the
winning of the mind from wickedness to
virtue; even as the child is often brought
to take most wholesome things by hiding
them in such other as have a pleasant
taste.

Sir Philip Sidney, The Defence of Poesy (1595);
Works ed. A. Feuillerat iii (Cambridge 1912)
20.

125

A good plot ... to my own feeling, is
the most significant part of a tale....

A novel should give a picture of common life enlivened by humour and sweetened by pathos. To make that picture worthy of attention, the canvas should be crowded with real portraits, not of individuals known to the world or to the author, but of created personages impregnated with traits of character which are known. To my thinking, the plot is but the vehicle for all this; and when you have the vehicle without the passengers, a story of mystery in which the agents never spring to life, you have but a wooden show. There must, however, be a story. You must provide a vehicle of some sort.

Anthony Trollope, *Autobiography* (1883) ch. vii; ed. M. Sadleir (1950) 126.

126

Yes—oh dear yes—the novel tells a story. That is the fundamental aspect without which it could not exist. That is the highest factor common to all novels, and I wish that it was not so, that it could be something different ... not this low atavistic form.

For the more we look at the story ... the more we disentangle it from the finer growths that it supports, the less shall we find to admire. It runs like a backbone—or may I say tape-worm, for its beginning and end are arbitrary. It is immensely old. ... The primitive audience was an audience of shock-heads, gaping round the camp-fire, fatigued with contending against the mammoth or the woolly rhinoceros, and only kept awake by suspense. What would happen next?

E. M. Forster, *Aspects of the Novel* (1927) ch. ii; (1949) 27f.

127

It is astonishing how little attention critics have paid to Story considered in itself. Granted the story, the style in which it should be told, the order in which it should be disposed, and (above all) the delineation of the characters, have been abundantly discussed. But the Story itself, the series of imagined events, is nearly always passed over in silence, or else treated exclusively as affording opportunities for the delineation of character.... This has had a curious result. Those forms of literature in which Story exists merely as a means to something else—for example, the novel of manners where the story is there for the sake of the characters, or the criticism of social conditions—have had full justice done to them; but those forms in which everything else is there for the sake of the story have been given little serious attention.... In talking of books which are 'mere stories' ... nearly everyone makes the assumption that 'excitement' is the only pleasure they ever give or are intended to give. *Excitement*, in this sense, may be defined as the alternate tension and appeasement of imagined anxiety. This is what I think untrue. In some such books, and for some readers, another factor comes in.... Something which the educated receive from poetry can reach the masses through stories of adventure, and almost in no other way. ... The re-reader is looking not for actual surprises (which can come only once) but for a certain ideal surprisingness.... It must be understood that this series—the *plot*, as we call it—is only really a net whereby to catch something else. The real theme may be, and perhaps usually is, something that has no sequence in it, something other than a process and much more like a state or quality. Giantship, otherness, the desolation of space, are examples.

C. S. Lewis, 'On Stories', *Essays Presented to Charles Williams* (Oxford 1947) 90, 92f, 102f.

128

I had so worked upon my imagination as really to believe that about the whole mansion and domain there hung an atmosphere peculiar to themselves and their immediate vicinity—an atmosphere which had no affinity with the air of heaven, but which had reeked up from the decayed trees, and the gray wall, and the silent tarn—a pestilent and mystic vapour, dull, sluggish, faintly discernible, and leaden-hued.

Edgar Allan Poe, 'The Fall of the House of Usher' (1839); *The Fall of the House of Usher and Other Tales* ed. R. P. Blackmur (New York 1960) 115.

129

It is, perhaps, not often that a map figures so largely in a tale, yet it is always important. The author must know his countryside, whether real or imaginary, like his hand.... With the map before him, he will scarce allow the sun to set in the east, as it does in *The Antiquary*. ... But it is my contention—my superstition, if you like—that who is faithful to his map, and consults it, and draws from it his inspiration, daily and hourly, gains positive support, and not mere negative immunity from accident. The tale has a root there; it grows in that soil; it has a spine of its own behind the words. Better if the country be real, and he has walked every foot of it and knows every milestone. But even with imaginary places, he will do well in the beginning to provide a map; as he studies it, relations will appear that he had not thought upon; he will discover obvious, though unsuspected, shortcuts and footprints for his messengers; and even when a map is not all the plot, as it was in *Treasure Island*, it will be found to be a mine of suggestion.

Robert Louis Stevenson, 'My First Book' (1894); *Works*, Vailima edn. v (1922-3) pp. xxxf.

130

As regards such things as landscape and scenery, I never feel inclined to describe them; indeed I tend to miss such writing out, when I am reading, which may be a sign that I am not fitted for it. I make an exception of Thomas Hardy, but surely his presentation of natural features almost as characters puts him on a plane of his own, and almost carries the thing into the human world. In the case of Jane Austen, I hurry through her words about Lyme and its surroundings, in order to return to her people.

It might be better to give more account of people's homes and intimate background, but I hardly see why the date and style of the Gavestons' house should be given, as I did not think of them as giving their attention to it, and as a house of a different date and style would have done for them equally well. It would be something to them that it was old and beautiful, but it would be enough.

Ivy Compton-Burnett, 'A Conversation Between I. Compton-Burnett and M. Jourdain', *Orion* (1945) 23.

131

POOH-BAH Merely corroborative detail, intended to give artistic verisimilitude to a bald and unconvincing narrative.

W. S. Gilbert, *The Mikado* (1885); *Original Plays* iii (1919) 209.

132

There is always, of course, for the story-teller, the irresistible determinant and the incalculable advantage of his interest in the story *as such*; it is ever, obviously, overwhelmingly, the prime and precious thing (as other than this I have never been able to see it); as to which what makes for it, with whatever headlong energy, may be said to pale before the energy with which it simply makes for itself. It rejoices, none the less, at its best, to seem to offer itself in a light, to seem to know, and with the very last knowledge, what it's about—liable as it yet is at moments to be caught by us with its tongue in its cheek and absolutely no warrant but its splendid impudence. Let us grant then that the impudence is always there—there, so to speak, for grace and effect and *allure*; there, above all, because the Story is just the spoiled child of art, and because, as we are always disappointed when the pampered don't 'play up', we like it, to that extent, to look all its character. It probably does so, in truth, even when we most flatter ourselves that we negotiate with it by treaty.

Henry James, Preface to *The Ambassadors* (1909); *The Art of the Novel* ed. R. P. Blackmur (New York 1934) 314f.

133

We have defined a story as a narrative of events arranged in their time-sequence. A plot is also a narrative of events, the emphasis falling on causality. 'The king died and then the queen died', is a story. 'The king died, and then the queen died of grief' is a plot. The time-sequence is preserved, but the sense of causality overshadows it. Or again: 'The queen died, no one knew why, until it was discovered that it was through grief at the death of the king.' This is a plot with a mystery in it, a form capable of high development. It suspends the time-sequence, it moves as far away from the story as its limitations will allow.... Mystery is essential to a plot, and cannot be appreciated without intelligence. To the curious it is just another 'and then—'. To appreciate a mystery, part of the mind must be left behind, brooding, while the other part goes marching on.

E. M. Forster, *Aspects of the Novel* (1927) ch. v; (1949) 82ff.

134

It is better for a novel to have a plot. Otherwise it has no shape, and incidents that have no part in a formal whole seem to have less significance.... And a plot gives rise to secondary scenes, that bring out personality, and give scope for revealing character. If the plot were taken out of a book, a good deal of what may seem unconnected with it, would have to go. A plot is like the bones of a person, not interesting like expression or signs of experience, but the support of the whole.... As regards plots I find

real life no help at all. Real life seems to
have no plots.

Ivy Compton-Burnett, 'A Conversation', *Orion*
(1945) 24f.

135

With regard to novels, I should like to
see one undertaken without any plot at
all. I do not mean that it should have no
story ... but avoiding all stage tricks and
strong situations, till some death or
marriage should afford a natural conclusion to the book.

Mary Russell Mitford, Letter to Sir William
Elford, 13 May 1815; *The Letters of Mary
Russell Mitford* ed. R. B. Johnson (1925) 129f.

136

What I should like to do is to write a
book about nothing, a book with no
reference to anything outside itself,
which would stand on its own by the
inner strength of its style, just as the
earth holds itself without support in space,
a book which would have hardly any
subject, or at any rate one that is barely
perceptible, if that were possible. The
best works are those with least matter;
the nearer the expression approaches
thought, the more the word is silenced
by it and disappears, then the more
beautiful the work becomes. I think the
future of art lies this way. I see it
growing more and more spiritualized.

Gustave Flaubert, Letter to Louise Colet, 16
January 1852; *Correspondance* i (Paris 1922)
417.

137

Why, sir, if you were to read Richardson
for the story, your impatience would be
so much fretted that you would hang
yourself.

Samuel Johnson, reported Boswell, *Life of
Samuel Johnson*, 6 April 1772; ed. G. B. Hill
and L. F. Powell ii (Oxford 1934) 175.

138

In order that the most banal event may
become an adventure, it is a necessary
and sufficient condition that one should
set about relating it. This is what deceives
people : a man is always a subject of
stories; he lives surrounded by his own
stories and the stories of others; he sees
what happens to him through them; and
he tries to live his life as if he narrated
it.

Jean-Paul Sartre, *La Nausée* (1934); tr. R. Baldick (Harmondsworth 1965) 61.

139

While in the life of the human race the
mythical is an early and primitive
stage, in the life of the individual it is a
late and mature one. What is gained is
an insight into the higher truth depicted
in the actual; a smiling knowledge of the
eternal, the ever-being and authentic; a
knowledge of the schema in which and
according to which the supposed
individual lives, unaware, in his naïve
belief in himself as unique in space and
time, of the extent to which his life is
but formula and repetition and his path
marked out for him by those who trod it
before him. His character is a mythical

role which the actor just emerged from the depths to the light plays in the illusion that it is his own and unique, that he, as it were, has invented it all himself, with a dignity and security of which his supposed unique individuality in time and space is not the source, but rather which he creates out of his deeper consciousness in order that something which was once founded and legitimized shall again be represented and once more for good or ill, whether nobly or basely, in any case after its own kind conduct itself according to pattern. Actually, if his existence consisted merely in the unique and the present, he would not know how to conduct himself at all; he would be confused, helpless, unstable in his own self-regard.

Thomas Mann, 'Freud and the Future' (1936); *Essays* tr. H. T. Lower-Porter (New York 1957) 317f.

140

Examine for a moment an ordinary mind on an ordinary day. The mind receives a myriad impressions—trivial, fantastic, evanescent, or engraved with the sharpness of steel. From all sides they come, an incessant show of innumerable atoms; and as they fall, as they shape themselves into the life of Monday or Tuesday, the accent falls differently from of old; the moment of importance came not here but there; so that, if a writer were a free man and not a slave, if he could write what he chose, not what he must, if he could base his work upon his own feeling and not upon convention, there would be no plot, no comedy, no tragedy, no love interest or catastrophe in the accepted style, and perhaps not a single button sewn on as the Bond Street tailors would have it. Life is not a series of gig lamps symmetrically arranged; life is a luminous halo, a semi-transparent envelope surrounding us from the beginning of consciousness to the end.... Let us record the atoms as they fall, let us trace the pattern, however disconnected and incoherent in appearance, which each sight or incident scores upon the consciousness.

Virginia Woolf, 'Modern Fiction' (1919); *Collected Essays* ii (1966) 106f.

141

We may define stream-of-consciousness fiction as a type of fiction in which the basic emphasis is placed on exploration of the prespeech levels of consciousness for the purpose, primarily, of revealing the psychic being of the characters.

When some of the novels which fall into this classification are considered, it becomes immediately apparent that the techniques by which the subjects are controlled and the characters are presented are palpably different from one novel to the next. Indeed, there is no stream-of-consciousness technique. Instead, there are several quite different techniques which are used to present stream of consciousness.

Robert Humphrey, *Stream of Consciousness in the Modern Novel* (Berkeley and Los Angeles 1958) 4.

142

This sort of romantic story used often to be very complicated formally. For it was customary in Spenser's time to use a poly-phonic technique, interweaving different narrative strands in an intricate way. The enjoyment of the story in this sense—of the interplay of stories—could be a very sophisticated response indeed. But such a response is always difficult for us to make now.

C. S. Lewis, *Spenser's Images of Life* (Cambridge 1967) 2.

143

Critics often complain of the ordinary length of novels,—of the three volumes to which they are subjected; but few novels which have attained great success in England have been told in fewer pages. The novel-writer who sticks to novel-writing as his profession will certainly find that this burden of length is incumbent on him. How shall he carry his burden to the end? How shall he cover his space? Many great artists have by their practice opposed the doctrine which I now propose to preach; but they have succeeded I think in spite of their fault and by dint of their greatness. There should be no episodes [digressions] in a novel. Every sentence, every word, through all those pages, should tend to the telling of the story. Such episodes distract the attention of the reader, and always do so disagreeably. Who has not felt this to be the case even with *The Curious Impertinent* and with the history of *The Man of the Hill*? And if it be so with Cervantes and Fielding, who can hope to succeed? Though the novel which you have to write must be long, let it be all one.

Anthony Trollope, *Autobiography* (1883) ch. xii; ed. M. Sadleir (1950) 237f.

144

The modes of telling a story founded in these processes of outward and inward life derive their effectiveness from the superior mastery of images and pictures in grasping the attention—or, one might say with more fundamental accuracy, from the fact that our earliest, strongest impressions, our most intimate convictions, are simply images added to more or less of sensation. These are the primitive instruments of thought. Hence it is not surprising that early poetry took this way—telling a daring deed, a glorious achievement, without caring for what went before. The desire for orderly narration is a later, more reflective birth. The presence of Jack in the box affects every child: it is the more reflective lad, the miniature philosopher, who wants to know how he got there.

George Eliot, 'Leaves from a Note-book: Storytelling' (1879); *Works* Copyright edn. (1908-11) 299.

145

This eternal time-question is accordingly, for the novelist, always there and always formidable; always insisting on the *effect* of the great lapse and passage, of the 'dark backward and abysm', by the terms of truth, and on the effect of compression, of composition and form, by the terms of literary arrangement. It is really a business to terrify all but stout hearts into abject omission and mutilation, though the terror would indeed be more general were the general consciousness of the difficulty greater.

Henry James, Preface to *Roderick Hudson* (1907); *The Art of the Novel* ed. R. P. Blackmur (New York 1934) 14.

I do not know why this double time-reckoning arrests my attention or why I am at pains to point out both the personal and the objective, the time in which the narrator moves and that in which the narrative does so. This is a quite extraordinary interweaving of time-units, destined, moreover, to include even a third: namely the time which one day the courteous reader will take for the reading of what has been written; at which point he will be dealing with a threefold ordering of time: his own, that of the chronicler, and historic time.

Thomas Mann, *Doctor Faustus*, cit. A. A. Mendilow, *Time and the Novel* (1952) 89f.

The time-sequence cannot be destroyed without carrying in its ruin all that should have taken its place; the novel that would express values only becomes unintelligible and therefore valueless.

E. M. Forster, *Aspects of the Novel* (1927) ch. ii; (1949) 42.

The novel is the representation of events which take place in time, a representation submitted to the conditions of apparition and development of these events.—The recital is the presentation of events which have taken place, and of which the reproduction is regulated by the narrator in conformity with the laws of exposition and persuasion.... Thus, the recital

tends to the substitution of an order of conceptual exposition for the order of living production, and of rational proofs for aesthetic proofs.

Ramón Fernández, *Messages*, tr. M. Belgion (1927) 63-5.

But let the gentle-hearted reader be under no apprehension whatsoever. It is not destined that Eleanor shall marry Mr Slope or Bertie Stanhope. And here, perhaps, it may be allowed to the novelist to explain his views on a very important point in the art of telling tales. He ventures to reprobate that system which goes so far to violate all proper confidence between the author and his readers.... Our doctrine is, that the author and the reader should move along together in full confidence with each other.

Anthony Trollope, *Barchester Towers* (1857) ch. xv; ed. M. Sadleir i (1953) 143f.

Certain accomplished novelists have a habit of giving themselves away which must often bring tears to the eyes of people who take their fiction seriously. I was lately struck, in reading over the pages of Anthony Trollope, with his want of discretion in this particular. In a digression, a parenthesis or an aside, he conceded to the reader that he and his trusting friend are only 'making believe'. He admits that the events he narrates have not really happened, and that he can give his narrative any turn the reader may like best. Such a betrayal of a sacred office seems to me, I confess, a terrible crime.... It implies that the novelist is less occupied in looking for the truth than the historian, and in doing so it deprives him at a stroke of all his standing-room. To represent and illustrate the past, the actions of men, is the task of either writer.

Henry James, 'The Art of Fiction' (1884); *Selected Literary Criticism* ed. M. Shapira (Harmondsworth 1968) 80.

151

I have ... constantly inclined to the idea of the particular attaching case *plus* some near individual view of it; that nearness quite having this to become an imagined observer's, a projected, charmed painter's or poet's—however avowed the 'minor' quality in the latter—close and sensitive contact with it. Anything, in short, I now reflect, must have seemed to me better— better for the process and the effect of representation, my irrepressible ideal —than the mere muffled majesty of irresponsible 'authorship'.

Henry James, Preface to *The Golden Bowl* (1909); *The Art of the Novel* ed. R. P. Black- mur (New York 1934) 328.

152

The novelist can assume the god-like creative privilege and simply elect to consider the events of the story in their various aspects—emotional, scientific, economic, religious, metaphysical, etc.

He will modulate from one to the other— as from the aesthetic to the psychico- chemical aspect of things, from the religious to the physiological or financial. But perhaps this is a too tyrannical imposition of the author's will. Some people would think so. But need the author be so retiring? I think we're a bit too squeamish about these personal appearances nowadays.

Put a novelist into the novel. He justifies aesthetic generalizations, which may be interesting—at least to me. He also justifies experiment. Specimens of his work may illustrate other possible or impossible ways of telling a story. And if you have him telling parts of the same story as you are, you can make a variation on the theme. But why draw the line at one novelist inside your novel? Why not a second inside his? And a third inside the novel of the second? ... At about the tenth remove you might have a novelist telling your story in algebraic symbols or in terms of variations in blood-pressure, pulse, secretion of ductless glands and reaction times.

Aldous Huxley, *Point Counter Point* (1928); (Harmondsworth 1955) 298f.

153

It happened to him (third-personal past); Here and now (third-personal present); Listen while I tell you (first-personal past, as if spoken); As I sit here at my desk (first-personal past, as if written); Opening another bottle, he continued (first-personal past, spoken, in third- or first-personal framework all-dialogue); Spotlight and flourish (in form of a play); One or two routine questions (catechetical); Dear Lovelace (epistolary); Dear me (in form of diary); Orderly scrapbook (documentary); Disorderly mind (stream of consciousness); String of pearls (series of first-personal narratives in third-personal framework); Known only to the Emperor?

Wallace Hildick, *Thirteen Types of Narrative* (1968), publishers' summary of contents.

154

Why is the present tense (not the 'historic present') not suitable for the extended novel? It is often used in the anecdote, and not infrequently in the short tale, and can here be perfectly suitable. Why not for the extended tale?

Roy Pascal, in *Modern Lang. Rev.* lvii (1962) 9.

155

The following work was found in the library of an ancient catholic family in the north of England. It was printed in Naples, in the black letter, in the year 1529.... The style is purest Italian.

William Marshall [Horace Walpole], Preface to the first edn. of *The Castle of Otranto* (1764); ed. W. S. Lewis (1964) 3.

The favourable manner in which this little piece has been received by the public, calls upon the author to explain the grounds on which he composed it.

H. W. [Horace Walpole], Preface to the second edn. of *The Castle of Otranto* (1765); ed. W. S. Lewis (1964) 7.

156

Here it is, this I toss and take again;
Small-quarto size, part print part manuscript:
A book in shape but, really, pure crude fact
Secreted from man's life when hearts beat hard,
And brains, high-blooded, ticked two centuries since.

. . . . .

Still read I on, from written title-page
To written index, on through street and street,
At the Strozzi, at the Pillar, at the Bridge;
Till, by the time I stood at home again
In Casa Guidi by Felice Church,
Under the doorway where the black begins
With the first stone-slab of the staircase cold,
I had mastered the contents, knew the whole truth
Gathered together, bound in this book,
Print three-fifths, written supplement the rest.

Robert Browning, *The Ring and the Book* (1868) 84-119.

An hour, once it lodges in the queer element of the human spirit, may be stretched to fifty or a hundred times its clock length; on the other hand, an hour may be accurately represented on the timepiece of the mind by one second. This extraordinary discrepancy between time on the clock and time in the mind is less known than it should be and deserves fuller investigation.... When a man has reached the age of thirty ... time when he is thinking becomes inordinately long, time when he is doing becomes inordinately short.

Virginia Woolf, *Orlando* (1928) (Harmonds-worth 1942) 58.

But little time will be left me to ponder upon my destiny! The circles rapidly grow small—we are plunging madly within the grasp of the whirlpool—and amid a roaring, and bellowing, and thundering of ocean and tempest, the ship is quivering—oh God! and—going down!

Edgar Allan Poe, 'Ms Found in a Bottle' (1833); *The Fall of the House of Usher and Other Tales* ed. R. P. Blackmur (New York 1960) 31.

Realism

159

Let us start with something very simple and say that realism is 'the objective representation of contemporary social reality'. This, I admit, says little and raises such questions as what is meant by 'objective' and what is meant by 'reality'. But we must not rush to consider ultimate questions but see this description in a historical context as a polemical weapon against romanticism, as a theory of exclusion as well as inclusion. It rejects the fantastic, the fairy-tale-like, the allegorical and the symbolic, the highly stylised, the purely abstract and decorative. It means that we want no myth, no *Märchen*, no world of dreams. It implies also a rejection of the improbable, of pure chance, and of extraordinary events, since reality is obviously conceived at that time, in spite of all local and personal differences, as the orderly world of nineteenth century science, a world of cause and effect, a world without miracle, without transcendence even if the individual may have preserved a religious faith. The term 'reality' is also a term of inclusion: the ugly, the revolting, the low are legitimate subjects of art. Taboo subjects such as sex and dying (love and death were always allowed) are now admitted into art.

René Wellek, *Concepts of Criticism* (New Haven and London 1963) 241.

160

In the worst inn's worst room, with mat half-hung,
The floors of plaster and the walls of dung,
On once a flock-bed, but repair'd with straw,
With tape-tied curtains, never meant to draw,
The George and Garter dangling from that bed
Where tawdry yellow strove with dirty red,
Great Villiers lies. . . .

Alexander Pope, *Moral Essays* iii (1732) 299-305.

161

Four storeys climbing to her bow'r;
Then, seated on a three-legg'd chair,

Takes off her artificial hair:
Now, picking out a crystal eye,
She wipes it clean, and lays it by.
Her eye-brows from a mouse's hide,
Stuck on with art on either side,
Pulls off with care, and first displays 'em,
Then in a play-book smoothly lays 'em.
Now dextrously her plumpers draws,
That serve to fill her hollow jaws.
Untwists a wire; and from her gums
A set of teeth completely comes.
Pulls out the rags contriv'd to prop
Her flabby dugs and down they drop.

· · · · ·

With gentlest touch, she next explores
Her shankers, issues, running sores,
Effects of many a sad disaster;
And then to each applies a plaster.

· · · · ·

Corinna wakes. A dreadful sight!
Behold the ruins of the night!
A wicked rat her plaster stole,
Half eat, and dragg'd it to his hole.
The crystal eye, alas, was missed;
And puss had on her plumpers pissed.
A pigeon pick'd her issue-peas;
And Shock her tresses fill'd with fleas.

Jonathan Swift, 'A Beautiful Young Nymph'
(1731); *Swift's Poems* ed. H. Williams ii
(Oxford 1958) 581 ff.

162

I hate vulgar realism in literature. The man who could call a spade a spade should be compelled to use one. It is all he is fit for.

Oscar Wilde, *The Picture of Dorian Gray*
(1891) ch. xvii; *Works* (1966) 147.

163

The charge of being 'too realistic' is easier to lay than to demonstrate. The charge can also lead easily to a philosophic and semantic shambles. If we think of some of the different uses of the word realism—as opposed to nominalism, or of realism as the antipode of idealism, of Courbet's realism, of social realism, magic realism, or the real McCoy—it is easy to understand why Ortega y Gasset maintained that to say simply that an art is realistic is the most emphatic way of saying nothing. Nevertheless, it seems reasonable to call Potter and most seventeenth-century Dutch painters realists. If we must have a label, 'realist' is a satisfactory one. Today, when it is no longer necessary to argue that the importance of a work of art *qua* work of art depends on the nobility or the meanness of its subject, 'realist' is no longer at all an opprobrious word.

Seymour Slive, *Delta* v (1962-3) 26f.

164

Still the arts are not to be slighted on the ground that they create by imitation of natural objects; for ... we must recognise that they give no bare reproduction of the thing seen but go back to the Ideas from which nature itself derives, and furthermore, that much of their work is all their own; they are moulders of beauty and add where nature is lacking. Thus Pheidias wrought the Zeus upon no model among things of sense but by apprehending what form Zeus must take if he chose to become manifest to sight.

Plotinus, *Enneads*, tr. S. Mckenna and B. S. Page (1926) V viii 1.

165

Baudelaire repudiated with indignation the charge that he was what is called a realist, and he was doubtless right in

doing so. He had too much fancy to embroiders and elaborates—endeavours to impart that touch of strangeness and mystery which is the very *raison d'être* of poetry. Baudelaire was a poet, and for a poet to be a realist is of course nonsense.

Henry James, 'Charles Baudelaire' (1876); *Selected Literary Criticism* ed. M. Shapira (Harmondsworth 1968) 57.

166

Language and science are abbreviations of reality; art is an intensification of reality. Language and science depend upon one and the same process of abstraction; art may be described as a continuous process of concretion. In our scientific description of a given object we begin with a great number of observations which at first sight are only a loose conglomeration of detached facts. But the farther we proceed the more these individual phenomena tend to assume a definite shape and become a systematic whole. What science is searching for is some central feature of a given object from which all its particular qualities may be derived. If a chemist knows the atomic number of a certain element he possesses a clue to a full insight into its structure and constitution. From this number he may deduce all the characteristic properties of the element. But art does not admit this sort of conceptual simplification and deductive generalisation. It does not inquire into the qualities or causes of things; it gives us the intuition of the form of things. But this too is by no means a mere repetition of something we had before. It is a true and genuine discovery. The artist is just as much a discoverer of the forms of nature as the scientist is a discoverer of facts or natural laws.

Ernst Cassirer, An Essay on Man (New Haven, Conn. 1944) 144f.

167

'Naturalism' ... was in constant competition with 'realism' and was often identified with it. It is an ancient philosophical term for materialism, epicureanism, or any secularism. In a literary sense it can be found again in Schiller, in the preface to the Bride of Messina (1803) as something which Schiller finds worth combating, as in poetry 'everything is a symbol of the real.' Heine, in a passage of the 1831 Salon which profoundly impressed Baudelaire, proclaimed himself a 'super-naturalist in art' in contrast to his 'naturalism' in religion. But again the term, widely used for faithful adherence to nature, crystallized as a specific slogan only in France. It was captured by Zola, and since the preface to the second edition of his novel Thérèse Raquin (1868) it became more and more identified with his theory of the scientific, experimental novel. But the distinction between 'realism' and 'naturalism' was not stabilized for a long time. Fernand Brunetière in his Le Roman Naturaliste (1893) discusses Flaubert, Daudet, Maupassant, George Eliot as well as Zola under this title. The separation of the terms is only a work of modern literary scholarship.

René Wellek, Concepts of Criticism (New Haven and London 1963) 233.

168

A contemptible reproach which they heap on us naturalistic writers is the desire to be solely photographers.... Well, with the application of the experimental method to the novel that quarrel dies out. The idea of experiment carries with it the idea of modification. We start, indeed, from the true facts, which are our indestructible basis; but to show the mechanism of these facts it is necessary for us to produce and direct the phenomena; this is our share of invention, here is the genius in the book.

Émile Zola, 'The Experimental Novel' (1880); The Modern Tradition ed. C. Feidelson and R. Ellmann (New York 1965) 274.

169

All these things—the decay of the bourgeoisie, the wretchedness of the common people, the resistance of the working class—Zola depicts in his novels, but without hope of a solution, as a nightmare never to be shaken off. In this 'objective' portrayal of appalling social conditions and in this refusal to describe them as changeable lie both the strength and the weakness of naturalism....

This photographic recording of conditions, thought of statically rather than dialectically, created a feeling of meaninglessness, an oppressive, discouraging atmosphere of passivity. In a certain sense naturalism anticipated the dehumanisation, the dull and despairing surrender of things made omnipotent by the inhuman laws of capitalist production.

Ernst Fischer, The Necessity of Art (Harmondsworth 1963) 78, 80.

170

But the world is neither significant nor absurd. It *is*, quite simply. That, in any case, is the most remarkable thing about it. And suddenly this evidence strikes us with irresistible force. All at once the beautiful construction collapses; opening our eyes to the unexpected, we have experienced once too often the shock of this stubborn reality we were pretending to have plumbed to its depths. Around us, defying the mob of our animistic or housewifely adjectives, things *are there*. Their surfaces are clear and smooth, intact, neither dubiously glittering, nor transparent. All our literature has not yet succeeded in penetrating their smallest corner, in softening their slightest curve.

Alain Robbe-Grillet, *Pour un nouveau roman* (Paris 1963) 21.

171

It was a headgear of a composite order, containing elements of an ordinary hat, a hussar's busby, a lancer's cap, a sealskin cap and a nightcap : one of those wretched things whose mute hideousness suggests un-plumbed depths, like an idiot's face. Ovoid and stiffened with whalebone, it began with three convex strips; then followed alternating lozenges of velvet and rabbit's fur, separated by a red band; then came a kind of bag, terminating in a cardboard-lined polygon intricately decorated with braid. From this hung a long, excessively thin cord ending in a kind of tassell of gold netting. The cap was new; its peak was shiny.

Gustave Flaubert, *Madame Bovary* (1856) ch. i; *Oeuvres* ed. A. Thibaudet and R. Dumesnil i (Paris 1951) 328.

172

He is to exhibit in his portraits of nature such prominent and striking features, as recall the original to every mind; and must neglect the minuter discriminations, which one may have remarked, and another have neglected, for those characteristics which are alike obvious to vigilance and carelessness.... He must divest himself of the prejudices of his age or country; he must consider right and wrong in their abstracted and invariable state; he must disregard present laws and opinions, and rise to general and transcendental truths, which will always be the same.

Samuel Johnson, *Rasselas* (1759) ch. x; ed. R. W. Chapman (Oxford 1927) 50f.

173

Imitation cannot serve as a standard of the value of art, because, if the chief property of art is the infection of others with the sensation described by the artist, the infection with the sensation not only does not coincide with the description of the details of what is being conveyed, but for the most part is impaired by a superabundance of details. The attention of him who received artistic impressions is distracted by all these well-observed details, and on account of them that author's feeling, if he has any, is not communicated.

Leo Tolstoy, 'What is Art?' (1897); *What is Art?* tr. A. Maud (Oxford 1930) 186f.

I think Mr Dickens has in many things quite a divine genius so to speak, and certain notes in his song are so delightful and admirable, that I should never think of trying to imitate him, only to hold my tongue and admire him. I quarrel with his art in many respects: which I don't think represented nature duly.... The art of novels *is* to represent nature: to convey as strongly as possible the sentiment of reality—in a tragedy or a poem or a lofty drama you aim at producing different emotions; the figures moving, and their words sounding, heroically: but in a drawing room drama a coat is a coat, and a poker a poker; and must be nothing else according to my ethics, not an embroidered tunic, nor a great red-hot instrument like the Pantomime weapon.

W. M. Thackeray, Letters to David Masson, 6 May 1851; *Letters* ed. G. N. Ray ii (1945) 772f.

One can speak best from one's own taste, and I may therefore venture to say that the air of reality (solidity of specification) seems to me to be the supreme virtue of a novel—the merit on which all its other merits (including that conscious moral purpose of which Mr Besant speaks) helplessly and submissively depend. If it be not there they are all as nothing, and if these be there, they owe their effect to the success with which the author has produced the illusion of life.

Henry James, 'The Art of Fiction' (1884); *Selected Literary Criticism* ed. M. Shapira (Harmondsworth 1968) 86f.

Formal realism is, of course, like the rules of evidence, only a convention, and there is no reason why the report on human life which is presented by it should be in fact any truer than those presented through the very different conventions of other literary genres.

Ian Watt, *The Rise of the Novel* (1957) 32.

I came to understand that modern realism in the form it reached in France in the early nineteenth century is, as an aesthetic phenomenon, characterised by a complete emancipation from the doctrine [of the ancients regarding the several levels of literary representation]. The emancipation is more complete, and more significant for later forms of the imitation of life, than the mixture of *le sublime* with *le grotesque* proclaimed by the contemporary romanticists. When Stendhal and Balzac took random individuals from daily life in their dependence upon historical circumstances and made them the subjects of serious, problematic, and even tragic representations, they broke with the classical rule of distinct levels of style, for according to this rule, everyday practical reality could find a place in literature only within the frame of a low or intermediate kind of style, that is to say, as either grotesquely comic or pleasant, light, colourful and elegant entertainment. They thus completed a development which had long been in preparation (since the time of the novel of manners and the *comédie larmoyante* of the eighteenth century, and more pronouncedly since the *Sturm und Drang* and early romanticism). They opened the way for modern realism, which has ever since developed in increasingly rich forms, in keeping with the constantly changing and expanding reality of modern life.

Erich Auerbach, *Mimesis* (1946); (Princeton, N.J. 1968) 554.

178

Absolute liberty is as meaningless as realism in a vacuum. Both are relative terms, referring us back to a definite series of restraints from which we have managed to secure some degree of release. When we call a book realistic, we mean that it is relatively free from bookish artificialities; it convinces us, where more conventional books do not. It offers us *realiora*, if not *realia*, as Eugene Zamyatin succinctly put it: not quite the real things, but things that seem more real than those offered us by others. By rereading these other books too and reconstructing their conventions, we can relate them to our comparatively realistic book and specify its new departures more precisely. We can define realism by its context.

Harry Levin, *The Gates of Horn* (New York 1966) 66.

Allegory and Symbolism

179

One has to realize that the meaning of this work [the *Divina Commedia*] is not simple, but rather to be termed polysemous—that is, having many meanings. The first meaning is that drawn from the letter, the second that drawn from things signified by the letter. The first is called literal, the second allegorical, moral, or anagogical. To illustrate the mode we may apply it to the following verses: 'When Israel went out of Egypt, the house of Jacob from a people of strange language, Judah was his sanctuary and Israel his dominion.' If we look only to the literal meaning, we see a reference to the departure of the children of Israel from Egypt in the time of Moses; if to the allegory, our redemption accomplished by Christ; if to the moral sense, the conversion of the soul from the woe and misery of sin to a state of grace; if to the anagogical sense, the departure of the consecrated soul from the slavery of this corruption to the liberty of eternal glory. And though these mystic senses may be called by various names, they can all in general be termed allegorical, since they are diverse from the literal or historical. For allegory is derived from *alleon* in Greek, which in Latin appears as *alienum*, or diverse.

In view of this, it is evident that the subject with which the alternative senses are concerned should be double. So one must regard the subject of this work as it is received according to the letter; then at the subject as it is understood allegorically. The subject of the whole work, then, taken merely in its literal sense, is simply the state of the souls after death: from that subject comes the whole action of the work and with that it is occupied. But if the entire work is taken allegorically the subject is man, in so far as through his free will he is liable by his merits and demerits to just rewards and punishments.

Dante, *Letter to Can Grande* vii-viii; *Literary Criticism: Plato to Dryden* ed. A. H. Gilbert (New York &c. 1940) 202f.

180

Allegories are the natural mirrors of ideology.

Angus Fletcher, *Allegory: The Theory of a Symbolic Mode* (Ithaca, N.Y. 1964) 368.

181

It is obvious that anything that is gained with fatigue seems sweeter than what is acquired without any effort. The plain truth, since it is quickly understood with little difficulty, delights us and passes from the mind. But, in order that it may be more pleasing, because acquired with labour, and therefore be better retained, the poets hide the truth beneath things apparently quite contrary to it. For that reason they produce fables, rather than some other covering, because their beauty attracts those whom neither philosophical demonstrations nor persuasions would have been able to allure. What then shall we say about the poets? Shall we hold that they are madmen, as their senseless adversaries, saying they know not what, have thought them? Certainly not; on the contrary they employ in their productions the most profound thought, which is equivalent to everything hidden in the fruit, and admirable and splendid language, which corresponds to the rind and the leaves.

Giovanni Boccaccio, *Life of Dante* xxii; *Literary Criticism: Plato to Dryden* ed. A. H. Gilbert (New York &c. 1940) 211.

182

As in a flourishing and ripe fruit tree
Nature hath made the bark to save the bole,
The bole the sap, the sap to deck the whole
With leaves and branches, they to bear and shield
The useful fruit, the fruit it self to yield
Guard to the kernel, and for that all those
(Since out of that again the whole tree grows):
So in our tree of man, whose nervy root
Springs in his top, from thence even to his foot
There runs a mutual aid through all his parts,
All joined in one to serve his queen of arts [side note: 'The soul'],
In which doth poesy like the kernel lie
Obscured, through her Promethean faculty
Can create men and make even death to live—
For which she should live honoured.

George Chapman, 'To Prince Henry' before *Iliads* (1609) 125-39; ed. A. Nicoll i (1957) 6.

183

That art is a mediocre art which demands from us an effort of reflection in order that we may be in a position to apprehend its images.

Ramón Fernández, 'On Philosophical Criticism', *Messages*, tr. M. Belgion (1927) 8.

184

Who that their fables can well moralize
The fruitful sentences are delectable;

Stephen Hawes, *Pastime of Pleasure* (1517) lines 947f.

185

All commentary, or the relating of the events of a narrative to conceptual terminology, is in one sense allegorical interpretation.

Northrop Frye, in *Encyclopedia of Poetry and Poetics* ed. A. Preminger (Princeton, N.J. 1965) 12.

186

It is plain that to fight against 'Temptation' is also to explore the inner world; and it is scarcely less plain that to do so is to be already on the verge of allegory. We cannot speak, perhaps we can hardly think, of an 'inner conflict' without a metaphor; and every metaphor is an allegory in little. And as the conflict becomes more and more important, it is inevitable that these metaphors should expand and coalesce, and finally turn into the fully-fledged allegorical poem. It would be a misunderstanding to suggest that there is another and better way of representing that inner world, and that we have found it in the novel and the drama. The gaze turned inward with a moral purpose does not discover *character*.

C. S. Lewis, *The Allegory of Love* (1938) 60f.

187

We may then safely define allegorical writing as the employment of one set of agents and images with actions and accompaniments correspondent, so as to convey, while in disguise, either moral qualities or conceptions of the mind that are not in themselves objects of the senses, or other images, agents, actions, fortunes, and circumstances so that the difference is everywhere presented to the eye or imagination, while the likeness is suggested to the mind; and this connectedly, so that the parts combine to form a consistent whole.

S. T. Coleridge, *Miscellaneous Criticism*, ed. T. M. Raysor (1936) 30.

188

A systematically complicated character will generate a large number of other protagonists who react against or with him in a syllogistic manner. I say 'generate', because the heroes in Dante and Spenser and Bunyan seem to create the worlds about them. They are like those people in real life who 'project', ascribing fictitious personalities to those whom they meet and live with. By analyzing the projections, we determine what is going on in the mind of the highly imaginative projector. By the same token, if the reader wants a sketch of the character of Redcrosse in Spenser, he lists the series of adventures and tests undergone by Redcrosse, not so much for the pleasure of seeing *how* Redcrosse reacts in each case, as to see, literally, what aspects of the hero have been displayed by the poet.... In this sense the subcharacters, the most numerous agents of an allegory, may be generated by the main protagonists, and the finest hero will then be the one who most naturally seems to generate subcharacters.

Angus Fletcher, *Allegory: The Theory of a Symbolic Mode* (Ithaca, N.J. 1964) 35f.

189

Allegory—a figure called inversion, where it is one in words, and an other in sentence and meaning.

Bibliotheca Eliotae ... enriched ... by Thomas Cooper (1552) Sig. D 6v.

190

An allegory is none other thing, but a metaphor, used throughout a whole sentence, or oration.

Thomas Wilson, *The Art of Rhetoric* (1560) iii; ed. G. H. Mair (Oxford 1909) 176.

191

Every speech wrested from his own natural signification to another not altogether so natural is a kind of dissimulation, because the words bear contrary countenance to the intent. But properly and in his principal virtue *allegoria* is when we do speak in sense translative and wrested from the own signification, nevertheless applied to another not altogether contrary, but having much conveniency with it as before we said of the metaphor: as for example if we should call the common wealth, a ship; the prince a pilot, the counsellors mariners, the storms wars, the calm and haven peace, this is spoken all in allegory: and because such inversion of sense in one single word is by the figure metaphor ... and this manner of inversion extending to whole and large speeches, it maketh the figure allegory to

be called a long and perpetual metaphor.

George Puttenham, *The Art of English Poesy* (1589) III xviii; ed. G. D. Willcock and A. Walker (Cambridge 1936) 186f.

192

Sometimes an allegory is mixed with some words retaining their proper and usual signification, whereof this may be an example: 'why dost thou covet the fruit, and not consider the height of the tree whereon it groweth? Thou dost not forethink of the difficulty in climbing, nor danger in reaching, whereby it cometh to pass, that while thou endeavourest to climb to the top, thou fallest with the bough which thou dost embrace.' This allegory describeth although somewhat obscurely, yet very aptly, the danger, vanity, and common reward of ambition. The words which retain their proper sense are these, *covet, consider,* and *forethink,* which words do make it a mixed allegory.

Henry Peacham, *The Garden of Eloquence* (1593) 26f.

193

Ironia ... continued maketh a most sweet allegory.

Abraham Fraunce, *The Arcadian Rhetoric* (1588); ed. E. Seaton (1950) 10.

194

Pushed to an extreme, this ironic usage would subvert language itself, turning everything into an Orwellian newspeak. In this sense we see how allegory is properly considered a mode: it is a fundamental process of encoding our speech. For the very reason that it is a radical linguistic procedure, it can appear in all sorts of different works.... The potential weaknesses of the mode are by now clear enough. They may be summed up in the one word 'anaesthesia'. The reader can be anaesthetized by the ritual order of enigma and romance. There is further a weakness inherent in the sublime and picturesque tendencies of the mode, namely a diffusion of inner coherence, since the typical allegory threatens never to end. The magnitude of the encyclopedic poem is controlled arbitrarily, which is to say it has no inherent limit. We need not be doctrinaire neo-Aristotelians to see the aesthetic virtues of the maintenance of 'proper magnitude', which allegories tend to violate. Their sublime magnitude disallows true organic form.

Angus Fletcher, *Allegory: The Theory of a Symbolic Mode* (Ithaca, N.Y. 1964) 2f., 367f.

195

The simpler the allegory, the more urgently the reader's attention is directed to the allegorical meaning. Hence simple or naïve moral allegory belongs primarily to educational literature: to the fables and moralities of the schoolroom, the parables and exempla of the pulpit, the murals and statuary which illustrate familiar ideas in official buildings. Often the allegorist is too interested in his additional meaning to care whether his fiction is consistent or not as a fiction. Bunyan, even Spenser, occasionally drop

into naïve allegory. In the first book of *The Faerie Queen*, the Redcross Knight is being taught by Faith, Hope and Charity, and Hope urges him to take hold of her anchor, the traditional emblem of hope. It is possible to think of Hope as a female teacher lugging this anchor into the lecture room to make her point —such emblems are still brought into classrooms—but it is simpler to think that the literal narrative is being naïvely distorted by the allegorical interest.

Northrop Frye in *Encyclopedia of Poetry and Poetics*, ed. A. Preminger (Princeton, N.J., 1965) 12.

196

All realism, in the medieval sense, leads to anthropomorphism. Having attributed a real existence to an idea, the mind wants to see this idea alive, and can only effect this by personifying it. In this way allegory is born. It is not the same thing as symbolism. Symbolism expresses a mysterious connexion between two ideas, allegory gives a visible form to the conception of such a connexion. Symbolism is a very profound function of the mind, allegory is a superficial one. It aids symbolic thought to express itself, but endangers it at the same time by substituting a figure for a living idea. The force of the symbol is easily lost in the allegory.

J. Huizinga, *The Waning of the Middle Ages*, tr. F. Hopman (1955) 206.

197

The symbolical cannot perhaps be better defined in distinction from the allegorical, than that it is always itself a part of that, of the whole of which it is representative. —'Here comes a sail',—(that is a ship) is a symbolic expression. 'Behold our lion!' when we speak of some gallant soldier, is allegorical. Of most importance to our present subject is this point, that the latter (allegory) cannot be other than spoken consciously;—whereas in the former (the symbol) it is very possible that the general truth may be unconsciously in the writer's mind during the construction of the symbol; and it proves itself by being produced out of his own mind,—as the Don Quixote out of the perfectly sane mind of Cervantes, and not by outward observation or historically. The advantage of symbolic writing over allegory is, that it presumes no disjunction of faculties, but simple dominance.

S. T. Coleridge, *Miscellaneous Criticism*, ed. T. M. Raysor (1936) 29.

198

Now an allegory is but a translation of abstract notions into a picture-language, which is itself nothing but an abstraction from objects of the senses; the principal being more worthless even than its phantom proxy, both alike unsubstantial, and the former shapeless to boot. On the other hand a symbol . . . is characterized by a translucence of the special in the individual, or of the general in the special, or of the universal in the general; above all by the translucence of the eternal through and in the temporal. It always partakes of the reality which it renders intelligible; and while it enunciates the whole, abides itself as a living part in that unity of which it is the

representative. The other are but empty echoes which the fancy arbitrarily associates with apparitions of matter, less beautiful but not less shadowy than the sloping orchard or hill-side pasture seen in the transparent lake below.

S. T. Coleridge, *The Statesman's Manual*, ed. W. G. T. Shedd (New York 1875) 437f.

199

True symbolism is where the particular represents the more general, not as a dream or a shadow, but as a living momentary revelation of the Inscrutable.

Johann Wolfgang von Goethe, *Maximen*, No. 314.

200

If our passions, being immaterial, can be copied by material inventions, then it is possible that our material world in its turn is the copy of an invisible world. As the god Amor and his figurative garden are to the actual passions of men, so perhaps we ourselves and our 'real' world are to something else. The attempt to read that something else through its sensible imitations, to see the archtype in the copy, is what I mean by symbolism or sacramentalism. . . . The difference between the two [allegory and symbolism] can hardly be exaggerated. The allegorist leaves the given—his own passions—to talk of that which is confessedly less real, which is a fiction. The symbolist leaves the given to find that which is more real. To put the difference in another way, for the symbolist it is we who are the allegory. We are the 'frigid personifications'; the heavens above us are the 'shadowy abstractions'; the world which we mistake for reality is the flat outline of that which elsewhere veritably is in all the round of its unimaginable dimensions.

C. S. Lewis, *The Allegory of Love* (1938) 45.

201

Thou heardest whilome, how Dame Penance
Made a declaration
Of six gates, in her sermon.
And five of hem, she saidë blive [quickly]
That they were the wittes five;

    . . . . .

'For these gates, I call "porters",
"Bringers-in and messagers"
Of eachë thing....
Eye is the gate, Looking porter;
Nose, the door and messager
Who can perceive is smelling;
And semblably in every thing,
Even like it doth be-fall
Of thine other wittes all,
Then when that Looking is porter
Of the Eye, and messager.'

Guillaume de Deguileville, *The Pilgrimage of the Life of Man*, tr. J. Lydgate (1426) ll. 6438-68.

202

Does the road wind up-hill all the way?
Yes, to the very end.
Will the day's journey take the whole long day?
From morn to night, my friend.

But is there for the night a resting place?
A roof for when the slow dark hours begin.
May not the darkness hide it from my face?
You cannot miss that inn.

Shall I meet other wayfarers at night?
Those who have gone before.
Then I must knock, or call when just in sight?
They will not keep you standing at that door.

Shall I find comfort, travel-sore and weak?
Of labour you shall find the sum.
Will there be beds for me and all who seek?
Yea, beds for all who come.

Christina Rossetti, 'Up-hill' (1858); ed. W. M. Rossetti
(1904) 339.

203

miles to go before I sleep

Robert Frost, 'Stopping by Woods', *New Hampshire*
(1923); *The Poetry of Robert Frost* (New York 1969)
224.

204

A symbol is, in sum, an extended comparison of which we are only given the second term; a system of connected metaphors. In brief, the symbol is the old 'allegory' of our fathers.

Jules Lemaître, 'Paul Verlaine et les poètes "symbolistes" et "décadents"', *Revue Bleue* xv (1888).

205

Although modern criticism demonstrates a fondness for symbolism in poetry and fiction, especially when it may be seen as a structural element, allegory is almost universally regarded with suspicion, if not with contempt. In the Middle Ages, on the other hand, the word *symbolism* was very seldom used, and poetry was thought of as being by nature allegorical. The difference is more than a difference in terminology, however; for the symbolism of modern poetry, which is most typically a vehicle for the expression of mood or emotion has no counterpart in the Middle Ages; and medieval allegory, which is a vehicle for the expression of traditional ideas has, with few exceptions, no counterpart in modern poetry.

D. W. Robertson, A *Preface to Chaucer* (Princeton N.J. 1963) 286.

206

Sophocles long ago
Heard it on the Aegaean, and it brought
Into his mind the turbid ebb and flow
Of human misery; we
Find also in the sound a thought,
Hearing it by this distant northern sea.
The Sea of Faith
Was once, too, at the full ...

Matthew Arnold, 'Dover Beach' (1867) ll. 15-22.

207

Nor need the relationship between what
is said and what is to be inferred be
based, as in metaphor and simile,
merely upon resemblance, for many
images have become potentially symbolic
not through likeness only but also
through one sort of association or
another.

Norman Friedman, in *Princeton Encyclopedia of
Poetry and Poetics*, ed. A. Preminger (Princeton, N.J. 1965) 833.

208

Why did Herbert call the poem ...
'Josephs coat'? ... Joseph's coat has a
very definite meaning in Christian
symbolism; any among a dozen treatises
will give it....

Rosemond Tuve, A *Reading of George Herbert*
(1952) 175f.

209

JAQUES   The sixth age shifts
    Into the lean and slipper'd pantaloon,
    With spectacles on nose and pouch on side,

William Shakespeare, *As You Like It* II vii 157-9.

The 'sixth act' of man's life as described by the melancholy Jaques
... belongs beyond doubt to Saturn, and not, as Boll thought, to
Jupiter.... The purse denotes not the joyous wealth of the 'Jovial'
period of life but the miserly riches of the Saturnine period.

R. Klibansky and others, *Saturn and Melancholy* (1964) 149 n 74.

210

This is *Turdus aonalaschkae pallasii*, the hermit thrush which I have heard in Quebec County. Chapman says (*Handbook of Birds of Eastern North America*) 'it is most at home in secluded woodland and thickety retreats.... Its notes are not remarkable for variety or volume, but in purity and sweetness of tone and exquisite modulation they are unequalled.' Its 'water-dripping song' is justly celebrated.

T. S. Eliot, note to *The Waste Land* (1922) l. 357.

211

e. e. cummings, 'anyone lived in a pretty how town', *Fifty Poems* (1940).

212

A symbol that cannot be separated from its sense cannot really be said to refer to something outside itself. 'Refer' is not the right word for its characteristic function. And where the symbol does not have an accepted reference, the use of it is not properly 'communication'. Yet its function *is* expression, in the logical, not the biological, sense.

Susanne K. Langer, *Feeling and Form* (1953) 380.

213

The yarns of seamen have a direct simplicity, the whole meaning of which lies within the shell of a cracked nut. But Marlow was not typical ... and to him the meaning of an episode was not inside like a kernel but outside, enveloping the tale which brought it out only as a glow brings out a haze, in the likeness of one of these misty halos that sometimes are made visible by the spectral illumination of moonshine.

Joseph Conrad, *Heart of Darkness* (1902) i;
Works, Collected edn. (1946) 48.

Imagery

214

By the pleasures of the imagination or fancy (which I shall use promiscuously) I here mean such as arise from visible objects, either when we have them actually in our view, or when we call up their ideas into our minds by paintings, statues, descriptions, or any the like occasion. We cannot indeed have a single image in the fancy that did not make its first entrance through the sight; but we have the power of retaining, altering and compounding those images, which we have once received, into all the varieties of picture and vision that are most agreeable to the imagination.... By the pleasures of the imagination, I mean only such pleasures as arise originally from sight, and ... I divide these pleasures into two kinds: my design being first of all to discourse of those primary pleasures of the imagination, which entirely proceed from such objects as are before our eyes; and in the next place to speak of those secondary pleasures of the imagination which flow from the ideas of visible objects, when the objects are not actually before the eye, but are called up into our memories, or formed into agreeable visions of things that are either absent or fictitious.

The pleasures of the imagination, taken in their full extent, are not so gross as those of sense, nor so refined as those of the understanding.

Joseph Addison, *Spectator* No. 411 (21 June, 1712); ed. D. F. Bond iii (Oxford 1965) 536f.

215

We all know fairly well what we mean by an image. We know that, roughly speaking, it is ... the little word-picture used by a poet or prose writer to illustrate, illuminate and embellish his thought....
        aged ears *play truant* at his tales,
those two metaphorical words call up a host of associations and emotions, and give us the picture of old grave men beguiled from their serious thoughts or labours by merry chatter of attractive and irresponsible youth, elders tempted from their grooves or their duty by fun and lightheartedness, as a boy is tempted to leave his lessons by the play of sunlight on a summer afternoon.

Caroline F. E. Spurgeon, *Shakespeare's Imagery and What it Tells Us* (Cambridge 1935) 9.

Peacham talks at length of the pleasures obtained from aptness of proportion and nearness of affinity; metaphors are ready pencils to line out and shadow any manner of proportion in Nature.... Assumptions that relate metaphor-making to the logical place *similitude* underlie his and others' discussions of it, rather than the modern assumption that metaphor-making is especially related to the play of association and to subconscious prepossessions for certain contents.

Rosemond Tuve, *Elizabethan and Metaphysical Imagery* (Chicago 1947) 122.

217

Similarity of imaginal elements would be disturbing and ridiculous: *lips like cherries, eyes like almonds, a skin like milk and strawberries, her beauty hangs upon the cheek of night as a rich jewel in an Ethiop's ear*—in every case it is the feeling that is the decisive element, not cognitive similarities. The feeling is intensified and expands in fresh, strongly emotive words, in order to reinforce and enhance the original emotion. The poetic figure exists to intensify emotion, not to supply the reader's imagination with more material.

Gustav Stern, *Meaning and Change of Meaning*, Göteborgs Högskolas Årsskrift xxxviii (Göteborg 1932) 307.

No doubt the seeing of the 'image' need not be done by a picture, but you do not even possess the almond simile till you 'see' (till you realise) that this eye is *shaped* like an almond; only in a parrot could the mere thought of an almond 'intensify emotion'.

W. Empson, *The Structure of Complex Words* (1951) 3.

219

Like most other words in literary criticism, *image* and *imagery* bear a wide range of meanings. Today they generally refer to any use of language that depends on concrete particulars rather than abstractions.... Each of the five senses has its own kind of image ... and there is the kinaesthetic image, which relates to our sense of movement or to our awareness of bodily effort.... When Donne, in 'A Valediction Forbidding Mourning', compares his mistress and himself to a pair of compasses, we are not meant to visualize the compasses. The comparison is an intellectual and not a sensory one.

R. L. Brett, *An Introduction to English Studies* (1965) 22.

220

The ingenious differentiating image, like the aptly brief defining
image, was genuinely regarded as an eloquent figure, the more
poetically fit for its logical usefulness. . . . Figures which point a
difference generally have the effect of sharp wit, since they cannot be
framed without the use of multiple predicaments and are usually
found from more than one of the places of invention. An example is
that image which King uses of . . . Ben Jonson. . . . The image not
only has the pun based on use, efficient cause, and different substance,
but adds the logical complication of a further differentiation through
extension of the similitude:

> And when more spreading titles are forgot,
> Or, spite of all their lead and cere-cloth, rot,
> Thou, wrapped and shrined by thine own sheets, wilt lie
> A relic famed by all posterity.
>
> Rosemond Tuve, *Elizabethan and Metaphysical Imagery* (Chicago
> 1947) 368.

221

> Thou on whose stream, mid the steep sky's commotion,
> Loose clouds like earth's decaying leaves are shed,
> Shook from the tangled boughs of Heaven and Ocean,
>
> P. B. Shelley, 'Ode to the West Wind'.

In what respects are the 'loose clouds' like 'decaying leaves'? The
correspondence is certainly not in shape, colour or way of moving. It
is only the vague general sense of windy tumult that associates
the clouds and the leaves; and, accordingly, the appropriateness of
the metaphor 'stream' in the first line is not that it suggests a surface
on which, like leaves, the clouds might be 'shed', but that it
contributes to the general 'streaming' effect in which the
inappropriateness of 'shed' passes unnoticed. What again, are those
'tangled boughs of Heaven and ocean'? They stand for nothing that
Shelley could have pointed to in the scene before him; the 'boughs',
it is plain, have grown out of the 'leaves' in the previous line, and we
are not to ask what the tree is.

F. R. Leavis, *Revaluation* (1936) 205.

222

Too much importance has always been attached to the sensory qualities of images.... An image may lose almost all its sensory nature to the point of becoming scarcely an image at all, a mere skeleton, and yet represent a sensation quite as adequately as if it were flaring with hallucinatory vividity. ... Care then should be taken to avoid the natural tendency to suppose that the more clear and vivid an image the greater will be its efficiency.

I. A. Richards, *Principles of Literary Criticism* (1924); (1967) 91f.

223

The fact that the 'argument from similars', analogy, similitude, was taught among the places of invention in all logics is partly responsible for the enormous favour in which such images were held and for the fact that similitudes are generally advanced not as illustrations but as arguments.... The Ramists' ... conception of 'arguments' and their faith in proof through the axiomatical disposition of truths gave the poetic analogy more dialectical validity. The particulars of a similitude 'argue' their generals; the similitude can be an axiom. When these and similar attitudes are imposed upon the general Elizabethan willingness to see universals in particular —in a period before scientific developments and habitual use of inductive reasoning had lessened men's respect for single 'significant' particulars—then the image functioning as analogy is bound to have considerable force to convince.

Rosemond Tuve, *Elizabethan and Metaphysical Imagery* (Chicago 1947) 371.

224

It is not rhyming and versing that maketh a poet ... but it is that feigning notable images of virtues, vices, or what else, with that delightful teaching, which must be the right describing note to know a poet by.

Sir Philip Sidney, *The Defence of Poesy* (1595); *Works* ed. A. Feuillerat iii (Cambridge 1912) 10f.

225

The image is not an idea. It is a radiant node or cluster; it is what I can, and must perforce, call a VORTEX, from which, and into which, ideas are continually rushing.

Ezra Pound, 'Vorticism', *The Fortnightly Review*, xcvi (1914) 469f.

226

The purpose of art, in the life of the poet, is to mitigate isolation by providing the Image which is the daily victory. 'I suffered continual remorse, and only became content when my abstractions had composed themselves into picture and dramatisation....' But the relief is impermanent; the poet discovers that 'he has made, after the manner of his kind, Mere images'. There is a tormenting contrast between the images (signified by the bronze and marble statuettes) and the living beauty. And out of this contrast grows the need for a poetic image which will resemble the living beauty rather than the marble or bronze. No static image will now serve.

Frank Kermode, *Romantic Image* (1961) 84f., citing W. B. Yeats.

The use of symbols is simply one aspect of language: the mistake lies in trying to invest them with some sort of transcendental significance instead of regarding them as a technical device of the same order as simile or metaphor. A symbol is nothing more than a vehicle for imaginative experience.

M. Turnell, 'Heirs of Baudelaire', *Scrutiny* xi (1942) 295.

Is there any important sense in which 'symbol' differs from 'image' and 'metaphor'? Primarily, we think, in the recurrence and persistence of the 'symbol'. An 'image' may be invoked once as a metaphor, but if it persistently recurs, both as presentation and representation, it becomes a symbol, may even become part of a symbolic (or mythic) system.

René Wellek and Austin Warren, *Theory of Literature* (rev. edn., Harmondsworth 1963) 189.

229

Of man's first disobedience, and the fruit
Of that forbidden tree, whose mortal taste
Brought death into the world ...

John Milton, *Paradise Lost* i 1-3.

All trees of noblest kind for sight, smell, taste;
And all amid them stood the tree of life,
High eminent, blooming ambrosial fruit
Of vegetable gold; and next to life
Our death the tree of knowledge grew fast by,

Ibid. iv 217-221.

Groves whose rich trees wept odorous gums and balm,
Others whose fruit burnished with golden rind
Hung amiable, Hesperian fables true,
If true, here only, and of delicious taste:

Ibid. iv 248-51.

Hail mother of mankind, whose fruitful womb
Shall fill the world more numerous with thy sons
Than with these various fruits the trees of God
Have heaped this table. . . .

Ibid. v 388-91.

Till body up to spirit work, in bounds
Proportioned to each kind. So from the root
Springs lighter the green stalk, from thence the leaves
More airy, last the bright consummate flower
Spirits odorous breathes : flowers and their fruit
Man's nourishment, by gradual scale sublimed
To vital spirits aspire, to animal,
To intellectual....

Ibid. v 478-85.

Fit vessel, fittest imp [sprig] of fraud....

Ibid. ix 89.

      them she upstays
Gently with myrtle band, mindless the while,
Her self, though fairest unsupported flower,

Ibid. ix 430-32

Serpent, we might have spared our coming hither,
Fruitless to me, though fruit be here to excess,

Ibid. ix 647f.

Forth reaching to the fruit, she plucked, she ate :

Ibid. ix 781.

Bad fruit of knowledge, if this be to know,

Ibid. ix 1073.

Thus they in mutual accusation spent
The fruitless hours....

Ibid. ix 1188f.

      they fondly thinking to allay
Their appetite with gust, instead of fruit
Chewed bitter ashes....

Ibid. x 564-6.

His promise, that thy seed shall bruise our foe

Ibid. xi 155.

      ages of endless date
Founded in righteousness and peace and love
To bring forth fruits joy and eternal bliss.

Ibid. xii 549-51.

At first glance it may seem that to these explicators [Brooks and Hardy] the poem [Lycidas] is not really about King, nor about Milton, but mainly about water.

M. H. Abrams, 'Five Types of Lycidas' in *Milton's 'Lycidas': The Tradition and the Poem* ed. C. A. Patrides (1961) 217.

An 'image' in the sense of a metaphor is not a likeness of anything. True, a metaphor depends on pointing to a likeness between heterogeneous things. But to say that courtiers fawning on a great man resemble spaniels fawning on their master is not saying that spaniels are a *likeness* of fawning courtiers, as Holbein's portrait is a likeness of Henry VIII.... If an image isn't necessarily a word-picture, or if it need not be a *picture* at all, isn't 'image' a rather awkward name for it?.... You can never stand back and scrutinize a mental image, since you are fully occupied in creating it—it represents your consciousness in action.

P. N. Furbank, *Reflections on the Word 'Image'* (1970) ch. 1 *passim.*

Metaphor

232

A metaphor is an alteration of a word, from the proper and natural meaning, to that which is not proper, and yet agreeth thereunto by some likeness, that appeareth to be in it.

Thomas Wilson, *The Art of Rhetoric* (1560) iii;
ed. G. H. Mair (Oxford 1909) 172.

233

There is a narrow sense of understanding a language in which one may be said to understand a language when he knows the grammar, the literal meanings of all the terms, and even the meaning of idioms. Such understanding does not suffice for the understanding of the metaphors of the language. In addition one must know something of the linguistic conventions— ... and even minor facets of the general culture, such as what characteristics of bears are uppermost in people's minds. This aspect is especially prominent in metaphors where an evaluation is the basis of the parallel. A popular song of some years ago praised a young lady by saying to her 'You're the cream in my coffee'. Entirely the wrong impression would be obtained in a community which drank its coffee black.

Paul Henle, ed., *Language Thought and Culture* (Ann Arbor, Mich. 1965) 185f.

234

The effect, then, of (metaphorically) calling a man a 'wolf' is to evoke the wolf-system of related commonplaces. If the man is a wolf, he preys upon other animals, is fierce, hungry, engaged in constant struggle, a scavenger, and so on. Each of these implied assertions has now to be made to fit the principal subject (the man) either in normal or in abnormal senses. If the metaphor is at all appropriate, this can be done—up to a point at least. A suitable hearer will be led by the wolf-system of implications to construct a corresponding system of implications about the principal subject. But these implications will *not* be those comprised in the commonplaces *normally* implied by literal uses of 'man'. The new implications must be determined by the pattern of implications associated with literal uses of the word 'wolf'. Any human traits that can without due strain be talked about in 'wolf language' will be rendered prominent, and any that cannot will be pushed into the background. The wolf metaphor suppresses some details, emphasises others—in short, *organizes* our view of man....

But ... reference to 'associated commonplaces' will fit the commonest cases where the author simply plays on the stock of common knowledge (and common misinformation) presumably shared by the reader and himself. But in a poem, or a piece of sustained prose, the writer can establish a novel pattern of implications for the literal uses of the key expressions, prior to using them as vehicles for his metaphors.... Metaphors can be supported by specially constructed systems of implications, as well as by accepted commonplaces; they can be made to measure and need not be reach-me-downs.

Max Black, 'Metaphor' in *Models and Metaphors* (Ithaca, N.Y. 1962) 41, 43.

235

I define a nose as follows—intreating only beforehand, and beseeching my readers, both male and female, of what age, complexion and condition whatsoever, for the love of God and their own souls, to guard against the suggestions and temptations of the devil, and suffer him by no art or wile to put any other ideas into their minds, than what I put into my definition—For by the word *Nose*, throughout all this long chapter of noses, and in every other part of my work, where the word *Nose* occurs—I declare, by that word I mean a nose, and nothing more, or less.... Now I find it needful to inform your reverences and worships, that besides the many nautical uses of long noses enumerated by *Erasmus*, the dialogist affirmeth that a long nose is not without its domestic conveniences also; for that in a case of distress—and for want of a pair of bellows, it will do excellently well *ad excitandum focum* (to stir up the fire).

Laurence Sterne, *Tristram Shandy* (1761) III, xxxi, xxxvii; i (Oxford 1926) 245f, 257f.

236

When a man has a wooden leg, is it a metaphoric or a literal leg? The answer to this ... is that it is both. It is literal in one set of respects, metaphoric in another. A word may be *simultaneously* both literal and metaphoric, just as it may simultaneously support many different metaphors, may serve to focus into one meaning many different meanings. The point is of some importance, since so much misinterpretation comes from supposing that if a word works one way it cannot simultaneously work in another and have simultaneously another meaning.

I. A. Richards, *The Philosophy of Rhetoric* (1936); (New York 1965) 118f.

237

One reason why metaphor is common in poetry is that metaphor vastly extends the language at the poet's disposal. Since metaphor uses terms in a transferred sense, this means that, subject to some not very serious limitations, a poet who wants to write about object X but finds its terminology defective or resistant to manipulation, can simply move over into the terminology of Y. By using Y-terminology to describe X, he opens to himself the linguistic resources available in connection with Y. The merit of a particular metaphor from the poet's point of view may be not simply that there are 'links' between love and a journey in a boat, but also that there is a much larger range of specialized terminology connected with boats and the sea than there is with love; once he chooses this as his analogy, he makes available to himself the whole terminology of seafaring—and, if he likes, of fishing and swimming and marine ecology too—

as in Dylan Thomas's *Ballad of the Long-Legged Bait*. The importance of this bare linguistic fact is inexhaustible. To look at metaphor as a linguistic phenomenon is to begin to suspect that the basic explanation of the prevalence of metaphor in poetry lies in the fact that metaphor, by extending the range of terminology at the poet's disposal, offers him a magnificent array of solutions to major problems of diction.

W. Nowottny, *The Language Poets Use* (1965) 67f.

238

The power of the pregnant image, its resonances and overtones, can be readily seen by contrast with 'flattened' and ineffective imagery, whatever the cause of its failure. Perhaps these most often come into the 'frigid' category of 'Longinus'; they lack vitality because they are both too 'literary', too obvious, too single moulded in their purpose. We may quote from Hardy's *Dynasts*:

> the enormous tale
> Of your campaign, like Aaron's serpent rod,
> Has swallowed up the smaller of its kind.
> Till dangerous ones drew near and daily sowed
> Those choking tares within your fecund brain.

When Hardy speaks of the accoutrements of cavalry flashing in the sun 'like a school of mackerel' we are conscious not only of the ineptness of the image but also of its inelasticity; as contrasted, say, with Vernon's description of the rebel army before Shrewsbury:

> All furnished, all in arms,
> All plumed like estridges that wing the wind,
> Bated like eagles having lately bathed ...

T. R. Henn, *The Harvest of Tragedy* (1966) 142.

239

Poetic language implicitly crossweaves multiplicity-in-unity and unity-in-multiplicity; it is tensive because of the precarious balance between two or more lines of association which it invites the imagination to contemplate.

Philip Wheelwright, *The Burning Fountain* (1968) 102.

240

Two technical terms ... assist us in distinguishing from one another what Dr Johnson called the two ideas that any metaphor, at its simplest, gives us. Let me call them the tenor and the vehicle.

I. A. Richards, *The Philosophy of Rhetoric* (1936); (New York 1965) 96.

241

It is an essential feature of metaphor that there must be a certain distance between tenor and vehicle. Their similarity must be accompanied by a feeling of disparity; they must belong to different spheres of thought. If they are too close to one another, they cannot produce the perspective of 'double vision' peculiar to metaphor.

Stephen Ullman, *Style in the French Novel* (Cambridge 1957) 214.

242

If, as in water stirred more circles be
Produced by one, love such additions take,
Those like so many sphears, but one heaven make,
For, they are all concentric unto thee;
And though each spring do add to love new heat,
As princes do in times of action get
New taxes, and remit them not in peace,
No winter shall abate the springs increase.

John Donne, 'Love's Growth' lines 21-8; *The Elegies and the Songs and Sonnets* ed. H. Gardner (Oxford 1965) 77.

243

As the two things put together are more remote, the tension created is, of course, greater. That tension is the spring of the bow, the source of the energy of the shot, but we ought not to mistake the strength of the bow for the excellence of the shooting; or the strain for the aim.

I. A. Richards, *The Philosophy of Rhetoric* (1936); (New York) 125.

244

I bridle in my struggling Muse with pain,
That longs to launch into a nobler strain.

To *bridle a goddess* is no very delicate idea; but why must she be bridled? because she *longs to launch*, an act which was never hindered by a *bridle*: and whither will she launch? Into a *nobler strain*. She is in the first line a horse, in the second a boat; and the care of the poet is to keep his *horse* or his *boat* from *singing*.

Samuel Johnson, Life of Addison, *Lives of the Poets* (1781); ed. G. B. Hill ii (Oxford 1935) 128.

245

I dream'd a banished Angel to me crept:
My feet were nourished on her breasts all night.

Meredith

The usual explanation of the grotesqueness of such lines is that mixed
metaphors are inevitably confusing and almost invariably comic.
This statement is untrue, for mixed metaphors can both enlarge our
understanding of a situation, and, strange as it may seem, clarify our
apprehension of its significance:

> Was the hope drunk
> Wherein you dress'd yourself? Hath it slept since
> And wakes now, to look so green and pale
> At what it did so freely?

Shakespeare

... the vital point is not so much the extent to which we unfold a
metaphor as the degree to which we visualize an image that is meant
to be primarily symbolical and non-visual. If Shakespeare's lines from
Macbeth awakened a series of visual images in our minds they would
leave us befuddled and bewildered. In fact, we grasp the implication
of each succeeding metaphor without being disturbed by irrelevant
mental pictures.

John Press, The Fire and the Fountain (1966) 148f.

246

It is an extremely important fact about
language that it is possible to use a word
intelligibly without using it in any of
its senses. There are other places in the
philosophy of language where this fact
has the effect of blurring sharp distinctions. 'Green ideas sleep furiously' is a
common example of a meaningless
sentence, one that is meaningless by
reason of a 'category mistake'. (Ideas
belong to the wrong category for being
qualified by colour terms.) But it is not
at all difficult to imagine a poetic context
in which this sentence would be quite
appropriate, in which it could be used
by the poet to communicate what he
wanted to communicate.

William Alston, Philosophy of Language
(Englewood Cliffs, N.J. 1964) 96f.

247

Poetic knowledge concerns matters
which through a deficiency in their
truth cannot be laid hold of by the
reason; hence the reason has to be
beguiled by means of certain similitudes

Theology, on the other hand, deals with matters which are above reason. So the symbolic mode is common to both types of discourse; neither type is suited to reasoning.

St Thomas Aquinas, *Commentary on the Sentences of Peter Lombard*, Prol. q.1, a5, ad 3m.

248

Metaphor ... is the synthesis of several units of observation into one commanding image; it is the expression of a complex idea, not by analysis, nor by direct statement, but by sudden perception of an objective relation.

Sir Herbert Read, *English Prose Style* (1952) 23.

249

If we allow ourselves to be misled by the heresy of paraphrase, we run the risk of doing even more violence to the internal order of the poem itself. By taking the paraphrase as our point of stance, we misconceive the function of metaphor and metre. We demand logical coherences where they are sometimes irrelevant, and we fail frequently to see the imaginative coherences on levels where they are highly relevant.

Cleanth Brooks, *The Well Wrought Urn* (New York 1947) 202.

250

I therefore suggest three divisions of the image: 1. The Dominants: that is, one or more images that, by specific statement or inference, provide a framework or theme for the play; and in terms of which part or all of the dramatic statement is made.... 2. 'Stream' images; that is a sequence or cluster of images which work through repetition, absolute or incremental, and thereby establish and reinforce their meaning in the body of the play. Such images may serve to communicate various forms of irony and ambiguity.... 3. 'Intermittent' images, establishing their validity through their context; usually unconscious in their origin; with functions—in addition to the excitement of sensibility proper to all such—of showing the impact of the relevant-irrelevant upon the design of the play.

T. R. Henn, *The Harvest of Tragedy* (1966) 135f.

251

Metaphor ... has a composite appeal. Through its use the imagination exploits the excitement of sensational experience and at the same time clarifies some idea. This is a very remarkable process because it runs counter to two pronounced tendencies in human nature. On the one hand physical and emotional excitement alone, even when only imagined, obscures the clearer faculties, as one sees in the effects of anger or passion, or even in simple self-abandonment or happiness; whilst on the other hand the rational faculty stakes its honour on the elimination of irrational factors in its attempts to state truth. In metaphor the excitements of experience are conjoined with clarity of statement.

Ronald Peacock, *The Art of Drama* (1957) 45.

252

The water, like a witch's oils,
Burnt green, and blue and white.
S. T. Coleridge, The Ancient Mariner (1798) ll. 125f.

VIOLA   And with a green and yellow melancholy,
She sat like patience on a monument,
William Shakespeare, Twelfth Night II iv 111.

CLEOPATRA   My salad days,
When I was green in judgment....
William Shakespeare, Antony and Cleopatra I v 73.

To lead an adventurous and honourable youth, and to settle when the
time arrives, into a green and smiling age, is to be a good artist
in life.
Robert Louis Stevenson, 'Crabbed Age and Youth' (1878); Works Vailima edn. ii
(1922-3) 80.

O pastoral heart of England ! Like a psalm
Of green days telling with a quiet beat
Sir Arthur Quiller-Couch, 'Ode upon Eckington Bridge', Poems (1929) 22.

Blown fields or flowerful closes,
Green pastures or grey grief.
A. C. Swinburne, 'A Match', Poems and Ballads (1866) ll. 5f.

Those eyes the greenest of things blue,
The bluest of things grey.
A. C. Swinburne, 'Félise', ibid. ll. 119f.

Annihilating all that's made
To a green thought in a green shade.
Andrew Marvell, 'The Garden'; ed. H. M. Margoliouth i (Oxford 1927) 49.

The idiot greens the meadow with his eyes.
Allen Tate, 'Idiot', Selected Poems (New York and London
1937) l.1.

253

The poetic end of the continuum is characterized by messages that are optimally organized, that is, maximum number of tendencies and constants plus optimum ungrammaticalness.... One possible view of degrees of grammaticalness is that the notion corresponds to the degree of difficulty with which a particular sentence be incorporated into the grammar.... Although grammaticalness may show correlations with statistical notions (like banality) or semantic notions (like literalness of meaning), the three are to be distinguished and measured independently.

Sol Saporta, in *Style in Language* ed. T. A. Sebeok (Cambridge, Mass. 1960) 92.

254

I am not of that opinion to conclude a poet's liberty within the narrow limits of laws, which either the grammarians or philosophers prescribe. For, before they found out those laws, there were many excellent poets, that fulfilled them. Amongst whom none more perfect than Sophocles, who lived a little before Aristotle.

Ben Jonson, *Timber; or Discoveries* (1640); *Ben Jonson* ed. C. H. Herford and others viii (Oxford 1947) 641.

255

In any language, stylistic inversion of 'major constituents' (in some sense to be defined) is tolerated up to ambiguity —that is, up to the point where a structure is produced that might have been generated independently by the grammatical rules.... In general, the rules of stylistic reordering are very different from the grammatical transformations, which are much more deeply embedded in the grammatical system. It might, in fact, be argued that the former are not so much rules of grammar as rules of performance.

Noam Chomsky, *Aspects of the Theory of Syntax* (Cambridge, Mass. 1965) 127.

256

In every speech community there are at least two competing norms, an innovating and a more archaic one.... The utilization of heterogeneous elements, pertaining to different systems or layers of language, often becomes in poetry a purposeful, artistically exploited device. In languages that have a variety of norms, each may be assigned a different poetic function.

Edward Stankiewicz, in *Style in Language* ed. T. A. Sebeok (Cambridge, Mass. 1960) 76.

257

It is evident ... that *ceteris paribus*, where rigidly regular metrical framework has to be applied to a language in which grammar is itself growing strict concerning the order in which words may be placed, it must become harder and harder for verse and poetry to keep house together. Nor is it without significance that we, today, should be more disgusted by 'inversions' ... and consequently more afraid of them, than our immediate ancestors; as a glance at contemporary verse will prove beyond dispute.

Owen Barfield, *Poetic Diction* (1952) 149.

258

What is common to all modern poetry is the assertion or the assumption (most often the latter) that syntax in poetry is wholly different from syntax as understood by logicians and grammarians.

Donald Davie, *Articulate Energy* (1955) 148.

259

Figurative speech is a novelty of language evidently (and yet not absurdly) estranged from the ordinary habit and manner of our daily talk and writing and figure it self is a certain lively or good grace set upon words, speeches and sentences to some purpose and not in vain, giving them ornament or efficacy by many manner of alterations in shape, in sound, and also in sense, sometime by way of surplusage, sometime by defect, sometime by disorder, or mutation, and also by putting into our speeches more pith and substance, subtility, quickness, efficacy or moderation, in this or that sort tuning and tempering them, by amplification, abridgement, opening, closing, enforcing, meekening or otherwise disposing them to the best purpose.

George Puttenham, *The Art of English Poesy* (1589) III x; ed. G. D. Willcock and A. Walker (Cambridge 1936) 159.

260

MACBETH   Come, seeling night,
    Scarf up the tender eye of pitiful day,
    And with thy bloody and invisible hand,
    Cancel and tear to pieces that great bond
    Which keeps me pale....

William Shakespeare, *Macbeth* III ii 46-50.

261

Sometime an allegory is mixed with some words retaining their proper and usual signification.

Henry Peacham, *The Garden of Eloquence* (1593) 26.

262

Follow thy fair sun, unhappy shadow.

Thomas Campion, in *A Book of Airs* (1601); *Works*, ed. W. R. Davis (Garden City, N.Y. 1967) 24.

263

In literature, the pure present can create the impression of an act, yet suspend the sense of time in regard to it. This explains its normal use in lyric poetry. Many critics, assuming that the present tense must refer to the present moment, have been led by this supposed grammatical evidence to believe that lyric poetry is always the utterance of the poet's own beliefs and actual feelings. But I maintain that lyric composition is art, and therefore creative; and the use of its characteristic tense must serve the creation that is peculiar to this kind of poetry.... Contemplation is the substance of the lyric, which motivates and even contains the emotion presented. And the natural tense of contemplation is the present. Ideas are timeless; in a lyric they are not said to have occurred, but are virtually occurring; the relations that hold them together are timeless, too. The whole creation in a lyric is an awareness of a subjective experience, and *the tense of subjectivity is the 'timeless' present.*

Susanne K. Langer, *Feeling and Form* (1953) 267f.

264

Strong is the lion—like a coal
His eye-ball—like a bastion's mole
   His chest against the foes :
Strong, the gier-eagle on his sail,
Strong against tide, th'enormous whale
   Emerges as he goes.

But stronger still, in earth and air,
And in the sea, the man of pray'r;
   And far beneath the tide;
And in the seat to faith assign'd,
Where ask is have, where seek is find,
   Where knock is open wide.

Beauteous the fleet before the gale;
Beauteous the multitudes in mail,
   Rank'd arms and crested heads :
Beauteous the garden's umbrage mild,
Walk, water, meditated wild,
   And all the bloomy beds.

Christopher Smart, from *A Song to David*
(1763) Sts. 76-8.

It seems to me that the normal and typical sentence in English as well as in Chinese expresses just this unit of natural process. It consists of three necessary words: the first denoting the agent or subject from which the act starts, the second embodying the very stroke of the act, the third pointing to the object, the receiver of the impact. Thus:

Farmer   pounds   rice

the form of the Chinese transitive sentence, and of the English (omitting particles), exactly corresponds to this universal form of action in nature. This brings language close to *things*, and in its strong reliance upon verbs it erects all speech into a kind of dramatic poetry....

I have seldom seen our rhetoricians dwell on the fact that the great strength of our language lies in its splendid array of transitive verbs, drawn both from Anglo-Saxon and from Latin sources. These give us the most individual characterizations of force. Their power lies in their recognition of nature as a vast storehouse of forces. We do not say in English that things seem, or appear, or eventuate, or even that they are; but that they *do*. Will is the foundation of our speech. We catch the Demi-urge in the act.

Ernest Fenollosa, *The Chinese Written Charac-ter as a Medium for Poetry* (1908); ed. Ezra Pound (1936) 16f., 33.

266

'Strength', in other words, is close and compact syntax, neither more nor less.

And it is too a virtue of authentic syntax, not of the pseudo-syntax that is music. For a verse is strong only if it has 'strong sense'. Let syntax be never so close, unless it is truly carrying 'weight of words', it cannot be 'strong'. To be 'strong', poetic syntax must bind as well as join, not only gather together but fetter too. The actual function of meaning, 'which calls for permanent contents', *must* be fulfilled. Verse may be 'strong' or it may 'aspire to the condition of music'; it cannot do both.

Donald Davie, *Articulate Energy* (1955) 60.

267

The next requisite is, that ... if his topics be probable and persuasory ... he be able to recommend them by the superaddition of elegance and imagery, to display the colours of varied diction, and pour forth the music of modulated periods.

Samuel Johnson, *The Adventurer* No. 115 (11 December 1753); *Works*, Yale edn. ii (New Haven and London 1963) 460.

268

It is only in the period that the wave-length of Milton's verse is to be found: it is his ability to give a perfect and unique pattern to every paragraph, such that the full beauty of the line is found in its context, and his ability to work in larger musical units than any other poet—that is to me the most conclusive evidence of Milton's supreme mastery. The peculiar feeling, almost a physical sensation of a breathless leap, communicated by Milton's long periods, and by his alone, is impossible to procure from rhymed verse.

T. S. Eliot, *Milton*, British Academy Lecture, 26 March 1947; *On Poetry and Poets* (1957) 157f.

269

No sooner had the almighty ceased, but all
The multitude of angels with a shout
Loud as from numbers without number, sweet
As from blest voices, uttering joy, heaven rung
With jubilee, and loud hosannas filled
The eternal regions: lowly reverent
Towards either throne they bow, and to the ground
With solemn adoration down they cast
Their crowns inwove with amarant and gold,
Immortal amarant, a flower which once
In Paradise, fast by the tree of life
Began to bloom, but soon for man's offence
To heaven removed where first it grew, there grows,
And flowers aloft shading the fount of life,
And where the river of bliss through midst of heaven
Rolls o'er Elisian flowers her amber stream;
With these that never fade the spirits elect
Bind their resplendent locks inwreathed with beams,
Now in loose garlands thick thrown off, the bright
Pavement that like a sea of jasper shone
Impurpled with celestial roses smiled.

John Milton, *Paradise Lost* iii 344-64.

270

To Bentley this was evidently not grammar, and he let in a couple of main verbs, like ferrets. Pearce could only save the text by putting brackets from *heaven* to *hosannas*, so that it is the angels who filled the regions, with a shout.... At the last moment, however, before his first edition was published, Pearce suddenly understood a Miltonic rhythm, and explained it at the end of the preface; a dramatic affair; it shows that Bentley was some use.... In the preface *angels uttering joy* becomes an ablative absolute, so that the sentence encloses the hierarchy as if with effort and rises through four lines to the main verb [rung].

W. Empson, *Some Versions of Pastoral* (1935) 160.

271

Their song was partial, but the harmony
(What could it less when spirits immortal sing?)
Suspended hell, and took with ravishment
The thronging audience.

John Milton, Paradise Lost ii 552-5.

The harmony suspended hell; but is it not much better with the parenthesis coming between? which suspends as it were the event, raises the reader's attention, and gives a greater force to the sentence.

Thomas Newton in Paradise Lost. A new edition. With notes of various authors,
by Thomas Newton i (1749) 118.

272

Though the *material* of poetry is verbal, its import is not the literal assertion made in the words, but *the way the assertion is made*, and this involves the sound, the tempo, the aura of associations of the words, the long and short sequences of ideas, the wealth or poverty of transient imagery that contains them, the sudden arrest of fantasy by pure fact, or of familiar fact by sudden fantasy, the suspense of literal meaning by a sustained ambiguity resolved in a long-awaited key-word, and the unifying, all-embracing artifice of rhythm. (The tension which music achieves through dissonance, and the reorientation in each new resolution to harmony, find their equivalents in the suspensions and periodic decisions of propositional sense in poetry. Literal sense, not euphony, is the 'harmonic structure' of poetry....)

Susanne K. Langer, *Philosophy in a New Key*
(Cambridge, Mass. 1942) 260f.

273

The medium is the message.

Marshall McLuhan, *Understanding Media*
(1964), title of ch. i.

274

In her [Susanne Langer's] view, the poet suspends the propositional sense through a long verse-period, not because the sense has to be qualified before it can be completed, but so as to achieve 'the tension which music achieves through dissonance'; and he decides the sense, bringing the period to a close, not because he is now prepared to commit himself to an assertion, but just to find an equivalent for music's 'reorientation in each new resolution to harmony'. The whole play of literal meaning, in fact, is a Swedish drill, in which nothing is being lifted, transported, or set down, though the muscles tense, knot, and relax as if it were.... It is plain that

Mrs Langer's sort of poetry, where it retains forms of prosaic syntax, only seems to make use of them. And to that extent the things it says are still, in the time-honoured phrase, pseudo-statements.

Donald Davie, *Articulate Energy* (1955) 21.

275

In the poetic approach the relevant consequences are not logical or to be arrived at by a partial relaxation of logic. Except occasionally and by accident logic does not enter at all. They are the consequences which arise through our emotional organization. The acceptance which a pseudo-statement receives is entirely governed by its effects upon our feelings and attitudes. Logic only comes in, if at all, in subordination, as a servant to our emotional response.... A pseudo-statement is 'true' if it suits and serves some attitude or links together attitudes which on other grounds are desirable.... A pseudo-statement is a form of words which is justified entirely by its effect in releasing or organizing our impulses and attitudes (due regard being had for the better or worse organizations of these *inter se*); a statement, on the other hand, is justified by its truth, *i.e.* its correspondence, in a highly technical sense, with the fact to which it points.

I. A. Richards, (1926); *Poetries and Sciences* (1970) 59f.

276

There is an important use of words—very frequent, I suggest, in poetry—which does not freeze its meanings but leaves them fluid, which does not fix an assertional clip upon them in the way that scientific prose and factual discourse must.... This is not to say, however, that the meanings in these fluid sentences are vague. They may or may not be—as meanings in rigid prose may or may not be. *Vagueness-precision* and *rigidity-fluidity*, as I am suggesting we use them here, are different dimensions. In fluid language a great many very precise meanings may be free to dispose themselves in a multiplicity of diverse ways.

I. A. Richards, *Speculative Instruments* (1955) 148f.

277

[Mallarmé] approached the attitude of men who in algebra have examined the science of forms and the symbolical part of the art of mathematics. This type of attention makes the structure of expressions more felt and more interesting than their significance or value. Properties of transformations are worthier of the mind's attention than what they transform; and I sometimes wonder if a more general notion can exist than the notion of a 'proposition' or the consciousness of thinking no matter what.

Paul Valéry 'Je disais quelquefois à Stéphane Mallarmé,' *Oeuvres completes* ed. J. Hytier i (Paris 1957) 658.

278

To the purist, wherever there is irony, there must be pseudo-syntax, because an ironical statement belies its own syntax, meaning something other than what the syntax says. The exaggerated value placed on irony in modern criticism is either a cause or a symptom of our dislike of authentic syntax in poetry.

Donald Davie, *Articulate Energy* (1955) 53.

279

Poetic reflections, therefore, are not essentially trains of logical reasoning, though they may incorporate fragments, at least, of discursive argument. Essentially they create the *semblance* of reasoning; of the seriousness, strain and progress, the sense of growing knowledge, growing clearness, conviction and acceptance—the whole experience of philosophical thinking.

Susanne K. Langer, *Feeling and Form* (1953) 219.

280

In prose as in algebra concrete things are embodied in signs or counters which are moved about according to rules, without being visualized at all in the process. There are in prose certain type situations and arrangements of words, which move as automatically into certain other arrangements as do functions in algebra. One only changes the Xs and the Ys back into physical things at the end of the process. Poetry, in one aspect at any rate, may be considered as an effort to avoid this characteristic of prose. It is not a counter language, but a visual concrete one. It is a compromise for a language of

intuition which would hand over sensations bodily. It always endeavours to arrest you, and to make you continuously see a physical thing, to prevent you gliding through an abstract process. It chooses fresh epithets and fresh metaphors, not so much because they are new, and we are tired of the old, but because the old cease to convey a physical thing and become abstract counters. A poet says a ship 'coursed the seas' to get a physical image, instead of the counter word 'sailed'.

T. E. Hulme, *Speculations* (1924) 134f.

281

The best part of human language, properly so called, is derived from reflection on the acts of the mind itself. It is formed by a voluntary appropriation of fixed symbols to internal acts, to processes and results of imagination.

S. T. Coleridge, *Biographia Literaria* (1817) ch. xvii; ed. J. Shawcross ii (Oxford 1907) 39f.

282

As Coleridge saw, syntax can have a place in poetry only when poetry makes use of what Hulme denied to it, a language of counters, of fiduciary symbols.... Hulme and Fenollosa in effect admit into poetry no words that are not whole images or parts of images. This is one of the reasons why they tend to exclude syntax, for syntax always needs some words sheerly as signs. On the other hand, older poets and critics often insisted on the necessity for spacing images, sewing them carefully into language of another sort.

Donald Davie, *Articulate Energy* (1955) 122.

283

... the assumption I am attacking. It leads us to think that a shift of meaning is a flaw in discourse, a regrettable accident, instead of a virtue. And therefore we neglect to study the plan of the shifts.

The assumption is that words have, or should have, proper meanings which people should recognize, agree about and stick to. A pretty programme, if it were possible. But, outside the technical languages of the sciences, it is not possible. For in the topics with which all generally interesting discussion is concerned, words must shift their meanings thus. Without these shifts such mutual understanding as we achieve would fail even within the narrowed resultant scope. Language, losing its subtlety with its suppleness, would lose also its power to serve us.

I. A. Richards, *The Philosophy of Rhetoric* (1936); (New York 1965) 72f.

284

Each mortal thing does one thing and the same:
Deals out that being indoors each one dwells;
Selves—goes itself; *myself* it speaks and spells;
Crying *What I do is me: for that I came.*

I say more: the just man justices;
Keeps grace....

Gerard Manley Hopkins, 'As Kingfishers Catch Fire' ed. W. H. Gardner and N. H. Mackenzie (1967) 90.

285

Langue, you will remember, is the speech-system, the vocabulary, accidence and syntax that a speech-group learns, adjusts and stores away in its individual memories for use when required....

Parole, on the other hand, is the particular speech-act.... The literary artifact ... is *parole.*

F. W. Bateson, *English Studies Today* ii (Bern 1961) 74f.

Appropriate Language

286

Lexicon is the choice of vocabulary, such as standard, learned, colloquial, neologist, including the appropriate (or clashing) grammar; very important for the connotative overtones in poetry is the nearness or distance from the etymology (like Dryden's beautiful 'deviate into sense'). In the English language we notice especially, in a subdued but ultimately powerful way, whether the words are Saxon, Norman, or Latin. The choice of words gives character and disposition, social status, the role assumed for the speech.

Paul Goodman, *The Structure of Literature* (Chicago 1962) 194.

287

Our maker therefore at these days shall not follow *Piers Plowman* nor Gower nor Lydgate nor yet Chaucer, for their language is now out of use with us; neither shall he take the terms of northern men, such as they use in daily talk ... ye shall therefore take the usual speech of the court, and that of London and the shires lying about London within sixty miles, and not much above.

George Puttenham, *Art of English Poesy* (1589) III iv; ed. G. D. Willcock and A. Walker (Cambridge 1936) 144f.

288

And first of the words to speak, I grant they be something hard, and of most men unused, yet both English, and also used of most excellent authors and most famous poets.... Having the sound of those ancient poets still ringing in his [Spenser's] ears, he mote needs in singing hit out some of their tunes. But whether he useth them by such casualty and custom, or of set purpose and choice, as thinking them fittest for such rustical rudeness of shepherds, either for that their rough sound would make his rhymes more ragged and rustical, or else because such old and obsolete wordes are most used of country folk, sure I think, and think I think not amiss, that they bring great grace and, as one would say, authority to the verse.... Yet neither every where must old words be stuffed in, nor the common dialect and manner of speaking so corrupted thereby, that as in old buildings it seem disorderly and ruinous. But all as in most exquisite pictures they use to blaze and portray not only the dainty lineaments of beauty, but also round about it to shadow the rude thickets and craggy clifts, that by the baseness of such parts, more excellency may accrue to the principal; for ofttimes we find ourselves, I know not how, singularly delighted with the show of such rudeness, and take great pleasure in that disorderly order. Even so do those rough and harsh terms enlumine and make more clearly to appear the brightness of brave and glorious words.

'E. K.', Epistle to Harvey, before *The Shepherd's Calender* (1579); *Elizabethan Critical Essays*, ed. G. G. Smith, i (Oxford 1904) 126f.

289

He [Spenser] is certainly inferior in his dialect. For the Doric had its brevity and propriety in the time of Theocritus; it was used in part of Greece, and frequent in the mouths of many of the greatest persons; whereas the old English and country phrases of Spenser were either entirely obsolete, or spoken only by people of the lowest condition. As there is a difference between simplicity and rusticity, so the expression of simple thoughts should be plain but not clownish.

Alexander Pope, A *Discourse on Pastoral Poetry* (1717); *Pastoral Poetry and An Essay on Criticism* ed. E. Audra and A. Williams (1961) 32.

290

Many words there are in every tongue, which are not used, except by illiterate persons, or on very familiar occasions, or in order to express what the decorum of polite society requires that we conceal: and these may be called *mean words*, and are never to be introduced in sublime description, in elegant writing, or on any solemn and serious topic.

James Beattie, *Dissertations Moral and Critical* (1783) 649.

291

Since it often happens that the most obvious phrases, and those which are used in ordinary conversation, become too familiar to the ear, and contract a kind of meanness by passing through the mouths of the vulgar, a poet should take particular care to guard himself against idiomatic ways of speaking.

Joseph Addison, *Spectator* No. 285 (26 January 1712); ed. D. F. Bond iii (Oxford 1965) 10.

292

Words become low by the occasion to which they are applied, or the general character of those who use them. . . .

> Come, thick night!
> And pall thee in the dunnest smoke of hell,
> That my keen knife see not the wound it makes;
> No heaven peep through the blanket of the dark,
> To cry, Hold, hold!

. . . The efficacy of this invocation is destroyed by the insertion of an epithet now seldom heard but in the stable, and *dun* night may come and go without any other notice than contempt. . . . [The] sentiment is weakened by the name of an instrument used by butchers and cooks in the meanest employments.... Who, without some relaxation of his gravity, can hear of the avengers of guilt *peeping through a blanket?*

Samuel Johnson, *Rambler* No. 168 (26 October 1751); *Works*, Yale edn. v (New Haven and London 1969) 126.

293

I hope it will be found that there is in these poems little falsehood of description, and that my ideas are expressed in language fitted to their respective importance. Something I must have gained by this practice, as it is friendly to one property of all good poetry, namely good sense; but it has necessarily cut me off from a large proportion of phrases and figures of speech which from father to son have long been regarded as the common inheritance of poets.

William Wordsworth, Preface to *Lyrical Ballads* (1800); ed. R. L. Brett and A. R. Jones (1963) 245.

294

Words too familiar, or too remote, defeat the purpose of a poet. From those sounds which we hear on small or on coarse occasions, we do not easily receive strong impressions or delightful images; and words to which we are nearly strangers, whenever they occur, draw that attention upon themselves which they should transmit to things.

Samuel Johnson, Life of Dryden, *Lives of the Poets* (1781); ed. G. B. Hill i (Oxford 1905) 420.

295

The language too of these men is adopted (purified indeed from what appear to be its real defects, from all lasting and rational causes of dislike or disgust) because such men hourly communicate with the best objects from which the best part of language originally derived; and because, from their rank in society and the sameness and narrow circle of their intercourse, being less under the action of social vanity they convey their feelings and notions in simple and unelaborate expressions. Accordingly, such a language arising out of repeated experience and regular feelings is a more permanent and a far more philosophical language than that which is frequently substituted for it by poets, who think that they are conferring honour upon themselves and their art in proportion as they separate themselves from the sympathies of men, and indulge in arbitrary and capricious habits of expression in order to furnish food and for fickle tastes and fickle appetites of their own creation.

William Wordsworth, Preface to *Lyrical Ballads* (1800); ed. R. L. Brett and A. R. Jones (1963) 239f.

296

The style in which a woman is called a nymph—and women generally are 'the fair'—in which shepherds are conscious swains, and a poet invokes the Muses and strikes a lyre, and breathes on a reed, and a nightingale singing becomes Philomel 'pouring her throat', represents a fashion as worn out as hoops and wigs. By the time of Wordsworth it was a mere survival—a dead form remaining after its true function had entirely vanished. The proposal to return to the language of common life was the natural revolt of one who desired poetry to be above all things the genuine expression of real emotion. Yet it is, I think, impossible to maintain that the diction of poetry should be simply that of common life.

Leslie Stephen, *Alexander Pope* (1880) 69.

297

The question of poetic diction was really a red herring which has misled many since Wordsworth's day. The real point is that Wordsworth wanted a minimum of stylisation because he was not working in any poetic tradition but kindling poetry from the naked experience, as it were. This is always a dangerous thing to do, for there is no conventional poetic effect (what Gerard Hopkins called 'parnassian', the language of great poets when they are not working under plenary inspiration) to fall back on if the kindling does not take place.

David Daiches, A *Critical History of English Literature* iv (1960) 877.

298

It seems to me that the poetical language of an age should be the current language heightened, to any degree heightened and unlike itself, but not (I mean normally: passing freaks and graces are another thing) an obsolete one. This is Shakespeare's and Milton's practice and the want of it will be fatal to Tennyson's *Idylls* and plays, to Swinburne, and perhaps to Morris.

Gerard Manley Hopkins, Letter to Robert Bridges, 14 August 1879; *Letters of Gerard Manley Hopkins to Robert Bridges* ed. C. C. Abbott (1955) 89.

299

Milton is using only a small part of the resources of the English language. The remoteness of his poetic idiom from his own speech is to be considered here.... A man's most vivid and sensuous experience is inevitably bound up with the language that he actually speaks.

F. R. Leavis, *Revaluation* (1936) 54.

300

There is no such thing as a poetic language, either as a diction or as a mode of sentential meanings. The nearest approach to this occurs when a tradition in poetry has so cut itself from the ordinary spoken language as to have a diction and grammar confined almost exclusively to itself. Whether or not the separation is always a death-bed phenomenon I leave the historians of literature to decide.

Isobel Hungerland, *Poetic Discourse* (Berkeley, Calif. 1958) 13.

In the ordinary transactions of daily life it does not matter very much that men use a restricted, impoverished vocabulary and a monotonously simple grammatical structure. This ironing out of all individual turns of phrase, this flattening of texture and dehydration of flavour enable us to digest speedily a mass of useful information. Demands from income-tax authorities, leading articles and the views of Her Majesty's Judges can be read and understood at a glance, because the mind need not dwell on the individual words of which they are composed. But poets are not content to use language as if it were a succession of vaguely emotive noises intended to prod the listener into taking some sort of action. They must, by their very nature, refuse to confine themselves to a standardized vocabulary and a conventional grammar which, adequate for the business of day-to-day living, are clumsy instruments for the delicate and difficult tasks that poets are called upon to perform.

John Press, *The Chequer'd Shade* (1963) 8f.

302

The linguist ... will want to recognize the principle of difference of style determined by difference of situation and function which is implied by such phrases as 'the language of sermons', 'the language of advertising'....

In order to accommodate such a flexible and potentially minute means of classification as a scale, we have to do away with the absolute distinction between literature and everything else.

Roger Fowler, in *Essays in Style and Language* ed. Roger Fowler (1966) 13.

303

Greek contains hundreds of words, verbal forms, and constructions found in verse alone and not in prose; similarly, to a smaller extent, with Latin.... Homer's language was a mixture of dialects, never spoken anywhere; Dante thought a similarly eclectic language right for Italian poetry. Spenser, Shakespeare and the Elizabethans, Milton and Herrick, Dryden and the Augustans, would have further shown that English poets have succeeded both with poetic diction and without, though mostly with .... Indeed, it might suffice, for answering Wordsworth, to ask oneself whether 'The Ancient Mariner' could be rechristened, without loss, 'The Old Sailor'. It is surely clear that 'poetic diction' is not always bad nor yet essential; without it poetry is still possible, but as a whole would be immensely poorer.

F. L. Lucas, *The Decline and Fall of the Romantic Ideal* (1948) 184f.

304

When words are selected and arranged in such a way that their meaning either arouses, or is obviously intended to arouse, aesthetic imagination, the result may be described as *poetic diction*

Owen Barfield, *Poetic Diction* (1952) 41.

Galbe. That was a good word; but it was French. *Le galbe évasé de ses hanches*: had one ever read a French novel in which that phrase didn't occur? Some day he would compile a dictionary for the use of novelists. *Galbe, gonflé, goulu; parfum, peau, pervers, potelé, pudeur; vertu, volupté.*

But he really must find that word. Curves, curves. . . . Those little valleys had the lines of cup moulded round a woman's breast; they seemed the dinted imprints of some huge divine body that has rested on these hills. Cumbrous locutions, these; but through them he seemed to be getting nearer to what he wanted. Dinted, dimpled, wimpled—his mind wandered down echoing corridors of assonance and alliteration ever further and further from the point. He was enamoured with the beauty of words.

Aldous Huxley, *Crome Yellow* (1921); (Harmondsworth 1955) 7.

The employment of a recondite vocabulary is a vicious trick when prompted by a modish desire to be clever:

> When once proleptic of the kiss
> Their parted lips stood poised in air
> No stellar parallax could tear
> Heart from heart in heniadys.

This is wit writing of the worst kind, a calculated euphuism parading in scientific plumage, frigid fancy masquerading as elegant precision. It illustrates the dangers that beset any poet who, departing from the commonly accepted speech of his own day, adopts an arcane vocabulary drawn from a remote age or from an unfamiliar branch of learning. Unless he commands sufficient poetic authority to compel the general acceptance of his minted coinage his work will inevitably be judged rebarbative and obscure, for although one may discover its meaning with the aid of a dictionary, it will be a dictionary, not a poetic, meaning.

John Press, *The Chequer'd Shade* (1963) 12f.

That miraculous line of Tennyson's 'And after many a summer dies the swan' loses all its radiance, as Aldous Huxley once remarked, if for *swan* we substitute the word *duck*. The word *swan* conjures up a visual image of exquisite whiteness, luminosity, and grace, whereas the vision produced by the word *duck* is of a small, waddling creature devoid of dignity and of pathos. . . . The swan brings with it an aura of mystery and of beauty as it sails down the reaches of the mind, recalling the silver-throated swans of the madrigalists and of Spenser, the swan which caressed Leda, the swans which haunt some of Yeats' finest poems, and those living birds which still glide unruffled on the backs at Cambridge. Tennyson's swan dies against the traditional background of English poetry, amid the lamenting music of five centuries.

John Press, *The Fire and the Fountain* (1966) 128.

308

The Augustan achievement was by shearing words of their secondary and irrelevant associations to release the full emphasis of their primary meanings. The connotations, instead of blurring the denotations, reinforced them. The poetry of Dryden and Pope differs therefore from earlier and later English poetry in that it is not a poetry of suggestion but of statement.

F. W. Bateson, *English Poetry and the English Language* (Oxford 1934) 58.

309

The relation of poetic diction to poetic thought is a comparatively unexplored subject; I am not sure that there is any necessary connection between them at all. His diction makes or mars the poet; it is the expression of his sensibility, and as such is unequivocal. The thought of a poet is a factor which will enhance his general 'value', but it does not alter his poetic value.

Sir Herbert Read, *Phases of English Poetry* (1928) 50.

310

For the past two hundred and fifty years it has been common to assume that abstract language is dead language, that poetry must depict particular actions, or if it be 'lyric' that it must reverie over remembered sensory impressions, according to the formula of the associationists. But these assumptions are false.... A race that has lost the capacity to handle abstractions with discretion and dignity may do well to confine itself to sensory impression, but our ancestors were more fortunate, and we ought to labour to regain what we have lost.

Yvor Winters, *The Function of Criticism: Problems and Exercises* (Denver, Colorado 1957) 61.

311

Let us look at the way the major language of poetry moves with its users, the adjectives, nouns, verbs most used by a poet, at least ten times or more in a representative thousand lines.... Consider the poetry of England in its first great era, the Elizabethan. The basic vocabulary was established by this time. Poets agreed largely on the emphasized terms for their religious, courtly, and pastoral worlds. Then Spenser, Sidney, Sylvester, Campion contributed an abundance of rich emotions and values in newly stressed words like *muse, virtue, joy, new, sad, happy*, so that those who wrote in the first years of the new century, Ben Jonson, John Donne, George Sandys, Fletcher, Wither, Herrick, Quarles, Herbert, Carew, Shirley, were able to look about them and to discard and to add frugally as they wished. They added a few verbs, *meet, appear, praise, write,* and discarded some courtly trappings from the past: *gold, fortune, hell, knight, lady, cruel, desire*. Their successors in turn dropped the formal feelings of the pastoral: *gentle, shepherd, faith, grief, woe*, and so on, to add a more classical vocabulary of *care, fate, soft, sense, shine*.... Then the poets ... publishing ... after the Restoration, set a new tone. They dropped little, but added much, a whole new set of meanings: Roscommon's *wild*, Oldham's *vain*, Blackmore's *human, various, land, sky*, Pomfret's *charm, mighty, delight*. Here, perhaps prepared for by the classical sensory terms, we have the beginnings of men's, of poets', sense of and response to the natural world in its scope and variety....

The next generation, turning into the eighteenth century, confirms this feeling ... in the face of the rich new natural vocabulary, the old terms of human concept and action go: *common, true, sin, town, sight, word, wit, begin, write*, these and others are lost to poetry—not so many to be lost again for another hundred years. It is a milestone of change, this abrupt abandoning of a conceptual vocabulary in favour of a sensory descriptive one. There is room in poetry now, through the eighteenth century, for new words, of nature ... and of an artifice in nature which will last not more than a century: *fool, maid, nymph, scene, behold*.... Now Crabbe, Bowles, Blake, make the step forward—this time into a new inner world: *cold, pale, black, white, grey, own, home, child, mother, morning, memory, foot, ear, pleasure, sorrow, wave, wood, feel, hold, sleep, turn, weep*. It is in this world, with its more recently added outward counterparts like *moon, star, water, body, bird, wing, shadow, house*, and especially with the innovations of the mid-nineteenth century, *dead, red, rain, stone*, that we still reside.... If the pattern continues, it will be the poets now growing up who will initiate a new central subject matter in primary vocabulary.

Josephine Miles, *Eras and Modes in English Poetry* (Berkeley and Los Angeles, Calif. 1964) 217ff.

Sound and Sense

312

The beauty of numbers consists in the grace or the propriety of 'em. The propriety of 'em consists in sounds adapted to the sense.

Samuel Say, *An Essay on the Harmony, Variety, and Power of Numbers* (1745) 97.

313

The sound must seem an echo to the sense.

Alexander Pope, *An Essay on Criticism* (1711) l. 365.

314

This notion of representative metre, and the desire of discovering frequent adaptations of the sound to the sense, have produced, in my opinion, many wild conceits and imaginary beauties. All that can furnish this representation are the sounds of the words considered singly, and the time in which they are pronounced. Every language has some words framed to exhibit the noises which they express, as *thump, rattle, growl, hiss*. These, however, are but few, and the poet cannot make them more, nor can they be of any use but when sound is to be mentioned. The time of pronunciation was in the dactylic measures of the learned languages capable of considerable variety; but that variety could be accommodated only to motion or duration, and different degrees of motion were perhaps expressed by verses rapid or slow, without much attention of the writer, when the image had full possession of his fancy; but our language having little flexibility, our verses can differ very little in their cadence. The fancied resemblances, I fear, arise sometimes merely from the ambiguity of words; there is supposed to be some relation between a *soft* line and *soft* couch, or between *hard* syllables and *hard* fortune.

Motion, however, may be in some sort exemplified; and yet it may be suspected that even in such resemblances the mind often governs the ear, and the sounds are estimated by their meaning.... Beauties of this kind are commonly fancied; and when real, are technical and nugatory, not to be rejected, and not to be solicited.

Samuel Johnson, Life of Pope, *Lives of the Poets* (1781); ed. G. B. Hill iii (Oxford 1905) 230-2.

315

A good poet will adapt the very sounds, as well as words, to the things he treats of. So that there is (if one may express it so) a style of sound: as in describing a gliding stream the numbers should run easy and flowing, in describing a rough torrent or deluge, sonorous and swelling.

And so of the rest. This is evident every where in Homer and Virgil, and no where else that I know of to any observable degree.

Alexander Pope, Letter to Cromwell, 25 Nov. 1710; Correspondence ed. G. Sherburn i (Oxford 1956) 107.

316

First march the heavy mules, securely slow,
O'er hills, o'er dales, o'er crags, o'er rocks, they go:
Jumping high o'er the shrubs of the rough ground,
Rattle the clattering cars, and the shocked axles bound.
But when arrived at Ida's spreading woods,
(Fair Ida, watered with descending floods)
Loud sounds the axe, redoubling strokes on strokes;
On all sides round the forest hurls her oaks
Headlong. Deep-echoing groan the thickets brown;
Then rustling, crackling, crashing, thunder down.
The wood the Grecians cleave, prepared to burn;
And the slow mules the same rough road return.

The numbers in the original of this whole passage are admirably adapted to the images the verses convey to us. Every ear must have felt the propriety of sound in this line,

Polla d'ananta, katanta, paranta te, dochmia t'ēlthon.

Alexander Pope, note to The Iliad of Homer (1720) xxiii 140-51.

317

Having thus represented the steady plod of the mules by a steadily-repeated grammatical construction, Pope goes on to represent by metrical dislocation the jolting of the chariots (an effect heightened by its contrast with the plod of the previous line).... What is ultimately done here may, from one point of view, be said to rank no higher than mimicry, or rather a succession of mimicries of successively-stated attributes of the scene that Pope is describing.

Though it is true that the corporeality of the words is used here to give the conceptual sense of the words a renewed contact with perceptual experience, yet, none the less, if the mimicries were removed (as some at least could be by rearranging the same words into an order not significant in relation to metrics and lineation) the conceptual meaning of the statement would survive unimpaired.

W. Nowottny, *The Language Poets Use* (1965) 3f.

318

Every element in a form, whether it be a musical form or any other, is capable of exciting a very intricate and widespread response. Usually the response is of a minimal order and escapes introspection. Thus a simple note or a uniform colour has for most people hardly any observable effect beyond the sensory characteristics. When it occurs along with other elements the form which they together make up may have striking consequences in emotion and attitude. If we regard this as an affair of mere summation of effects it may seem impossible that the effect of the form can be the result of the effects of the elements.... But ... the effects of happenings in the mind rarely add themselves up. Our more intense experiences are built up of less intense experiences as a wall is built up of bricks.... The separate responses which each element in isolation would tend to excite are so connected with one another that their combination is, for our present knowledge, incalculable in its effects.

I. A. Richards, *Principles of Literary Criticism* (1924); (1967) 132f.

319

Language is spoken before it is written; even after it is written it is implicitly spoken; and language as sound has potentialities far beyond those of language as written or visual. Sound is in some sense the medium of literature, no matter how words are considered as expressive. What is more questionable is how near this medium can ever come to being that of music. Sound in its conventional semantic value is certainly not a musical medium. Further it is not musical in its whole complex of suggestive or directly imitative values, onomatopoeia, and all the more mysteriously felt shades of sound propriety....

The notion of a separate music is further crippled if we consider that it is impossible for any system of sound in prose to be unconnected with its meaning —that is, neither contribute to it nor detract from it. Suppose a man to be writing a double composition, both prose and music; then in the use of any given piece of language he must, consciously or unconsciously, choose for the meaning or for the music. (It is impossible that two such disconnected effects should often coincide.) Or, to change the sense of 'must', he must choose for the meaning and sacrifice the music, for the meaning of the words is their nature, while the music of the words is negligible.

W. K. Wimsatt, Jr, *The Prose Style of Samuel Johnson* (New Haven, 1963) 5, 7f.

320

As an aesthetic instrument, language is not sound to which meaning can be assigned, but sound which IS meaning.

Lascelles Abercrombie, *Principles of English Prosody* (1923) 17.

321

In the vast majority of those words which can be said to have an independent musical value, the musical suggestion is at odds with the meaning. When the musical suggestion is allowed to predominate, decadence of style has begun.

J. Middleton Murry, *The Problem of Style* (Oxford 1922) 86.

322

There is no denying, however, that there are words which we feel instinctively to be adequate to express the ideas they stand for, and others the sounds of which are felt to be more or less incongruous with their signification.

Otto Jesperson, *Language: Its Nature Development and Origin* (1922) 398.

323

Evidently there is here another field for the future analysis of poetry; when it becomes possible to list the root-notions that the words must by their own nature be suggesting, it will be possible and profitable to discuss in some detail how far their sound is an echo to their sense. But such a process will always be subject to curious limitations; 'owing to the comparative paucity of different mouth-gestures, each mouth-gesture—which produces its own particular sound or root-word—has to stand for a considerable number of hand- (or other bodily) gestures; to put it in another way, each root word is naturally liable to bear many different meanings.... Any of these meanings may be used figuratively or objectively.'

William Empson, *Seven Types of Ambiguity* (1930); (Harmondsworth 1961) 15, citing Sir Richard Paget, *Human Speech*.

324

It must be remembered, too, that many sounds that are more justly claimed to be direct reflectors of nature or man's feelings, according to present-day pronunciation, have changed to what they now are from older sounds quite unlike them. *Thud* itself probably developed out of a word with a mild initial [t], unvoiced and unaspirated, in prehistoric times.... What symbolism does exist is based on objective, measureable factors in articulation—friction, explosion, hissing of consonants, etc.—which may be brought into relationship with subjective psychological factors. Vowel sounds as well as consonants have some obvious physical characteristics that invite poetic exploitation. The physiological apparatus of speech becomes tenser for the production of some of these—[i] and [e], for instance—than for others such as [o] and [a] and [ɔ]. The differentiation has been noticed by linguists, and even some of the most cautious have speculated on the psychological traits in language sounds.

The high, front, tense vowels have been associated with nearness and immediacy, while the back, relaxed vowels suggest distance in time or space or urgency, in more than one language.

Margaret Schlauch, *Modern English and Ameri can Poetry* (1956) 145f.

325

Now do they raise ghastly lightnings, now grisly reboundings
Of ruff raff roaring, men's hearts with terror agrising.
With pell mell ramping, with thwick thwack sturdily thundering.

Richard Stanyhurst, 'The description of Liparen, in Aeneis viii' (1582); *Transla tion of the First Four Books of the Aeneis ... With other Poetical Devices* ed. E. Arber (1880) 138.

326

The double double double beat
Of the thundering drum.

John Dryden, *A Song for St Cecilia's Day*, 1687 ll. 29f.

327

Puffs, powders, patches, bibles, billet-doux.

Alexander Pope, *The Rape of the Lock* (1714) i 138.

328

The baiting place of wit, the balm of woe,
The poor man's wealth, the prisoner's release,

Sir Philip Sidney, *Astrophil and Stella* (1598) xxxix.

329

A needless alexandrine ends the song,
That like a wounded snake, drags its slow length along.

Alexander Pope, *An Essay on Criticism* (1711) ll. 356f.

330

So glides some trodden serpent on the grass,
And long behind his wounded volume trails.

John Dryden, Annus Mirabilis (1667) st. 123.

331

Gold are their vests: long Alpine spears they wield:
And their left arm sustains a length of shield.

John Dryden, Aeneis viii 877l.

332

The merchant from th'Exchange returns in peace,
And the long labours of the *toilette* cease—

Alexander Pope, The Rape of the Lock (1714) iii 23f.

333

O'er bog or steep, through straight, rough, dense, or rare,

John Milton, Paradise Lost ii 948.

334

Thrice rung the bell, the slipper knocked the ground,
And the press'd watch returned a silver sound.

Alexander Pope, The Rape of the Lock (1714) i 17f.

335

I know a bank whereon the wild thyme blows,
Where oxlips and the nodding violet grows
Quite over-canopied with luscious woodbine,
With sweet musk-roses, and with eglantine.

William Shakespeare, A *Midsummer Night's Dream* II i 249-52.

336

OBERON White hawthorn, and the pastoral eglantine;
Fast fading violets covered up in leaves;
And mid-May's eldest child,
The coming musk-rose, full of dewey wine,
The murmurous haunt of flies on summer eves.

John Keats, 'Ode to a Nightingale' (1819) ll. 46-50.

337

Music that gentlier on the spirit lies,
Than tired eyelids upon tired eyes;

Alfred, Lord Tennyson, 'The Lotus-Eaters' (1832) ll. 50f.

Metrical Structure

338

Sighs are my food, drink are my tears;

Sir Thomas Wyatt; *Collected Poems* ed. K. Muir and P. Thomson (Liverpool 1969) 242 (accentual).

Reading the *Odyssey*
   in my rock garden

Robert Bridges, 'Cheddar Pinks', *New Verse* (1921) (alternating six- and five-syllable lines).

Cease then, nor order imperfection name:

Alexander Pope, *An Essay on Man* (1733) i 281 (accentual plus syllabic).

Cast their eyes hitherward; lo, in an agony,

Thomas Campion, 'Canto Secundo' (1591); *Works*, ed. W. R. Davis (Garden City, N.Y. 1967), (quantitative: $-\cup\cup- -\cup\cup- \cup-$).

Changing kisses alike; straight with a false alarm,

Thomas Campion, 'Canto Secundo' (accentual plus quantitative: $-- -\cup\cup-$).

Rocks, caves, lakes, fens, bogs, dens, and shades of death,

John Milton, *Paradise Lost* (1667) ii 621 (how many stresses?).

Savage, extreme, rude, cruel, not to trust;

William Shakespeare, *Sonnets* (1609) cxxix (scansion?).

339

Metre, like every other form of speech, is variable rhythm, and can never be otherwise. It differs from every other form of speech in being rhythm *varying over a constancy*. It may be summarily defined thus: *Metre is the modulated repetition of a rhythmical pattern....*

Metre is rhythm, the variation of which constantly suggests its reference to one ideal pattern; and if this reference is not constantly made in the act of hearing the variable rhythm, there is no metre.

Lascelles Abercrombie, *Principles of English Prosody* (1923) 42.

340

The very notion that he [Wyatt] progressed slowly, with laborious practice, towards metre is unplausible. Emphatic metrical schemes are among the earliest forms of composition, and both children and 'primitive' peoples master them readily. It is true that exceptional polish of simple metres may represent one form of literary sophistication, as in Dryden and Pope, but advancing skill and command of language may equally lead to increasing irregularity, as of course in Shakespeare.

D. W. Harding, *Scrutiny* xiv (1946) 93.

341

'And thé rewárd littlé trust fór evér' ... 'Now sínce in thée is nóne othér reasón.' All these examples show definite rules of construction followed by Wyatt.

A. K. Foxwell, A *Study of Sir Thomas Wyatt's Poems* (1911) 24.

342

Which syllables should be regarded as long or short was clear enough in grammar from the vowels, which we defined as long or short. Poets, however, shorten long syllables freely in final positions; since in the flow of speech the accent on the next syllable absorbs its length. But if a syllable is influenced by any grammatical or rhetorical accent, it is not shortened; as *my money*—⌣⌣

Alexander Gil, *Logonomia anglica* (1621) 132.

343

'Nor can the glory contain it self in th'endless space'. It is not by negligence that this verse is so loose, long, and as it were, vast; it is to paint in the number [rhythm] the nature of the thing which it describes, which I would have observed in divers other places of this poem, that else will pass for very careless verses: as before, 'And over-runs the neighb'ring fields with violent course'. In the Second Book, 'Down a precipice deep, down he casts them all'— and 'And fell adown his shoulders with loose care'. In the 3. 'Brass was his helmet, his boots brass, and o'er his breast a thick plate of strong brass he wore'. In the 4. 'Like some fair pine o'erlooking all th'ignobler wood'; and, 'Some from the rocks cast themselves down headlong'; and many more: but it is enough to instance in a few. The thing is, that the disposition of words and numbers should be such, as that out of the order and sound of them, the things themselves may be represented.

Abraham Cowley, *Davideis* (1668) i, n 25; *Poems* ed. A. R. Waller (Cambridge 1905) 273.

344

Compare for example:— 'Deep into a gloomy grot' with 'Peep into a roomy cot'. The ascribed rhythm, the movement of the words, trivial though it be ... is different, though almost every prosodist would have to scan them in the same fashion, and the kymograph would, I think, for most readers, show few important differences.... 'J. Drootan-Sussting Benn/Mill-down Leduren N.' ... If the reader has any difficulty in scanning these verses, reference to Milton, *On the Morning of Christ's Nativity*, xv, will prove of assistance, and the attempt to divine the movement of the original before looking it up will at least show how much the sense, syntax and feeling of verse may serve as an introduction to its form. But the illustration will also support a subtler argument against anyone who affirms that the mere sound of verse has *independently* any considerable aesthetic virtue.

I. A. Richards, *Practical Criticism* (1929) 231f.

345

Presaged by wondrous signs, and mostly by flocks of wild pigeons,

Henry Wadsworth Longfellow, *Evangeline* II v; *Works* iv (1886) 100.

346

Triple metres (anapestic, dactylic) tend to have something vaguely comic, light, or superficial about them.

Paul Fussell, *Princeton Encyclopedia of Poetry and Poetics*, ed. A. Preminger (Princeton, N.J. 1965) 498.

347

It is when words sing that they give that absolute moving attention which is beyond their prose powers.

R. P. Blackmur, 'Lord Tennyson's Scissors', *Form and Value in Modern Poetry* (Garden City N.Y. 1957) 369.

348

However minute the employment may appear, of analysing lines into syllables, and whatever ridicule may be incurred by a solemn deliberation upon accents and pauses, it is certain, that without this petty knowledge no man can be a poet; and that from the proper disposition of single sounds results that harmony that adds force to reason, and gives grace to sublimity; that shackles attention, and governs passions.

Samuel Johnson, *Rambler* No. 88 (19 Jan. 1751); *Works*, Yale edn. iv (New Haven and London 1969) 99.

349

La Liberté la plus grand : qu'importe le nombre de vers, si le rythme est *beau*?

H. de Regnier, *cit.* P. M. Jones, *The Background of Modern French Poetry* (Cambridge 1951) 94.

350

Vers libre is a battle-cry of freedom and there is no freedom in art.... The division between Conservative Verse and Vers libre does not exist, for there is only good verse, bad verse, and chaos.

T. S. Eliot 'Reflections on Vers libre' (1917)
To Criticize the Critic (1965) 184, 189.

351

T. S. Eliot, The Waste Land (1922).

352

Only a bad poet could welcome free verse as a liberation from form. It was a revolt against dead form, and a preparation for new form or for the renewal of the old; it was an insistence upon the inner unity which is unique to every poem, against the outer unity which is typical.

T. S. Eliot, 'The Music of Poetry' (1942); On
Poetry and Poets (1957) 37.

353

A signal refusal to follow a literary convention is in itself significant with respect to it. The practice of the Imagist poets, for example, of not capitalizing the initial letters of lines of verse had as strictly a signifying or labelling effect as does the conventional capitalization: the sign read 'This is an Imagist poem',

rather than merely 'This is verse'.

John Hollander, in Style in Language, ed. T. A.
Sebeok (Cambridge, Mass. 1960) 405.

354

No unit can be kept in mind as a constant norm, unless it is grouped in a perceptible way. We do not remember or 'feel' any constant number (say, sixteen syllables) unless it is so grouped.

Benjamin Hrushovski, 'On Free Rhythms in
Modern Poetry', ibid. 188.

355

If free verse had form in any real sense, its form would be detectable.

D. A. Stauffer, The Nature of Poetry (New York
1946) 204.

356

It is strange that a generation of critics so sensitive and ingenious as ours should have turned out very backward, indeed phlegmatic, when it comes to hearing the music of poetry, or at least, to avoid misunderstanding, to hearing its metres. The only way to escape the sense of a public scandal is to assume that the authority of the metres is passing, or is past, because we have become jaded by the metres; which would mean that something else must be tried.

John Crowe Ransom, 'The Strange Music of
English Verse', Kenyon Review xviii (1956) 460.

357

Contents of the Phrase.—Here is a great deal of talk about rhythm—and naturally; for in our canorous language, rhythm is always at the door. But it must not be forgotten that in some languages this element is almost, if not quite, extinct, and that in our own it is probably decaying. The even speech of many educated Americans sounds the note of danger. I should see it go with something as bitter as despair, but I should not be desperate. As in verse no element, not even rhythm, is necessary, so, in prose also, other sorts of beauty will arise and take the place and play the part of those that we outlive.

Robert Louis Stevenson, 'On Some Technical Elements of Style in Literature' (1885) Works, Vailima edn. iv (1922-3) 441.

358

Prosody ... must be 'oriented' not toward phonetics, that is, the physical and physiological description of speech-sounds, but towards phonemics, which examines the speech sounds *sub specie* of their linguistic function, that is, their capacity for differentiating word meanings.

Victor Erlich, *Russian Formalism—History—Doctrine* (1955) 188.

359

Although intonation patterns often have independent meanings of their own, their use in confirming segmental meanings (plain-sense meanings, roughly, or the meanings of the sequences of words by themselves) is perhaps most significant for metrics. In the first place, prosody may clarify a meaning which has become obscured by the synactic compression so frequently found in poetry, particularly in lyric poetry. It is, I am sure, a common experience for many readers suddenly to grasp the meaning of a difficult line upon hearing it read aloud for the first time.

Seymour Chatman, 'Robert Frost's "Mowing": an Inquiry into Prosodic Structure', *Discussions of Poetry: Rhythm and Sound*, ed. G. Hemphill (Boston, Mass. 1961) 85.

360

Basic to all discussion of these matters is Trager and Smith's *An Outline of English Structure (Studies in Linguistics, Occasional Paper No. 3, Buffalo 1951)*, because it contains the most authoritative account of the sounds of modern spoken English.... Their phonology ... involves (1) Four kinds of *stress* (primary/, secondary^, tertiary\, weak˘). (2) Four degrees of *pitch*, ranging from low to high. (3) Four significant *junctures* between the syllables of the language.... The proposition that metre and language are two different things ... is a dangerous one.... Language, he [John Thompson] allows, following Trager and Smith, has four stresses, but metre, he claims, has only two. In poetry, he says, it is the 'tension' existing between the language stresses and the metrical stresses which is peculiar to the art, and which is 'usually highly prized'.... Yet Mr Thompson does not convince me.... If poetry is written in English, then it must have *four* stresses, because English has four stresses. If it does not have them, then it is not English.

Terence Hawkes, in *Essays in Criticism* xii (1962) 413-5.

The notion of an accentual spondee (or 'level' foot) in English would seem to be illusory, for the reason that it is impossible to pronounce any two successive syllables in English without some rise or fall of stress—and *some* rise or fall of stress is all that is needed for a metrical ictus. This fact produces in English iambic metre two kinds of ambiguous situations or metrical choices, that of two weak syllables coming together, and that of two strong syllables coming together. In each of these situations, the iambic principle is saved merely by the fact that certain unhappy choices are impossible.

W. K. Wimsatt Jr. and Monroe C. Beardsley, 'The Concept of Metre: an Exercise in Abstraction', *Publications of the Modern Language Association* lxxiv (1959) 594.

There is more to English verse than a simple alternation of two stresses, or of stressed and unstressed syllables in the traditionally stated patterns. English has *four* degrees of significant stress and the poet who hears all four when he composes verse, makes his metrical patterns out of various sequences and combinations of these four stresses.... When two instances of the same stress phoneme occur on syllables immediately following each other, the occurrence of the second in the sequence will be phonetically more 'prominent' than the first. So in *ănĭmăl* the weak stress over the *final* syllable is phonetically stronger—perceived as 'louder'—than that of the *second* syllable. Likewise in the case of the secondary stresses, in *ăn + ôld + stône + hóuse*, the stress on *stone* is louder than that on *old*.

Henry Lee Smith, *Studies in Linguistics Occasional Papers* No. 7 (Buffalo, N.Y. 1959) 7.

'Shoot, if you must, this old gray head,

John Greenleaf Whittier, 'Barbara Frietchie', *In War Time* (1864) l. 34.

If the real point about this house is its antiquity, wouldn't *old* get more stress than *stone*? If the *stone* is the aspect to be emphasized, it will naturally be more heavily stressed by the speaker or reader. If both qualities are of equal importance, 'good English' will allot them an equal degree of stress.

F. W. Bateson, in *Essays in Criticism* xiii (1963) 200.

The Smith hypothesis—as between syllables of equal stress—of a shade more emphasis in the second than the first and in the third than the second has no practical prosodic importance, if it exists at all (no statistical evidence has been provided so far). It is difficult enough to reach agreement as between the four standard degrees of stress; further subdivision, though no doubt theoretically possible, will be too ghostly to affect aurally recognizable patterns.... What might be called the prosodic fallacy is to detach metre from poetry. A poem's scansion is necessarily *subsequent* to its meaning (its literary meaning, its significance as poetry). In other words, the degree of stress a particular syllable is to receive is less a matter of phonology than of rhetoric .

F. W. Bateson, in *Essays in Criticism* xii (1962) 423.

... the *metrum* or accentual pattern underlying ordinary English metrics. I suspect myself that this basic pattern is not to be found in the foot but in the line—and that the recurring element which is the distinguishing characteristic of English verse (as syllabic regularity is of French verse) is the *total stress-weight of the line.*

F. W. Bateson, in *Essays in Criticism* xiii (1963) 200f.

Unity

367

Accordingly, just as in the other imitative arts the object of each imitation is a unit, so, since the fable is an imitation of an action, that action must be a complete unit, and the events of which it is made up must be so plotted that if any of these elements is moved or removed the whole is altered and upset.

Aristotle, *Poetics* viii; tr. L. J. Potts (Cambridge 1959) 28.

368

Every work of genius is a whole, made up of the regular combination of different parts, so organized as to become altogether subservient to a common end.... But however perfectly the associating principles perform this part of their office, a person will scarce reckon himself certain of the propriety of that disposition, till it has been authorised by judgment. Fancy forms the plan in a sort of mechanical or instinctive manner: judgment on reviewing it, perceives its rectitude or its errors, as it were scientifically; its decisions are founded upon reflection, and produce a conviction of their justness.

Alexander Gerard, *Essay on Genius* (1774) 84f.

369

Still follow sense, of ev'ry art the soul,
Parts answ'ring parts shall slide into a whole,

Alexander Pope, 'Epistle to Burlington' (1744 edn.) ll. 65f.

370

First, then, we warn thee not too hastily to condemn any of the incidents in this our history as impertinent and foreign to our main design, because thou dost not immediately conceive in what manner such incident may conduce to that design. This work may, indeed, be considered as a great creation of our own; and for a little reptile of a critic to presume to find fault with any of its parts, without knowing the manner in which the whole is connected, and before he comes to the final catastrophe, is a most presumptuous absurdity. The allusion and metaphor we have here made use of, we must acknowledge to be infinitely too great for the occasion; but there is, indeed, no other, which is at all adequate to express the difference between an author of the first rate and a critic of the lowest.

Henry Fielding, *Tom Jones* (1749) X i; *Works* ed. W. E. Henley iv (1903) 193f.

371

I was just going, for example, to have given you the great outlines of my uncle Toby's most whimsical character;—when my aunt Dinah and the coachman came across us, and led us a vagary some millions of miles into the very heart of the planetary system: Notwithstanding all this, you perceive that the drawing of my uncle Toby's character went on gently all the time;—not the great contours of it,—that was impossible,—but some familiar strokes and faint designations of it, were here and there touched on, as we went along, so that you are much better acquainted with my uncle Toby now than you was before.

By this contrivance the machinery of my work is of a species by itself; two contrary motions are introduced into it, and reconciled, which were thought to be at variance with one another. In a word, my work is digressive, and it is progressive too,—and at the same time....

Digressions, incontestably, are the sunshine;—they are the life, the soul of reading!

Laurence Sterne, *Tristram Shandy* (1759) I xxii; i (Oxford 1926) 76f.

372

Nuns fret not at their convent's narrow room;
And hermits are contented with their cells;
Maids at the wheel, the weaver at his loom,
Sit blithe and happy; bees that soar for bloom,
High as the highest peak of Furness-fells,
Will murmur by the hour in foxglove bells:
In truth the prison, into which we doom
Ourselves, no prison is: and hence for me,
In sundry moods, 'twas pastime to be bound
Within the sonnet's scanty plot of ground;
Pleased if some souls (for such there needs must be)

Who have felt the weight of too much liberty,
Should find brief solace there, as I have found.

William Wordsworth, 'Nuns Fret Not' (1807).

373

The form is mechanic when on any given material we impress a determined form, not necessarily arising out of the properties of the material.... The organic form, on the other hand, is innate; it shapes as it develops itself from within, and the fullness of its development is one and the same with the perfection of the outward form.

S. T. Coleridge, *Shakespearian Criticism* ed. T. M. Raysor, i (Cambridge, Mass. 1930) 224.

374

Really, universally, relations stop nowhere, and the exquisite problem of the artist is eternally but to draw, by a geometry of his own, the circle within which they shall happily *appear* to do so.

Henry James, Preface to *Roderick Hudson* (1907); *The Art of the Novel* ed. R. P. Blackmur (1934) 5.

375

A powerfully imaginative mind seizes and combines at the same instant all the important ideas of its poem or picture, and while it works with one of them, it is at the same instant working with and modifying all in their relation to it and never losing sight of their bearings on

each other—as the motion of a snake's body goes through all parts at once and its volition acts at the same instant in coils which go contrary ways.

T. E. Hulme, *Speculation* (1924) 139f.

376

When a poet's mind is perfectly equipped for its work, it is constantly amalgamating disparate experience; the ordinary man's experience is chaotic, irregular, fragmentary. The latter falls in love, or reads Spinoza, and these two experiences have nothing to do with each other, or with the noise of the typewriter or the smell of the cooking; in the mind of the poet these experiences are always forming new wholes.

T. S. Eliot, 'The Metaphysical Poets' (1921); *Selected Essays* (1951) 287.

377

How can one say, Mozart has composed [*componirt*] *Don Juan*! Composition! As if it were a piece of cake or biscuit, which had been stirred together out of eggs, flour, and sugar! It is a spiritual creation, in which the details, as well as the whole, are pervaded by *one* spirit, and by the breath of *one* life; so that the producer did not make experiments, and patch together, and follow his own caprice, but was altogether in the power of the demonic spirit of his genius, and acted according to his orders.

Johann Wolfgang von Goethe, *Conversations with Eckermann*, 20 June 1831; tr. J. Oxenford (1930) 415.

378

There was a time when I saw (*je voyais*). I saw or wished to see the patterns or relations between things, not the things themselves. *Things* made me smile with pity. Persons who stopped at things were for me no better than idolaters. I *knew* that the essential *thing* was pattern.

Paul Valéry, 'Propos me concernant', *Présence de Valéry* ed. J. Berne-Joffroy (Paris 1944) 55.

379

The spirit of poetry like all other living powers ... must embody in order to reveal itself; but a living body is of necessity an organized one,—and what is organization, but the connection of parts to a whole, so that each part is at once end and means!

S. T. Coleridge, *Shakespearian Criticism* ed. T. M. Raysor, i (Cambridge, Mass. 1930) 223.

380

I should like to commit myself to the view that for a poem to exist as a unity more than merely bibliographical, we need the sense of one voice speaking, as in lyric or elegaic verse; or of several voices intelligibly related to one another, as in narrative with dialogue or drama: that what these voices say needs a principle of connection no different from that which is acceptable in any other kind of discourse; that the collocation of images is not a method at all but the negation of a method. In fact, to expose oneself completely, I want to say that a poem, internally considered, ought to make the same kind of sense as any other discourse.

Graham Hough, *Image and Experience* (1960) 25.

381

But to deny that the coherence of a poem is reflected in a logical paraphrase of its 'real meaning' is not, of course, to deny coherence to poetry; it is rather to assert that its coherence is to be sought elsewhere. The characteristic unity of a poem (even of those poems that may accidentally possess a logical unity as well as a poetic unity) lies in the unification of attitudes into a hierarchy subordinated to a total and governing attitude.

Cleanth Brooks, *The Well Wrought Urn* (New York 1947) 207.

382

The cement which binds any artistic production into one whole and therefore provides the illusion of being a reflection of life is not the unity of persons or situations, but the unity of the author's independent moral relation to his subject.

Leo Tolstoy, 'Guy de Maupassant' (1894); *What is Art?* tr. A. Maud (Oxford 1930) 38.

383

All happy families resemble one another, but each unhappy family is unhappy in its own way.

Everything was upset in the Oblonsky's house.

Leo Tolstoy, *Anna Karenina* (1877), opening sentence.

It is a truth universally acknowledged, that a single man in possession of a good fortune, must be in want of a wife.

Jane Austen, *Pride and Prejudice* (1813), opening sentences.

384

If there is one gift more essential to a novelist than any other it is the power of combination—the single vision. The success of the masterpieces seem to be not so much in their freedom from faults —indeed we tolerate the grossest errors in them all—but in the immense pervasiveness of a mind which has completely mastered its perspective.

Virginia Woolf, 'The Novels of E. M. Forster' (1942); *Collected Essays* i (1966) 344f.

385

We cannot know too much about the remarkable *inclusiveness* of the book [A *Passage to India*]. We continue to have our illusion of order, and clever faking; but this book reminds us how vast the effort for totality must be; nothing is excepted, the extraordinary is essential to order.

Frank Kermode, *Puzzles and Epiphanies* (1962) 85.

386

But as to amplitude, the invariable rule dictated by the nature of the action is, the fuller the more beautiful so long as the outline remains clear; and for a simple rule of size, the number of happenings that will make a chain of probability (or necessity) to change a given situation from misfortune to good fortune or from good fortune to misfortune is the minimum.

Aristotle, *Poetics* vii; tr. L. J. Potts (Cambridge 1959) 28.

387

It surely is an easy thing to bring it about that in many and separate actions there should be a variety of events, but that the same variety should be furnished by one sole action, *hoc opus, hic labor est*. In that variety which arises from the multitude of the plots in themselves, no art or ingenuity of the poet is to be observed, and it is common to both learned and ignorant. Variety in the unified plot depends on the skill of the poet, and when it is attained is recognized as the result of his skill and as not to be achieved by any moderate capacities. The multiple plot will delight the less in proportion as it is more confused and less intelligible; the unified plot because of its arrangement and the binding together of its parts will not merely be more clear and distinct but will appear much more novel and marvellous. The plot and form should then be one in every sort of poem, including those that treat of arms and the loves of heroes and of errant knights, which generally are called heroic poems.

Torquato Tasso, *Discorsi del Poema Eroico* (Naples n.d.) iii; *Literary Criticism: Plato to Dryden* ed. A. H. Gilbert (New York &c. 1940) 501.

388

Upon the same scale we may compare Sophocles with Shakespeare; in the one there is a completeness, a satisfying, an excellence, on which the mind can rest; in the other we see a blended multitude of materials, great and little, magnificent and mean, mingled, if we say so, with a dissatisfying, or falling short of perfection, yet so promising of our progression that we would not exchange it for the repose of the mind which dwells on the forms of symmetry in acquiescent admiration of grace.

S. T. Coleridge, *Miscellaneous Criticism*, ed. T. M. Raysor (1936) 190.

389

Form in literature is an arousing and fulfilment of desires. A work has form in so far as one part of it leads a reader to anticipate another part, and to be gratified by the sequence.

Kenneth Burke, *Counterstatement* (Los Altos, Calif. 1953) 147.

390

A poem is that species of composition, which is opposed to works of science, by proposing for its *immediate* object pleasure, not truth; and from all other species (having *this* object in common with it) it is discriminated by proposing to itself such delight from the *whole*, as is compatible with a distinct gratification from each component *part*.

S. T. Coleridge, *Biographia Litteraria* (1817) ch. xiv; ed. J. Shawcross ii (Oxford 1907) 10.

391

... a feeling we have all had: that the study of mediocre works of art remains a random and peripheral form of critical experience, whereas the profound masterpiece draws us to a point at which we seem to see an enormous number of converging patterns of significance.

Northrop Frye, *Anatomy of Criticism* (Princeton, N.J. 1957) 17.

392

The degree of beauty manifested by any work of art will be a resultant of two factors: (a) the richness, complexity or subtlety of the configurational organization; and (b) the completeness or compactness of the organization for experience.

Harold Osborne, *The Theory of Beauty* (1952) 126.

Speculative Instruments

393

We passed through Glen Shiel, with prodigious mountains on each side. We saw where the battle was in 1715. Mr Johnson owned he was now in a scene of as wild nature as he could see. But he corrected me sometimes in my observations. 'There,' said I, 'is a mountain like a cone.' 'No Sir,' said he, 'it would be called so in a book; and when a man comes to look at it, he sees 'tis not so. It is indeed pointed at the top. But one side of it is much longer than the other.' Another mountain I called immense. 'No,' said he, 'but it is a considerable protuberance.'

James Boswell, *Journal of a Tour to the Hebrides*, 1 September 1773; ed. R. W. Chapman (Oxford 1924) 249.

394

Nature never set forth the earth in so rich tapestry as divers poets have done, neither with so pleasant rivers, fruitful trees, sweet-smelling flowers, nor whatsoever else may make the too much loved earth more lovely : her world is brazen, the poets only deliver a golden.

Sir Philip Sidney, *The Defence of Poesy* (1595); Works ed. A. Feuillerat iii (Cambridge 1912) 8.

395

My own experience is that the more we study Art, the less we care for Nature. What Art really reveals to us is Nature's lack of design, her curious crudities, her extraordinary monotony, her absolutely unfinished condition. Nature has good intentions of course, but as Aristotle once said, she cannot carry them out. When I look at a landscape I cannot help seeing all its defects. It is fortunate for us, however, that Nature is so imperfect, as otherwise we should have no art at all. Art is our spirited protest, our gallant attempt to teach Nature her proper place.

Oscar Wilde, 'The Decay of Lying' (1889); *Works* (1966) 970.

396

If your everyday life seems poor to you, do not accuse it; excuse yourself, tell yourself that you are not poet enough to summon up its riches, since for the creator there is no poverty and no poor or unimportant place.

R. M. Rilke, *Letters to a Young Poet*, 17 February 1903; tr. R. Snell (1945) 12.

397

Gwendolen's uncontrolled reading, though consisting chiefly in what are called pictures of life, had somehow not prepared her for this encounter with reality. Is that surprising? It is to be believed that attendance at the *opéra bouffe* in the present day would not leave men's minds entirely without shock, if the manners observed there with some applause were suddenly to start up in their own families.... What hymning of cancerous vices may we not languish over as sublimest art in the safe remoteness of a strange language and artificial phrase! Yet we keep a repugnance to rheumatism and other painful effects when presented in our personal experience.

George Eliot, *Daniel Deronda* (1876) ch. xiv; ed. B. Hardy (Harmondsworth 1967) 193.

398

For its nature is to be not a part, nor yet a copy, of the real world ... but to be a world by itself, independent, complete, autonomous; and to possess it fully you must enter that world, conform to its laws, and ignore for the time the beliefs, aims, and particular conditions which belong to you in the other world of reality.

A. C. Bradley, *Oxford Lectures on Poetry* (1909) 5.

399

There is continual spring, and harvest there
Continual, both meeting at one time:
For both the boughs do laughing blossoms bear,
And with fresh colours deck the wanton prime,
And eke at once the heavy trees they climb,
Which seem to labour under their fruits load:
The whiles the joyous birds make their pastime
Amongst the shady leaves, their sweet abode,
And their true loves without suspicion tell abroad.

Edmund Spenser, *The Faerie Queen* III vi 42.

400

In the afternoon they came unto a land
In which it seemed always afternoon.

Alfred, Lord Tennyson, 'The Lotos-Eaters' 3f

If poetry is a dream, the business of life is much the same. If it is a fiction, made up of what we wish things to be, and fancy that they are, because we wish them so, there is no other nor better reality.

William Hazlitt, 'On Poetry in General' (1818); *Complete Works* ed. P. P. Howe v (1930) 3.

402

Poetry acts in another and diviner manner. It awakens and enlarges the mind itself by rendering it the receptacle of a thousand unapprehended combinations of thought. Poetry lifts the veil from the hidden beauty of the world, and makes familiar objects to be as if they were not familiar.

P. B. Shelley, A *Defence of Poetry* (1821); *Works* ed. R. Ingpen and W. E. Peck vii (1930) 116.

With regard to poetry in general, I am convinced, the more I think of it ... that *all* of us, Scott, Southey, Wordsworth, Moore, Campbell, and I,—are all in the wrong ... that we are upon a wrong revolutionary poetic system. I was really astonished and mortified at the ineffable distance in point of sense, harmony, effect, and even *imagination*, passion and *invention*, between the little Queen Anne's man, and us of the Lower Empire.... To the question, 'whether the description of a game of cards be as poetical, supposing the execution of the artist equal, as a description of a walk in the forest?' [asked by William Bowles] it may be answered, that the *materials* are certainly not equal; but that the artist which who has rendered the game of cards poetical, is by *far the greater* of the two.

George Gordon, Lord Byron, *cit.* J. D. Hunt, *The Rape of the Lock* (1968) 100f.

404

Belinda now, whom thirst of fame invites,
Burns to encounter two adventurous knights,
At ombre singly to decide their doom;
And swells her breast with conquests yet to come.
Straight the three bands prepare in arms to join,
Each band the number of the sacred nine.
Soon as she spreads her hand, th'aerial guard
Descend, and sit on each important card :
First Ariel perched upon a matador,
Then each according to the rank he bore;
For sylphs, yet mindful of their ancient race,
Are, as when women, wondrous fond of place.

Alexander Pope, *The Rape of the Lock* (1714) iii 25-36.

405

He spoke slightingly of Dyer's *Fleece*.—'The subject, Sir, cannot
be made poetical. How can a man write poetically of serges and
druggets! Yet you will hear many people talk to you gravely of
that *excellent* poem, *The Fleece*.' Having talked of Grainger's
Sugar-Cane, I mentioned to him Mr Langton's having told me, that
this poem, when read in manuscript at Sir Joshua Reynolds's, had
made all the assembled wits burst into a laugh, when, after much
blank verse pomp, the poet began a new paragraph thus: 'Now, Muse,
let's sing of *rats*.' And what increased the ridicule was, that
one of the company, who slyly overlooked the reader, perceived
that the word had been originally *mice*, and had been altered to
rats, as more dignified.

   This passage does not appear in the printed work, Dr Grainger,
or some of his friends, it would seem, having become sensible that
introducing even *rats*, in a grave poem, might be liable to banter.
He, however, could not bring himself to relinquish the idea; for
they are thus, in a still more ludicrous manner, periphrastically
exhibited in his poem as it now stands:

<blockquote>
Nor with less waste the whisker'd vermin race
A countless clan despoil the lowland cane.
</blockquote>

James Boswell, *Life of Samuel Johnson* (1791), ed. G. B. Hill and L. F. Powell ii
(Oxford 1934) 453f.

406

<blockquote>
a day will come,
When, through new channels sailing, we shall clothe
The Californian coast, and all the realms
That stretch from Anian's straits to proud Japan;
And the green isles, which on the left arise
Upon the glassy brine, whose various capes
Not yet are figur'd on the sailors chart:
Then ev'ry variation shall be told
Of the magnetic steel; and currents mark'd,
Which drive the heedless vessel from her course.
</blockquote>

John Dyer, *The Fleece* (1757) iv 673-82.

407

I SING THE SOFA. I who lately sang
Truth Hope and Charity, and touch'd with awe
The solemn chords, and with a trembling hand,
Escap'd with pain from the advent'rous flight,
Now seek repose upon an humbler theme.

William Cowper, The Task (1785) i 1·5.

408

High on a mountain's highest ridge,
Where oft the stormy winter gale
Cuts like a scythe, while through the clouds
It sweeps from vale to vale,
Not five yards from the mountain-path,
This thorn you on your left espy;
And to the left, three yards beyond,
You see a little muddy pond,
Of water, never dry;
I've measured it from side to side:
'Tis three feet long, and two feet wide.

William Wordsworth, 'The Thorn' 23-33, Lyrical Ballads (1798).

409

There are no noble subjects or ignoble subjects; from the standpoint of pure Art one might almost establish the axiom that there is no such thing as subject, style in itself being an absolute manner of seeing things.

Gustave Flaubert, Letter to Louise Colet, 16 January 1852; *Correspondance* i (Paris 1922) 417.

410

'What I want to do is represent reality on the one hand, and on the other that effort to stylise it into art of which I have just been speaking.'

'My poor dear friend, you will make your readers die of boredom,' said Laura; as she could no longer hide her smile, she had made up her mind to laugh outright.

'Not at all. In order to arrive at this effect—do you follow me?—I invent the character of a novelist, whom I make my central figure; and the subject of the book, if you must have one, is just that very struggle between what reality offers him and what he himself desires to make of it.'

André Gide, *The Counterfeiters* (1925); (Paris 1943) 239.

411

But what we can't say, we can't say, and we can't whistle it either.

F. P. Ramsay, *Foundations of Mathematics* (1931) 238.

412

Let but Sophocles bring you Ajax on a stage, killing and whipping sheep and oxen, thinking them the Army of Greeks, with their Chieftains Agamemnon, and Menelaus: and tell me if you have not a more familiar insight into anger, than finding in the Schoolmen his Genus and Difference.

Sir Philip Sidney, *The Defence of Poesy* (1595); *Works* ed. A. Feuillerat iii (Cambridge 1912) 14f.

413

Poetry has to be something more than a conception of the mind. It has to be a revelation of nature. Conceptions are artificial. Perceptions are essential.... Metaphor creates a new reality from which the original appears to be unreal. ... Poetry is often a revelation of the elements of experience.

Wallace Stevens, 'Adagia', *Opus Posthumous* (1959) 164, 169, 177.

414

Art is a way of knowing. We learn about the universe of experience through our perceptions quite as much as through the exercise of discursive reason.... The devaluing of immediate perceptions, to which the whole modern intellectual process tends, is a great misfortune, since it results in the partial closing of one of our two main windows on the universe.... The typical imaginative or 'creative' work, in contrast, makes most of its statements about experience not by logical propositions but by presenting the experience itself so that the reader can sense its meanings directly as percepts. The difference between art and nonart might indeed, be precisely located here: a literary work is art in so far as its meanings are presented as percepts; nonart (the word is not to be taken as depreciatory) so far as its meanings are defined in ratiocinative terms.

Wayne Shumaker, *Elements of Critical Theory* (Berkeley and Los Angeles, Calif. 1964) 68f.

415

The great power of poetry is its interpretative power: by which I mean, not a power of drawing out in black and white an explanation of the mystery of the universe, but the power of so dealing with things as to awaken in us a wonderfully full, new, intimate sense of them, and of our relations with them. When this sense is awakened in us, as to objects without us, we feel ourselves to be in contact with the essential nature of those objects, to be no longer bewildered and oppressed by them, but to have their secret, and to be in harmony with them; and this feeling calms and satisfies us as no other can. Poetry, indeed, interprets in another way besides this; but one of its two ways of interpreting, of exercising its highest power, is by awakening this sense in us. I will not enquire whether this sense is illusive, whether it can be proved or not, whether it does absolutely make us possess the real nature of things; all I can say is, that poetry can awaken it in us, and that to awaken it is one of the highest powers of poetry.

Matthew Arnold, 'Maurice de Guérin' (1863); *Lectures and Essays in Criticism* ed. R. H. Super (Ann Arbor, Mich. 1962) 12f.

416

It may be that the imagination is a miracle of logic and that its exquisite divinations are calculations beyond analysis, as the conclusions of the reason are wholly within analysis.

Wallace Stevens, *The Necessary Angel* (1960) 154.

417

I am certain of nothing but of the holiness of the heart's affections and the truth of imagination—What the imagination siezes as beauty must be truth—whether it existed before or not—for I have the same idea of all our passions as of love they are all in their sublime, creative of essential beauty.... The imagination may be compared to Adam's dream—he awoke and found it truth. I am the more zealous in this affair, because I have never yet been able to perceive how anything can be known for truth by consequitive reasoning—and yet it must be.

John Keats, Letter to Benjamin Bailey, 22 November 1817; ed. H. E. Rollins i (Cambridge 1958) 184f.

418

Do not all charms fly
At the mere touch of cold philosophy?
We know her woof, her texture; she is given
In the dull catalogue of common things.
Philosophy will clip an angel's wings,
Conquer all mysteries by rule and line,
Empty the haunted air, and gnomèd mine—
Unweave a rainbow, as it erewhile made
The tender person'd Lamia melt into a shade.

John Keats, *Lamia* (1820) ii 229-38.

419

Poetry begins where matter of fact or science ceases to be merely such, and to exhibit a further truth; that is to say, the connection it has with the world of emotion, and its power to produce imaginative pleasure. Inquiring of a gardener, for instance, what flower it is we see yonder, he answers, 'a lily'. This is matter of fact. The botanist pronounces it to be of the order of 'Hexandria Monogynia'. This is matter of science.... 'The plant and flower of *light*', says Ben Jonson; and poetry shows us the beauty of the flower in all its mystery and splendour.

Leigh Hunt, Review of *Lamia* in *The Indicator*
(2 August 1820).

420

The romantic image is a means of exploring reality, by which the poet is in effect asking imagery to reveal to him the meaning of his own experience.

C. Day Lewis, *The Poetic Image* (1947) 58.

421

Their language is vitally metaphorical; that is, it marks the before unapprehended relations of things and perpetuates their apprehension, until the words which represent them become, through time, signs for portions or classes of thought instead of pictures of integral thoughts; and then if no new poets should arise to create afresh the

associations which have thus been disorganised, language will be dead to all the nobler purposes of human intercourse.

P. B. Shelley, A *Defence of Poetry* (1821); *Works* ed. R. Ingpen and W. E. Peck vii (1930) 111.

422

Many of the beauties of poetry and even of eloquence are founded on falsehood and fiction, on hyperboles, metaphors, and an abuse or perversion of terms from their natural meaning. To check the sallies of the imagination, and to reduce every expression to geometrical truth and exactness, would be most contrary to the laws of criticism; because it would produce a work which, by universal experience, has been found the most insipid and disagreeable. But though poetry cannot submit to exact truth, it must be confined by rules of art, discovered to the author either by genius or by observation.

David Hume, 'Of the Standard of Taste' (1757);
Essays (Oxford 1963) 2.

423

[Pope's *Essay on Man*] affords an egregious instance of the predominance of genius, the dazzling splendour of imagery, and the seductive powers of eloquence. Never were penury of knowledge and vulgarity of sentiment so happily disguised....

Surely a man of no very comprehensive search may venture to say that he has heard all this before, but it was never till now recommended by such a blaze of embellishment or such sweetness of melody. The vigorous contraction of some thoughts, the luxuriant amplification of others, the incidental illustrations, and sometimes the dignity, sometimes the softness of the verses, enchain philosophy, suspend criticism, and oppress judgment by overpowering pleasure.

Samuel Johnson, Life of Pope, *Lives of the Poets* (1781); ed. G. B. Hill iii (Oxford 1905) 243f.

424

I think that poetry should surprise by a fine excess and not by singularity—it should strike the leader as a wording of his own highest thoughts, and appear almost a remembrance.

John Keats, Letter to John Taylor, 27 Feb. 1818; ed. H. E. Rollins i (Cambridge 1958) 238.

425

There is a kind of phenomenal feeling of acceptance—Russell has called it an 'ah yes' feeling—that a poem or speech may move us to momentarily. It is hard, sometimes impossible, to distinguish this feeling from sheer intensity of participation or outgoing sympathy.... But wallowing in a feeling of pleasure at hearing something said, or letting go of your critical faculties completely, is not believing.

M. C. Beardsley, *Aesthetics* (New York 1958)

426

That which we call taste in writing, is but a fine discernment of truth. But as truth must be always one, and always the same to all who have eyes to discern it; he who pleases one of a true taste at first, is sure of pleasing all the world at last.

John Dennis, Epistle Dedicatory to *Liberty Assured* (1704).

427

This therefore is the praise of Shakespeare, that his drama is the mirror of life; that he who has mazed his imagination, in following the phantoms which other writers raise up before him, may here be cured of his delirious ecstasies, by reading human sentiments in human language, by scenes from which a hermit may estimate the transactions of the world, and a confessor predict the progress of the passions.

Samuel Johnson, *Preface to Shakespeare* (1765); *Works*, Yale edn. vii (New Haven and London 1968) 65.

428

Whether we deal with syllogisms or poems, we deal with dialectic—with, that is, a developing series of statements. Or if the word 'statements' seems to prejudge the question so far as literature is concerned, let us say merely that we can deal with a developing series—the important word is 'developing'. We judge the value of the development by judging the interest of its several stages and the propriety and the relevance of their connection among themselves. We make the judgment in terms of the implied purpose of the developing series.

Dialectic, in this sense, is just another word for form, and has for its purpose, in philosophy or in art, the leading of the mind to some conclusion. Greek drama, for example, is an arrangement of moral and emotional elements in such a way as to conduct the mind—'inevitably' as we like to say—to a certain affective condition. This condition is a quality of personal being which may be judged by the action it can be thought ultimately to lead to.

Lionel Trilling, 'The Meaning of a Literary Idea', *The Liberal Imagination* (1951) 283.

Serious art implies a view of life which can be stated in philosophical terms, even in terms of systems. Between artistic coherence (what is sometimes called 'artistic logic') and philosophical coherence there is some kind of correlation. The responsible artist has no will to confuse emotion and thinking, sensibility and intellection, sincerity of feeling with adequacy of experience and reflection. The view of life which the responsible artist articulates perpetually is not, like most views which have popular success as propaganda 'simple'; and an adequately complex vision of life cannot, by hypnotic suggestion, move to premature or naïve action.

René Wellek and Austin Warren, *Theory of Literature* (rev. edn., Harmondsworth 1963) 36.

The Editorial Art

430

It is something strange that of all the commentators upon Homer, there is hardly one whose principal design is to illustrate the poetical beauties of the author. They are voluminous in explaining those sciences which he made but subservient to his poetry, and sparing only upon that art which constitutes his character. This has been occasioned by the ostentation of men who had more reading than taste, and were fonder of showing their variety of learning in all kinds, than their single understanding in poetry. Hence it comes to pass that their remarks are rather philosophical, historical, geographical, allegorical, or in short rather anything than critical and poetical. Even the grammarians, though their whole business and use be only to render the words of an author intelligible, are strangely touched with the pride of doing something more than they ought. The grand ambition of one sort of scholars is to increase the number of various lections; which they have done to such a degree of obscure diligence, that we now begin to value the first editions of books as most correct, because they have been least corrected. The prevailing passion of others is to discover new meanings in an author, whom they will cause to appear mysterious purely for the vanity of being thought to unravel him. These account it a disgrace to be of the opinion of those that preceded them; and it is generally the fate of such people who will never say what was said before, to say what will never be said after them. If they can but find word that has once been strained by some dark writer to signify anything different from its usual acceptation, it is frequent with them to apply it constantly to that uncommon meaning, whenever they meet it in a clear writer: for reading is so much dearer to them than sense, that they will discard it at any time to make way for a criticism.... Where they cannot contest the truth of the common interpretation, they get themselves room for dissertation by imaginary amphibiologies, which they will have to be designed by the author. This disposition of finding out different significations in one thing, may be the effect of either too much, or too little wit: for men of a right understanding generally see at once all that an author can reasonably mean, but others are apt to fancy two meanings for want of knowing one. Not to add, that there is a vast deal of difference between the learning of a critic, and the puzzling of a grammarian.

Alexander Pope, Preliminary note to *The Iliad of Homer* (1715) i; ed. M. Mack i (1967) 82.

431

The art of writing notes is not of difficult attainment. The work is performed, first by railing at the stupidity, negligence, ignorance, and asinine tastelessness of the former editors, and showing, from all that goes before and all that follows, the inelegance and absurdity of the old reading; then by proposing something, which to superficial readers would seem specious, but which the editor rejects with indignation; then by producing the true reading, with a long paraphrase, and concluding with loud acclamations on the discovery, and a sober wish for the advancement and prosperity of genuine criticism. . . .

Notes are often necessary, but they are necessary evils. Let him, that is yet unacquainted with the powers of Shakespeare, and who desires to feel the highest pleasure that the drama can give, read every play from the first scene to the last, with utter negligence of all his commentators. When his fancy is once on the wing, let it not stoop at correction or explanation. When his attention is strongly engaged, let it disdain alike to turn aside to the name of Theobald and of Pope. Let him read on through brightness and obscurity, through integrity and corruption; let him preserve his comprehension of the dialogue and his interest in the fable. And when the pleasures of novelty have ceased, let him attempt exactness, and read the commentators.

Particular passages are cleared by notes, but the general effect of the work is weakened. The mind is refrigerated by interruption; the thoughts are diverted from the principal subject; the reader is weary, he suspects not why; and at last throws away the book, which he has too diligently studied.

Parts are not to be examined till the whole has been surveyed; there is a kind of intellectual remoteness necessary for the comprehension of any great work in its full design and its true proportions; a close approach shows the smaller niceties, but the beauty of the whole is discerned no longer.

It is not very grateful to consider how little the succession of editors has added to this author's power of pleasing. He was read, admired, studied, and imitated, while he was yet deformed with all the improprieties which ignorance and neglect could accumulate upon him.

Samuel Johnson, *Preface to Shakespeare* (1765); *Works*, Yale edn. vii (New Haven and London 1968) 108, 111.

432

Every writer knows how diaries and articles are utilized as material for books, and no ordinary reader knows or cares. What is important is the finished work by which the author wishes to stand. . . . We are told in these introductions [to the Centenary edition of *The Marble Faun*], in accordance with the MLA formula, that, in the course of writing the book, the author, as novelists often do, changed the names of certain of the characters; and that many of the descriptions in it—as has been noted, also a common practice—have been taken from his Italian notebooks. This information is of no interest whatever. Nor is it of any interest to be told that Hawthorne's wife corrected certain inaccuracies in the Roman descriptions and otherwise made occasional suggestions, which Hawthorne did not always accept. It has evidently been trying for Mr Bowers to find that, in the original manuscript, the author had been so inconsiderate as usually to make his changes 'by wiping out with a finger while the ink was still wet and writing over the same space.' But the places where these smudges occur have been carefully noted and listed.

Edmund Wilson, *The Fruits of the MLA* (New York 1968) 13, 18.

433

It should always be with some misgivings that an editor presents to the public materials which the author has discarded. By returning the materials to his files, the author has voted against publication. By resurrecting them, the editor risks exposing the author to the adverse criticism which he wished to avoid. But, at the same time, the resurrection serves a valuable purpose by making available almost indispensable evidence to be used by those seeking to understand the creative process.

Franklin R. Rogers, Introduction to *Mark Twain's Satires and Burlesques* (Berkeley and Los Angeles, Calif. 1967) 1.

434

Beyond this, for the ordinary reader, who is not obliged to use them for a Ph.D. thesis, these papers have no interest whatever. If he has already looked into this author's complete works, he knows that Mark Twain, during his lifetime, had already published so much now uninteresting clowning that there can be very little point in salvaging any he rejected.

Edmund Wilson, *The Fruits of the MLA* (New York 1968) 21f.

435

Any book, any essay, any note in *Notes and Queries* which produces a fact even of the lowest order about a work of art is a better piece of work than nine-tenths of the most pretentious critical journalism, in journals or in books. We assume, of course, that we are masters and not servants of facts, and that we know that the discovery of Shakespeare's laundry bills would not be of much use to us, but we must always reserve final judgment as to the futility of the research which has discovered them, in the possibility that some genius will appear who will know of a use to which to put them. Scholarship, even in its humblest forms, has its rights; we assume that we know how to use it, and how to neglect it. Of course the multiplication of critical books and essays may create, and I have seen it create, a vicious taste for reading about works of art instead of reading the works themselves, it may supply opinion instead of educating taste. But *fact* cannot corrupt taste.... The real corrupters are those who supply opinion or fancy.... What is Coleridge's *Hamlet*: is it an honest inquiry as far as the data permit, or is it an attempt to present Coleridge in an attractive costume?

T. S. Eliot, 'The Function of Criticism' (1923); *Selected Essays* (1951) 33.

436

An emendatory critic would ill discharge his duty, without qualities very different from dulness. In perusing a corrupted piece, he must have before him all possibilities of meaning, with all possibilities of expression. Such must be his comprehension of thought, and such his copiousness of language. Out of many readings possible, he must be able to select that which best suits with the state of opinions, and modes of language prevailing in every age, and with his author's particular cast of thought, and turn of expression. Such must be his knowledge, and such his taste. Conjectural criticism demands more than humanity possesses, and he that exercises it with most praise has very frequent need of indulgence. Let us now be told no more of the dull duty of an editor.... When he succeeds best, he produces perhaps but one reading of many probable, and he that suggests another will always be able to dispute his claims.

It is an unhappy state, in which danger is hid under pleasure. The allurements of emendation are scarcely resistible. Conjecture has all the joy and all the pride of invention.

Samuel Johnson, *Preface to Shakespeare* (1765); *Works*, Yale edn. vii (New Haven and London 1968) 94f., 109.

437

The eighteenth-century editor had none of this indifferentism; his object was to unmix the metaphors as quickly as possible, and generally restore the text to a rational and shipshape condition. We have no longer enough faith to attempt such a method, but its achievements must be regarded with respect, both because it has practically invented some of Shakespeare's most famous passages and because, in its more naïve forms, it may often show how the word it supplants came into Shakespeare's mind.

Thus, to take one of the famous cruces in *Macbeth*,
My way of life
Is falne into the Seare, the yellow Leafe,

is an achievement we must allow no emendation to remove; but Johnson's *May of life* seems to me a valuable piece of retrospective analysis, because it shows how the poetry was constructed; first, there would be an orderly framework of metaphor, then any enrichment of the notion which kept to the same verbal framework and was suggested easily by similarity of sound.

W. Empson, *Seven Types of Ambiguity* (1930); (Harmondsworth 1961) 82f.

I wondered whether I was yet dead, or still dying. But of a sudden some fashionless form brushed my side—some inert, soiled fish of the sea; the thrill of being alive again tingled in my nerves, and the strong shunning of death shocked me through.

Herman Melville, *White-Jacket* (1850) xcii; *Works*, Standard edn. vi (1922) 497.

Hardly anyone but Melville could have created the shudder that results from calling this frightening vagueness some 'soiled fish of the sea.' The *discordia concors*, the unexpected linking of the medium of cleanliness with filth, could only have sprung from an imagination that had apprehended the terrors of the deep, of the immaterial deep as well as the physical.

F. O. Matthiesen, in *American Literature* xxi (1949) 338.

The only difficulty with this critical *frisson* about Melville's imagination, and undemonstrable generalisations such as 'nobody but Melville could have created the shudder', and so on, is the cruel fact that an unimaginative typesetter inadvertently created it, not Melville; for what Melville wrote, as is demonstrated in both the English and American first editions, was *coiled* fish of the sea.

Fredson Bowers, *Textual and Literary Criticism* (Cambridge 1959) 30.

439

As time goes on, textual criticism will have less and less to do. In the old texts its work will have been performed so far as it is performable. What is left will be an obstinate remainder of difficulties, for which there is no solution or only too many. In the newer texts, on the other hand, as experience has already shown, it will have from the outset but a very contracted field.

John Percival Postgate, 'Textual Criticism', *Encyclopedia Britannica* (1911) xxvi 715.

440

The aim of a critical edition should be to present the text, so far as the available evidence permits, in the form in which we may suppose that it would have stood in a fair copy, made by the author himself, of the work as he finally intended it.

W. W. Greg, *The Editorial Problem in Shakespeare* (rev. edn. Oxford 1954) p. x.

441

Granting that the fact of revision (or correction) is established, an editor should in every case of variation ask himself (1) whether the original reading is one that can reasonably be attributed to the author, and (2) whether the later reading is one that the author can reasonably be supposed to have substituted for the former. If the answer to the first question is negative, then the later reading should be accepted as at least possibly an authoritative correction (unless, of course, it is itself incredible). If the answer to (1) is affirmative and the answer to (2) is negative, the original reading should be retained. If the answers to both questions are affirmative, then the later reading should be presumed to be due to revision and admitted into the text, whether the editor himself considers it an improvement or not.

W. W. Greg, 'The Rationale of Copy-Text' (1949); *Collected Papers* ed. J. C. Maxwell (Oxford 1966) 387.

442

She took me to her elfin grot,
    And there she wept, and sigh'd full sore,
And there I shut her wild wild eyes
    With kisses four.

John Keats, 'La Belle Dame Sans Merci' (1819) ll. 29-32.

She took me to her elfin grot,
    And there she gaz'd and sighed deep
And there I shut her wild sad eyes
    So kiss'd to sleep.

John Keats, 'La Belle Dame Sans Merci', *Indicator* (10 May 1820).

443

My judgement (he says) is as active while I am actually writing as my imagination. In fact, all my faculties are strongly excited and in their full play. And shall I afterwards, when my imagination is idle and the heat in which I wrote has gone off, sit down coldly to criticize when in possession of only one faculty what I have written when almost inspired?

Keats to Woodhouse, *The Keats Circle*, ed. H. E. Rollins, (1948) 59.

444

If ... we were to assure ourselves ... that certain corrections found in a later edition of a play were of Shakespearian authority, it would ... undoubtedly be necessary to incorporate these corrections in our text, but unless we could show that the edition in question (or the copy from which it had been printed) had been gone over and corrected throughout by Shakespeare ... the nearest approach to our ideal of an author's fair copy of his work in its final state will be produced by using the earliest 'good' print as copy-text and inserting into it, from the earliest edition which contains them, such corrections as appear to us to be derived from the author.... We are ... to consider whether a particular edition taken *as a whole* contains variants ... which ... seem likely to be the work of the author: and once having decided this to our satisfaction we must accept *all* the alterations of that edition, saving any which seem obvious blunders or misprints.

R. B. McKerrow, *Prolegomena for the Oxford Shakespeare* (Oxford 1939) 17f.

eschew the excesses of eclecticism, any attempt to evade the responsibility of individual judgement is an abdication of the editorial function.

W. W. Greg, in *The Works of Thomas Nashe*, ed. R. B. McKerrow, rev. F. P. Wilson, v (1958) Supplement, 33.

445

This will have struck many as doubtful, and it seems to me definitely perverse. It admittedly belongs to what is commonly called the 'conservative reaction' against the unprincipled eclecticism of most editors of the eighteenth and nineteenth centuries, and it forms, indeed, but an element in the concerted attempt of a later generation to substitute objective or mechanical rules in place of personal judgement. It seems to me, however, that any such attempt is in its nature mistaken and bound to lead to uncritical results. Judgement must inevitably be exercised alike to detect the presence of authorial alterations and to eliminate 'obvious blunders and misprints', and there can be no logical reason for refusing to exercise it likewise to discriminate between alterations for which the author must be considered responsible and those due to some other agency.... There is surely something wrong with an editorial principle that faces [?forces] the editor to include in his text admitted corruptions as well as authorized corrections.... The truth is that no critical principle can be devised that will relieve an editor of ultimate responsibility, and the risk of overlooking some authorial corrections is no excuse for an editor including in his text readings that he himself believes to be of no authority at all. Essential as it is to

446

What is it that enables an editor to detect the presence of 'obvious blunders and misprints'? The fact that blunders and misprints don't make sense! What is it that enables him to distinguish between 'alterations for which the author must be considered responsible and those due to some other agency'? The fact that an author's alterations make *better* sense! And what finally is it that makes an author's last or intermediate readings preferable, or not preferable, to his original text? The fact that they too do, or do not, make better sense.

F. W. Bateson, *Essays in Criticism* xvii (1967) 387.

447

The reading of the ancient books is probably true, and therefore is not to be disturbed for the sake of elegance, perspicuity, or mere improvement of the sense. For though much credit is not due to the fidelity, nor any to the judgement of the first publishers, yet they who had the copy before their eyes were more likely to read it right, than we who read it only by imagination.

Samuel Johnson, *Preface to Shakespeare* (1765); *Works*, Yale edn. vii (New Haven and London 1968) 106.

448

Whatever practice may be thought desirable in a popular or reading
edition, in a critical—that is, a critics'—edition modern
opinion is unanimously in favour of preserving the spelling and
punctuation of the original authority, at least so far as they are
not actually misleading....

What alternative is there, assuming that nothing must be done
in any way to distort the author's language? That modernization
on the lines usually followed does quite seriously misrepresent
Elizabethan English, experience has amply proved. To print
banquet for *banket*, *fathom* for *faddom*, *lantern* for *lanthorn*, *murder*
for *murther*, *mushroom* for *mushrump*, *orphan* for *orphant*, *perfect*
for *parfit*, *portcullis* for *perculace*, *tattered* for *tottered*, *vile* for
vild, *wreck* for *wrack*, and so on, and so on, is sheer perversion.
And how, in modern spelling, are we to render Spenser's rime?—

> By this arriued there
> Dame V*na*, wearie Dame, and entrance did requere....

In favour of normalization something might no doubt be said, since
it was after all the aim of contemporary printers: nevertheless
the objections to it appear to be conclusive. Today a standard
orthography masks quite a wide divergence of pronunciation even
among people of the same local and social surroundings. In
Shakespeare's day a writer's individualities of speech reflected
themselves naturally in his spelling, and to alter his spelling is
to destroy a clue to his language.... So long as there is any chance
of an edition preserving some trace, however faint, of the author's
individuality, the critic will wish to follow it.

W. W. Greg, *The Editorial Problem in Shakespeare* (rev. edn. Oxford 1954) **pp. l-lii.**

449

Old-spelling editors are traditionally
allowed intervals in which they may be
permitted to be mere copyists of the
unintelligible.

George Watson, *The Study of Literature* (1969)
131.

450

The real objection to an Old Spelling Shakespeare—or to any Old
Spelling edition of any author whatsoever (including the spelling

cranks like Spenser and Milton)—is the theoretical or artifactual one. An editor's duty is to establish his author's text, and since that text was originally oral and becomes oral again whenever it is properly read, what theory requires is a written text so spelled and punctuated that it can be translated back into an approximation of the oral original with the maximum certainty and the minimum difficulty or delay....

But is the project sound theoretically? Does the oral substratum in the literary artifact commit us to a historical reconstruction of either the author's or the original performers' or readers' pronunciations? The former possibility is particularly intriguing. Since William Blake and John Keats both spoke English with a cockney accent it is conceivable that we ought to read 'The Tiger' as follows: 'Toiger, toiger, burnin' broight...' and 'Ode to a Nightingale' as follows:

> Theow was not born for death, himmortal bird;
> Now 'ungry generitions tread thee deown!

Indeed the 'individualities of speech' Greg was so anxious to retain ... were *simply* eccentricities of authorial pronunciation. ...The sounds and half-sounds that constitute the physical substratum of the literary artifact originate in the speech of the society to which the author belongs. As such they are public (not private). A particular speaker's private idiosyncrasies ... are extraneous to the public communication he engages in whenever he speaks.

F. W. Bateson, 'The Literary Artifact', *Penn. State Univ. Journal of Gen. Educ.* xv (July 1963) [unpaginated].

451

It is worth noticing what is commonly overlooked: that all problematical texts tend to be edited in such a way as to produce a mixed result. The nature of the mixture may differ widely: but purity is not obtainable in the more difficult cases by any means whatever. When the old-spelling editor edits a Renaissance text by basing himself upon a copy-text such as the first printed edition, while correcting misprints and clearing up the outmoded confusion between i : j and u : v, he may offer his edition to the world in good conscience as the nearest approach to editorial purity that the example allows. But his text is likely to be a mixture of several elements: the accidentals of the author himself, those of one or more compositors (in so far as these differ from the author's, and from one another's), the editor's emendations (which may conform to modern practice, or to a normalized view of Renaissance practice, or to the author's, or to one or another of his compositor's); together with certain features of modern printing practice such as using 'j' for a consonantal 'i'. Such an editor may have produced this result honestly and in good faith, but he is not in a strong position in accusing others of eclecticism.

The plain fact is that mixture is usually inevitable and a degree of eclecticism an unavoidable duty. Once this is seen to be so, a still more radical prospect is opened to the editor: not only the prospect of scholarly modernized texts but one of texts which are partly or largely modernized while yet retaining such features characteristic of their period or author as can be shown to be significant.

George Watson, *The Study of Literature* (1969) 131f.

452

O that this too much grieu'd and sallied flesh
Would melt to nothing, or that the vniversall
Globe of heauen would turne al to a Chaos!

William Shakespeare, *Hamlet* First Quarto (1603) I ii 129-31,

O that this too too sallied flesh would melt,
Thaw, and resolue it self into a dewe,
Or that the euerlasting had not fixt
His cannon gainst seale slaughter, ô God, God,

Hamlet Second Quarto (1604-5) I ii 129-32.

Oh that this too too solid Flesh, would melt,
Thaw, and resolue it selfe into a Dew:
Or that the Euerlasting had not fixt
His Cannon 'gainst Selfe-slaughter. O God, O God!

Hamlet First Folio (1623) I ii 129-32.

453

But he [Shakespeare] surely had no hand in the 'too too solid Flesh'. A vision of Burbage's waist-band should suffice to prove that, editors notwithstanding, Shakespeare can never have meant to write 'solid' here. It is a desperate guess for the unintelligible 'sallied' of the quartos. The problem is therefore one of emendation.... The folio's 'solid' is a guess we must reject: the 'sallied' of the quartos is unintelligible. But 'sallies' occurs elsewhere in the second quarto as a misprint for 'sullies', showing that the words could be easily confused in Shakespeare's hand. Thus, when he intended 'sullied' flesh, it was twice misread as 'sallied' and finally misemended to 'solid'. Of this explanation I have little doubt.

W. W. Greg, 'Principles of Emendation in Shakespeare', *Proceedings of the British Academy* (1928) 169, 171f.

454

Sisson plumps for *solid flesh* in *Hamlet* and—ignoring all the important bibliographical evidence—hinges his case on the probability (as he takes it) that *s-o-l-l-i-d* was misread as *sallied*. I must say, to misread a very rare word indeed like *sallied* as *sollid* would not in my view be at all impossible; but for this Q 2 compositor to misread a common simple word and in the process somehow to arrive by chance at the peculiar word remembered by the Q 1 actor-reporter and the word used later by Polonius only in the good text (and set by a different compositor) is to argue what seems to be the impossible.

Fredson Bowers, *Textual and Literary Criticism* (Cambridge 1959) 72.

455

It is certainly not sufficient to state that the postulated *sally* can 'be explained as a borrowing from French *sale*, and its later disappearance in turn is explained by its homonymity with *sally* "issue forth to attack".' This kind of etymologizing used to be practised before the birth of modern philology and is still indulged in freely by philological dilettantes....

Since there never was such an etymological variant of *sully*, Bowers's argument with its string of hypotheses built one upon another is completely invalid.

... The word was either *solid* or *sullied*. ... Orthographically the following variants of the two words can be reconstructed for Elizabethan English: (1) *sullied* may have been written *sullied, sullyed, sullid(e), sulled, sulleyed*, and further *sollied, sollyed, sollid(e), solled, solleyed*, each with one or two l's; (2) *solid* may have been written *sol(l)id(e), sol(l)ied, sol(l)ed* as well as *sallid(e), sallied, salled*. There was consequently an area of graphic overlapping within which the two words could be spelled alike. If Shakespeare had written, say, *sollied*, this form could easily have been rendered *solid* in F and *sallied* in Q 1, 2; in the latter case we should have to assume a well-evidenced *a : o* misprint. Such a hypothesis, which alone would account for both textual variations, would not bring us appreciably nearer a semantic solution, since it would be impossible to determine whether this postulated longhand form *sollied* stood for *solid* or *sullied*.... I am afraid that the problem of *solid-sallied* will never be solved.

Helge Kökeritz, *Studia Neophilologica* xxx (1958) 8-10.

456

It is surely obvious that in dealing with such a rare word appearing twice in one play, we may not appeal to separate and divided error. It seems incredible that there is no connection between *sallied* at I ii 129 and sallies at II i 39. Hence if *sallies* means *sullies*, as it surely does, *sallied* must mean *sullied.* . . . No reason exists to suppose that the first could have influenced the second. . . . We can now prove on physical evidence that no connection can possibly obtain. Bibliographical analysis now shows not only that sheet E in which (sig. E 1ᵛ) the second *sally* appears in the Second Quarto was printed on a different press from Sheet C containing on sig C 1 'this too too sallied flesh', each being machined at approximately the same time, but also (as necessarily follows), that each was set by a different compositor. Since the second *sally* was set by the second compositor from manuscript, the appearance of the first *sally* in *sallied flesh*, set by the first workman, can have had no possible influence on the other. Hence if one word is right, as must be so, the other must also be right as well, and the contamination explanation for *sallied flesh* fails as a matter of simple logical impossibility. If we cannot believe that *sallied* was picked up from the First Quarto in error, there is no argument by which *solid* can be maintained.

It stands that bibliographical research separating the typesetting and the printing of the two sheets as the work of two different compositors and presses can be applied directly to settle this celebrated Shakespearian crux.

Fredson Bowers, *Shakespeare Survey* ix (1956) 46f.

French *sale*) that is identical in meaning with *sully* (from French *souiller*). . . . But apart from this Bowers seems to be guilty of a *suppressio veri*. He conveniently forgets that, though Polonius uses the *a*-form in Q 2, he has the *u*-form in F. And as it happens the F compositor responsible for *solid flesh* was not the compositor who set *slight sulleyes*. Supposing Bowers is right in thinking Shakespeare used the *a*-form, what happens now to his criterion of two compositors not making the same mistake? . . . . Even if we accept *sally* as a genuine form and drop the point about the F compositors, the bibliographical solution propounded by Bowers will still be invalid. This is because the premiss that two compositors working separately will not make the same misprint is a psychological probability and not a typographical law. Bowers is not claiming that two compositors *never* make the same misprints. And in that case neither he nor anyone else can distinguish *a priori* between the rare occasions when they do and the more frequent occasions when they do not. Unless such a criterion can be produced, one which will enable an editor to distinguish between the Bowers rule and its exception, the rule is not worth having.

F. W. Bateson, *English Studies Today* ii (Bern 1961) 69-71.

457

This is ingenious, but far from conclusive. For one thing it commits Bowers to the desperate hypothesis of a hitherto unrecorded word *sally* (from

458

too too sullied. . . . 'Sullied flesh' is the key to the soliloquy and tells us that Hamlet is thinking of the 'kindless' incestuous marriage as a personal defilement. Further, 'sullied' fits the immediate context as 'solid' does not.

There is something absurd in associating
'solid flesh' with 'melt' and 'thaw';
whereas Shakespeare always uses 'sully'
or 'sullied' elsewhere ... with the image,
implicit or explicit, of dirt upon a surface
of pure white; and the surface Hamlet
obviously has in mind here is snow,
symbolical of the nature he shares with
his mother, once pure but now
befouled.

Hamlet, ed. J. Dover Wilson (Cambridge 1934)
151f.

459

The crux needs to be tackled with the
appropriate tools, which are stylistic
rather than bibliographical or
philological. Let us start with Coleridge's
formula. The image of Hamlet's flesh
melting, thawing and resolving (=
dissolving) into dew requires, to be
metaphorically effective, an opposite or
discordant quality against which the
imagination can balance or reconcile it.
But *flesh*, in ordinary usage, is not the
opposite of dew. Flesh at once suggests
blood, which is already liquid, whereas
the metaphor requires a substance that
has *not* already melted, thawed and
dissolved, though capable of melting,
thaw and dissolution. And since the
process of liquefaction is described in
three main verbs and a noun, the
preceding non-liquid condition needs, to
achieve balance, an equally emphatic

description; Hamlet's flesh must be
supremely rigid, *frozen stiff*. 'too too
solid' is therefore exactly what the
immediate verbal context requires: it
provides the right amount of emphasis,
and it prevents *flesh* from suggesting
softness or liquidity. On the other hand,
'too too sullied', though defensible in
general terms of the play, lets the
metaphor down here by removing any
effective relationship between its two
terminal points; flesh that is sullied calls
for *cleaning*, not *melting*....

All in all the stylistic conclusion
must be that, though 'sullied flesh' is
a possible reading (unlike 'sallied flesh'),
it weakens the metaphor disastrously:
'solid flesh' is better English, better
Shakespeare, better poetry....
Bibliographical considerations have not
entered in any way into the solution I
have just proposed, which is entirely
stylistic.

F. W. Bateson, *English Studies Today* ii (Bern
1961) 69f.

460

A single emendation or choice of variants,
even at times the position of a comma or
semicolon, may involve first-class issues
of poetic criticism or dramatic
interpretation.

J. Dover Wilson, *The Manuscript of Shakespeare's 'Hamlet'* i (Cambridge 1934) p. xii.

Criticism

461

Ill writers are commonly the sharpest censors for they (as the
best poet, and the best patron [Dorset] said)

> When in the full perfection of decay
> Turn vinegar, and come again in play.

Thus the corruption of a poet is the generation of a critic: I
mean of a critic in the general acceptation of this age: for
formerly they were quite another species of men. They were
defenders of poets, and commentators on their works: to
illustrate obscure beauties; to place some passages in a better
light, to redeem others from malicious interpretations: to help
out an author's modesty, who is not ostentatious of his wit; and
in short, to shield him from the ill-nature of those fellows, who
were then called *Zoili*, and *Momi*, and now take upon themselves the
venerable name of censors.... Are our auxiliary forces turned our
enemies? Are they, who, at best, are but wits of the second order,
and whose only credit amongst readers, is what they obtained by
being subservient to the fame of writers, are these become rebels
of slaves, and usurpers of subjects; or to speak in the most
honourable terms of them, are they from our seconds, become
principals against us? Does the ivy undermine the oak, which
supports its weakness? What labour would it cost them to put
in a better line, than the worst of those which they expunge in
a true poet?

John Dryden, Dedication to *Examen poeticum* (1693); *Essays* ed. W. P. Ker ii
(New York 1961) 2f.

462

If, on Parnassus' top you sit,
You rarely bite, are always bit:
Each poet of inferior size
On you shall rail and criticize;
And strive to tear you limb from limb,
While others do as much for him.

The vermin only tease and pinch
Their foes superior by an inch.
So, nat'ralists observe, a flea
Hath smaller fleas that on him prey,
And these have smaller fleas to bite 'em,
And so proceed *ad infinitum*:
Thus ev'ry poet in his kind,
Is bit by him that comes behind;
Who, though too little to be seen,
Can tease, and gall, and give the spleen;
Call dunces, fools, and sons of whores,
Lay Grubstreet at each others' doors:
Extol the Greek and Roman masters,
And curse our modern poetasters.
Complain, as many an ancient bard did
How genius is no more rewarded;
How wrong a taste prevails among us;
How much our ancestors out-sung us;
Can personate an awkward scorn
For those who are not poets born:
And all their brother dunces lash,
Who crowd the press with hourly trash.

Jonathan Swift, 'On Poetry: a Rhapsody' (1733)
ll. 329-56; *Swift's Poems* ed. H. Williams ii
(Oxford 1958) 651f.

463

There spoke up a brisk little somebody,
Critic and whippersnapper, in a rage
To set things right.

Robert Browning, *Balaustion's Adventure* (1871)
I i 308.

464

Criticism is a natural activity for the literate man; hence the number and diversity of those who have practised it. It is a normal prolongation of intelligent reading and, we may add, the necessary accompaniment of all intelligent writing.

Whoever compares what he finds in a book with the content of his own experience, whoever compares one book with another, has begun to be a critic.

Graham Hough, *An Essay on Criticism* (1966)
4f.

465

Over everything stands its demon, or soul, and, as the form of the thing is reflected by the eye, so the soul of the thing is reflected by a melody. The sea, the mountain ridge, Niagara, and every flower-bed, pre-exist, or super-exist, in pre-cantations, which sail like odours in the air, and when any man goes by with an ear sufficiently fine, he overhears them and endeavours to write down the notes, without diluting or depraving them. And herein is the legitimation of criticism, in the mind's faith, that the poems are a corrupt version of some text in nature, with which they ought to be made to tally.

Ralph Waldo Emerson, 'Shakespeare, or, The Poet' (1850); *Complete Prose Works* ed. G. T. Bettany (1889) 97.

466

Literary criticism has in the present day become a profession,—but it has ceased to be an art. Its object is no longer that of proving that certain literary work is good and other literary work is bad, in accordance with rules which the critic is able to define. English criticism at present rarely even pretends to go so far as this. It attempts, in the first place, to tell the public whether a book be or be not worth public attention; and, in the second place, so to describe the purport of the work as to enable those who have not time or inclination for reading it to feel that by a short cut they have become acquainted with its contents. Both these objects, if fairly well carried out, are salutary.

Anthony Trollope, *Autobiography* (1883), ch. xiv; ed. M. Sadleir (1950) 261.

467

He dreaded, as if it were a dwelling-place of lost souls, that dead anatomy of culture which turns the universe into a mere ceaseless answer to queries, and knows not everything, but everything else about everything—as if one should be ignorant of nothing concerning the scent of violets except the scent itself for which one had no nostril.

George Eliot, *Daniel Deronda* (1876) ch. xxxii; ed. B. Hardy (Harmondsworth 1967) 413.

468

The critics aim is, first, to realize as sensitively as possible this or that which claims his attention; and a certain valuing is implicit in the realizing.

F. R. Leavis, *The Common Pursuit* (1952); (Harmondsworth 1962) 213.

469

For critical judgement not only grows out of the critic's experience of objective matter, and not only depends upon that for validity, but has for its office the deepening of just such experience in others. Scientific judgements not only end in increased control but for those who understand they add enlarged meanings to the things perceived and dealt with in daily contact with the world. The function of criticism is the re-education of perception of works of art; it is an auxiliary in the process, a difficult process, of learning to see and hear. The conception that its business is to appraise, to judge in the legal and moral sense, arrests the perception of those who are influenced by the criticism that assumes this task.

John Dewey, *Art as Experience* (New York 1934) 324f.

470

We wish to ask whether poems should be criticized by criteria which are so specific as to apply simply to poems themselves, or whether they may be criticized by criteria which are generic enough to include other arts. The question might be broadened to read: Are specific situations ever illuminated by our turning to principles which are more abstract than the situations themselves? The answer must be, I believe, that they always are. Such is the character of theorizing, a character not invalidated even by the high degree of relevant individuality found in works of art. The unit and wholeness of a poem, for example, are concepts which the literary critic will do well to pursue not only in Aristotle's *Poetics* but in his *Physics* and *Metaphysics*—and in the *Enneads* of Plotinus and the *Introduction* to the philosophy of fine art by Hegel.

W. K. Wimsatt, 'The Domain of Criticism' in *Aesthetic Inquiry* ed. M. C. Beardsley (Belmont, Calif. 1967) 26.

471

What modern criticism is could be defined crudely and somewhat inaccurately as *the organized use of non-literary techniques and bodies of*

knowledge to obtain insights into literature. The tools are these methods or 'techniques', the nuggets are 'insights', the occupation is mining, digging, or just plain grubbing. The non-literary techniques are things like psychoanalytic associations or semantic translations, the non-literary bodies of knowledge range from the ritual patterns of primitives to the nature of capitalist society. And all of these result in a kind of close reading and detailed attention to the text that can only be understood on the analogy of microscopic analysis.

S. E. Hyman, *The Armed Vision* (New York 1955) 3.

472

'Close analysis' is useful to critics and readers. But for the poet there is the danger of disintegration of poetry into paraphrase, examination of technique, influences, all analyzed in the vocabulary of criticism. The poem risks becoming fragmented into the words explaining what it means and how it is written, and although critics would be the first to admit that the poem is different from and never can be even the most complete analysis, the modern student often reads the analysis into the poem, rather than the poem first and then the analysis. If he himself becomes a poet, he may proceed from critical analysis of his projected poem to the writing of the poetry.

Stephen Spender, *The Struggle of the Modern* (1963) 189.

Without the critical faculty, there is no artistic creation at all worthy of the name. You spoke a little while ago of that fine spirit of choice and delicate instinct of selection by which the artist realizes life for us and gives to it a momentary perfection. Well, that spirit of choice, that subtle tact of omission, is really the critical faculty in one of its most characteristic moods, and no one who does not possess this critical faculty can create anything at all in art. Arnold's definition of literature as a criticism of life was not very felicitous in form, but it showed how keenly he recognized the importance of the critical element in all creative work.

Oscar Wilde, 'The Critic as Artist' (1890); *Works*, (1966) 1020.

474

The spontaneous lover of literature and art, the boy or youth who discovered it for himself, without sponsoring or solicitude, the 'wild flower', whose rarity (or even disappearance) Mr Lewis so regrets, was, unknown to himself, the product of a tradition, a way of life. Nothing that the professional educator, the schoolmaster or university teacher, can do, will restore that tradition; all he can hope to do is to find some sort of substitute, and to remind others of the former reality to which it so inadequately corresponds. And as to Mr Lewis's fears lest the lively genius be lulled to sleep in the critical feather-bed : it is not the real critic, the genuine 'appreciator', who is the enemy of the nascent creative mind, the future

Traherne or Wordsworth. The true opposite of the creative is not the *critical* but the *academic*.

W. W. Robson, *The Twentieth Century* clvii (1955) 546.

475

Nothing, of course will ever take the place of the good old fashion of 'liking' a work of art or not liking it; the most improved criticism will not abolish that primitive, that ultimate test. I mention this to guard myself from the accusation of intimating that the idea, the subject, of a novel or picture, does not matter. It matters, to my sense, in the highest degree, and if I might put up a prayer, it would be that artists should select none but the richest.

Henry James, 'The Art of Fiction' (1884); *Selected Literary Criticism* ed. M. Shapira (Harmondsworth 1968) 90.

476

Every voice is united in applauding elegance, propriety, simplicity, spirit in writing; and in blaming fustian, affectation, coldness, and a false brilliancy : but when critics come to particulars, this seeming unanimity vanishes; and it is found, that they had affixed a very different meaning to their expressions. In all matters of opinion and science, the case is opposite. The difference between men is there oftener found to lie in generals than in particulars; and to be less in reality than in appearance. An explanation of the terms commonly ends the controversy, and the disputants are surprised to find, that they had been quarrelling, while at bottom they agreed in their judgment.

David Hume, 'Of the Standard of Taste' (1757); *Essays* (Oxford 1963) 231f.

477

Criticism has ever lacked its own philosophy, without which research must continue always inconclusive, having no touch-stone or relevance nor any criterion to distinguish failure from success.... Every formulation of doctrine ... inescapably implies theoretical assumptions which belong to the province of aesthetics.... As long as aesthetics remains inchoate criticism must needs be muddled and confused.

Harold Osborne, *Aesthetics and Criticism* (1955) 6.

478

Dr Wellek points out, justly, that in my dealings with English poetry I have made a number of assumptions that I neither defend nor even state.... After offering me a summary of these assumptions, he asks me to 'defend this position abstractly and to become conscious that large ethical, philosophical and, of course, ultimately, also aesthetic *choices* are involved.' ... Even if I had felt qualified to satisfy Dr Wellek on his own ground I should have declined to attempt it in that book [*Revaluation*].

Literary criticism and philosophy seem to me to be quite distinct and different kinds of discipline....

Unfairness to poets out of lack of interest in their philosophy he does, of course, in general charge me with.... I will only comment ... that Dr Wellek seems to me to assume too easily that the poet's essential 'belief' is what can be most readily extracted as such from his works by a philosopher.

F. R. Leavis, *Scrutiny* vi (1937) 59f., 70.

479

[Coleridge's] opinion is a safe guide ... only if we know Coleridge the critic as well as we know *Hamlet*, the play criticized. Such examples of the necessity of rectifying a critical pronouncement by some inquiry into the critic's character and bias and intention might be multiplied. They show that the question, 'What is the intent of the critic?' may be as important to the reading public as the prior question 'What is the intent of the artist?' is to the critic himself.'

D. A. Stauffer, *The Intent of the Critic* (Princeton, N.J. 1941) 5.

480

It is clear that criticism cannot be a systematic study unless there is a quality in literature which enables it to be so. We have to adopt the hypothesis, then, that just as there is an order of nature behind the natural sciences, so literature is not a piled aggregate of 'works' but an order of 'words'.

Northrop Frye, *Anatomy of Criticism* (Princeton, N.J. 1957) 17.

481

Recognition of the methodological differences between systems of criticism, and of their consequent respective powers and limitations, quickly establishes the fact that twenty-five centuries of inquiry have not been spent in vain. On the contrary, the partial systems of criticism correct and supplement one another, the comprehensive intertranslate, to form a vast body of poetic knowledge; and contemporary theorists, instead of seeking new bases for criticism, would do better to examine the bases of such criticisms as we have and so avail themselves of that knowledge.

Elder Olson, *Critics and Criticism*, ed. R. S. Crane (Chicago 1952) 552.

482

It is of the last importance that English criticism should clearly discern what rule for its course, in order to avail itself of the field now opening to it, and to produce fruit for the future, it ought to take. The rule may be summed up in one word,—*disinterestedness*. And how is criticism to show disinterestedness? By keeping aloof from what is called 'the practical view of things'; by resolutely following the law of its own nature, which is to be a free play of the mind on all subjects which it touches. By steadily refusing to lend itself to any of those ulterior, political, practical considerations about ideas, which plenty of people will be sure to attach to them, which perhaps ought to be attached to them, which in this country at any rate are certain to be attached to them quite sufficiently, but which criticism has really nothing to do with. Its business is, as I have said, simply to know the best that is known and thought in the world, and by in its turn making this known, to create a current of true and fresh ideas.

Matthew Arnold, 'The Function of Criticism at the Present Time', (1865); *Lectures and Essays in Criticism* ed. R. H. Super (Ann Arbor, Mich. 1962) 269f.

483

Although the formulae of the aestheticians are useless for the role usually assigned to them, we must not ignore the live purpose they frequently serve as slogans in the effort to change taste and as instruments for opening up new avenues of appreciation.

W. E. Kennick, 'Does Traditional Aesthetics Rest on a Mistake?', *Collected Papers in Aesthetics* ed. C. Barrett (Oxford 1965) 21.

484

It is ... the task of criticism to establish principles; to improve opinion into knowledge; and to distinguish those means of pleasing which depend upon known causes and rational deduction, from the nameless and inexplicable elegancies which appeal wholly to the fancy.... Criticism reduces those regions of literature under the dominion of science, which have hitherto known only the anarchy of ignorance, the caprices of fancy, and the tyranny of prescription.

Samuel Johnson, *Rambler* No. 92 (2 February 1751); *Works*, Yale edn. iv (New Haven and London 1969) 122.

Any critic, no matter what his method, needs the intelligence to adapt it specifically to the work with which he is dealing: the knowledge, both literary and otherwise, to be aware of the implications of what he is doing; the skill to keep from being picked up and carried away by his method to one or another barren and mechanical monism; the sensibility to remain constantly aware of the special values of the work he is criticising as a unique aesthetic experience; and the literary ability to express what he has to say.

S. E. Hyman, *The Armed Vision* (New York 1955) 10.

No work of criticism is final. Criticism is never done once and for all. It is always contingent on the historical process and the state of social evolution. With every change of historical phase the literature of the past requires to be reinterpreted, and critical questions are never closed because the existing literary canon is not a closed series.

Graham Hough, An *Essay on Criticism* (1966) 6.

Intention

487

As a series of digits or an arrangement of points comes closer and closer to satisfying all tests for randomness it begins to exhibit a very rare and unusual type of statistical regularity that in some cases even permits the prediction of missing portions.... We thus face a curious paradox. The closer we get to an absolutely patternless series, the closer we get to a type of pattern so rare that if we came on such a series we would suspect it had been carefully constructed by a mathematician rather than produced by a random procedure.

Martin Gardner, 'On the Meaning of Randomness and Some Ways of Achieving It', *Scientific American* (July 1968) 119.

488

Order and disorder are purely human inventions.... If I should throw down a thousand beans at random upon a table, I could doubtless, by eliminating a sufficient number of them, leave the rest in almost any geometrical pattern you might propose to me, and you might then say that that pattern was the thing prefigured beforehand, and that the other beans were mere irrelevance and packing material. Our dealings with Nature are just like this. She is a vast *plenum* in which our attention draws capricious lines in innumerable directions. We count and name whatever lies upon the special lines we trace, whilst the other things and the untraced lines are neither named nor counted.

William James, *The Varieties of Religious Experience* (1902); (1960) 421 n 1.

489

'Intention', as we shall use the term, corresponds to *what he intended* in a formula which more or less explicitly has had wide acceptance. 'In order to judge the poet's performance, we must know *what he intended.*' Intention is design or plan in the author's mind. Intention has obvious affinities for the author's attitude toward his work, the way he felt, what made him write....

A poem does not come into existence by accident. The words of a poem, as Professor Stoll has remarked, come out of a head, not out of a hat. Yet to insist on the designing intellect as a cause of a poem is not to grant the design or intention as a *standard* by which the critic is to judge the worth of the poet's performance.

One must ask how a critic expects to get an answer to the question about intention. How is he to find out what the poet tried to do? If the poet succeeded in doing it, then the poem itself shows what he was trying to do. And if the poet did not succeed, then the poem is not adequate evidence, and the critic must go outside the poem—for evidence of an intention that did not become effective in the poem.

W. K. Wimsatt and Monroe C. Beardsley, *The Verbal Icon* (New York 1958) 4.

The theme of the role and the ordeal of the artist which figures in *Rewards and Fairies* suffers from being treated in the vein of *Stalky & Co.* In the story called *The Wrong Thing*, he embarks on a promising subject: the discrepancy between the aim of the artist who is straining to top the standards of his craft, and the quite irrelevant kinds of interest that the powers that employ him may take in him; but he turns it into a farce and ruins it.

Edmund Wilson, 'The Kipling that Nobody Read', *The Wound and the Bow* (Cambridge, Mass. 1929) 159.

491

If we could determine the success of Gide in fulfilling his intention, if, for example, we take his word that he was content with his novel, we are no further along toward an evaluation of that work, for the question immediately arises whether it was *worth* intending. . . . When we speak of a 'skilful work', this is a judgment about the producer, and is logically irrelevant to the question whether the product is good or bad.

M. C. Beardsley, *Aesthetics* (New York 1958) 459.

492

There is something very odd about speaking of bad literature. . . . If we speak of someone as a bad father, we mean not that he is not a father biologically, but that he is not a father socially. He doesn't play his role in education, in rearing, and, in consequence, he just is not a father. To that extent, 'bad' works like the word 'false' (a false friend, a false poem). . . . Now for the reasons why it should be odd to speak of a bad poem, or a bad father—the reason why we are tempted to is that we use another criterion for poetry or fatherhood, as the case may be, the criterion of intention. Something is a poem . . . or is a father if it is designed to be one—if it claims to be one. So . . . in agreeing that it is odd to speak of a bad poem, I do so on the ground that it involves the intentional fallacy. It makes reference to intention. To speak of a bad poem is to say that this is a poem as shown by its intention (its intended purpose), but that it carries out the purpose badly.

Rulon Wells, in *Style in Language*, ed. T. A. Sebeok (Cambridge, Mass. 1960) 425f.

493

Hollywood critics applauded what they thought was far-out avant-garde technique for title credits of the new Peter Sellers film *Bo bo*. Then they realized a gaping 15ft hole had been torn in the screen.

Daily Express, 'This is America'.

494

There is always a silent reference of human works to human abilities, and . . . the enquiry, how far man may extend his designs, or how high he may rate his native force, is of far greater dignity

than in what rank we shall place any
particular performance.

Samuel Johnson, *Preface to Shakespeare* (1765);
Works, Yale edn. vii (New Haven and London
1968) 81.

495

The original structure of the poem
[*Absalom and Achitophel*] was defective;
allegories drawn to great length will
always break; Charles could not run
continually parallel with David.

Samuel Johnson, Life of Dryden, *Lives of the
Poets* (1781); ed. G. B. Hill i (Oxford 1905) 436f.

496

It is notable that good critics often
demand of an author, and with good
reason, that he should have written a
different book. And it is not at all
obvious that in principle they should
not. When Dr Johnson, in his Life of
Dryden, complained of *Absalom and
Achitophel* ... he is certainly regretting
that Dryden had not written a radically
different poem, and to object that he
should accept the poem for what it is
amounts to a demand that he
should abdicate his function altogether.
But then to fulfil an intention,
in literature as in life, is not necessarily
to behave as one should. If a man sets
out to shoot his mother-in-law, and
does so, one may applaud his marksman-
ship but not the deed itself.... The
probability that *Samson* was written for
the study rather than for the stage is a
major fact about *Samson*. Anyone who
supposed that Milton was attempting a
theatrical rival to Dryden's *Conquest
of Granada*, for example, would probably
prove an unreceptive reader of Milton's
play. It is said that Tibetan tea, which is
partly composed of rancid butter, is
revolting to Western tastes if considered
as tea but acceptable if considered as
soup. When we ask of a poem questions
of the order of 'What did the poet intend
it for?'—whether stage or study,
whether court audience or popular—the
answer seems in principle likely to be
useful to the extent that it is accurate.
This is surely a good question to ask, and
anybody who objects at this point that
the search for the author's intention is
necessarily a fallacy should be sent about
his business.

George Watson, *The Study of Literature* (1969)
72f.

497

The verb 'to mean' conveys two senses,
often simultaneously: that of intending,
and that of signifying.... Practical
intentions can be directed to the most
diverse ends: such as arousing an
emotion, justifying the ways of God to
man, wooing the fair sex, obtaining a
pension for the author, or purging the
audience of pity and terror. And although
the critic will judge the poem as a poem,
not as a means of achieving any of these
objects, his understanding of it may be
greatly influenced by what he knows of
the poet's practical intentions.... Where
we find it difficult to construct a
practical intention, as for example with
Shakespeare's sonnets, we may find it
exceedingly difficult to know in what
tone, with what degree of seriousness
or irony, we are to read the poem:

criticism which evades these questions, while it may be the only kind possible here, is thin and unsatisfactory.... I have said that we could suppose a literary intention, as well as a practical one, for whatever is written or spoken. But can we, in fact, construct such an intention? Whenever something is quite plainly and unambiguously said, it hardly makes sense to ask the speaker what he intended his words to signify.... The object of a literary intention is a significance: yet it is only where significance is in doubt that it makes sense to ask what the intention is.... Nor can we evade this dilemma by thinking of the poet's intention otherwise than as a construct. We know from experience how often we have no clear idea what we want to say until we have said it; how rhymes will determine sense.

T. M. Gang, 'Intention', *Essays in Criticism* vii (1957) 176-9.

498

Milton only discovered the totality of what he meant by *Lycidas* in the act of writing it. But the poem is in no way less Miltonic for that reason. Because a man alters his intention in the course of action, it can hardly be said of him that he is acting other than according to intention.

George Watson, *The Study of Literature* (1969) 80.

499

This is the true and objective way of criticism, as contrasted to ... genetic

inquiry, in which, taking advantage of the fact that Eliot is still alive, and in the spirit of a man who would settle a bet, the critic writes to Eliot and asks what he meant, or if he had Donne in mind. We shall not here weigh the probabilities—whether Eliot would answer that he meant nothing at all, had nothing at all in mind—a sufficiently good answer to such a question—or in an unguarded moment might furnish a clear and, within its limit, irrefutable answer. Our point is that such an answer to such an inquiry would have nothing to do with the poem 'Prufrock'; it would not be a critical inquiry. Critical inquiries, unlike bets, are not settled by consulting the oracle.

W. K. Wimsatt and Monroe C. Beardsley, *The Verbal Icon* (New York 1958) 18.

500

I am not familiar with the exact constitution of the Tarot pack.

T. S. Eliot, note to *The Waste Land* (1922) i 46.

501

'Is not a critic', asks Professor Stoll 'a judge, who does not explore his own consciousness, but determines the author's meaning or intention, as if the poem were a will, a contract, or the constitution? The poem is not the critic's own.' He has accurately diagnosed two forms of irresponsibility, one of which he prefers. Our view is yet different. The poem is not the critic's own and not the author's (it is detached from the author at birth and goes about the world beyond his power to intend about it or control it). The poem belongs to the public. It is embodied in language, the peculiar possession of the public.... The history of words *after* a poem is written may contribute meanings which if relevant to the original pattern should not be ruled out by a scruple about intention.

W. K. Wimsatt and Monroe C. Beardsley, *The Verbal Icon* (New York 1958) 5, 281.

502

DUNCAN What bloody man is that?

William Shakespeare, *Macbeth* I ii 1.

And did the Countenance Divine
Shine forth upon our clouded hills?
And was Jerusalem builded here
Among these dark Satanic Mills?

William Blake, Preface to *Milton* (1804) ll. 5-8.

503

No piece of critical reasoning which ignores, or begs the question of, 'intention' can really stand up. A good recent example occurs on p.7 of Mr Bateson's *English Poetry: A Critical Introduction*.... We are told ... that by 'dark Satanic Mills' Blake refers to the altars of the Churches.... I am far from wishing to dispute that this is the real meaning of Blake's verses—if we reserve the term 'real' for the meaning which the author himself attaches to the work. But are we to do so? The lines themselves would never, in a thousand years, yield this meaning; it has to be supplied from outside. But few would oppose Coleridge's 'Every work of art must contain within itself the reason why it is thus and not otherwise'.... The usual objection to a reading of a poem which obfuscates, or ignores, the author's meaning, is that it is an injustice to the merit of the poem. But in this case it seems to be rather an improvement.

John Wain, *Essays in Criticism* ii (1952) 105f.

504

If the test of a poem's meaning is simply the degree of its attractiveness to the reader, the number of meanings need only be limited by the number of readers. In the last resort, *any* work can mean *any* thing. What hinders, Mr. Wain asks? Why, only that if the meaning of the poet's words is to be entirely at this or that reader's beck and call, there ceases to be any point at this stage in reading the poem at all!

If the criterion is not the individual reader's preference, what is it? Are the intentionalists right after all in referring us, when we run into difficulties, to what was going on in the poet's mind? The compromise that I tried to elaborate ... was to identify the meaning of a poem with the interaction of four constant factors: (i) the poet, (ii) the poet's original audience, (iii) their common language, (iv) their inherited literary conventions. In terms of this formula the poet's intentions are relevant only to the extent to which the audience, the language and the literary tradition permit their expression. Anything that is not directly or indirectly implicit in the actual words of the poem must therefore be eliminated. But this does not mean that a phrase or a poem is restricted to what Mr. Wain calls its 'simple surface meaning'.... For a precise understanding the poem's exact position, chronological and qualitative, within the particular tradition must also be known—a process that inevitably entails the accumulation of as much relevant information as possible about the poem's author and its original audience. I conclude, indeed, that these two participants in the poetic act are not really separable. The proper question to put is not 'What did Blake mean?', but 'What meaning did Blake succeed in conveying to the best of his early readers?'

F. W. Bateson, *Essays in Criticism* ii (1952) 108f.

505

Eliot's allusions work when we know

them—and to a great extent even when we do not know them, through their suggestive power.

W. K. Wimsatt and Monroe C. Beardsley, *The Verbal Icon* (New York 1958) 15.

506

We must remember that every part that catches the reader's attention and enters into the reality of his experience will be expressive in some way, either controlled or uncontrolled. Therefore, if the poet does not need this particular implication for his whole, he must try to neutralize or even delete the part.

Paul Goodman, *The Structure of Literature* (Chicago 1962) 16.

507

Theoretically there can be no objection, from the synchronic point of view, if one author patches another author's work—as Wordsworth patched 'The Ancient Mariner' and Coleridge patched 'We are Seven'. An extreme case of this process is the familiar line in *The Revenger's Tragedy* 'The poor benefit of a bewitching minute'. T. S. Eliot preferred 'bewildering', the reading of the 'Mermaid' edition of Webster and Tourneur, as 'much the richer word here' in spite of the fact that there is no other authority for the change. According to Addington Symonds, the editor of the 'Mermaid' edition, the text that he used for *The Revenger's Tragedy* was that in W. C. Hazlitt's re-edition of Dodsley's *Old Plays*. But Hazlitt's Dodsley has 'bewitching' like all the earlier editions that I have seen. The 'richer reading' was therefore in this case, if Eliot's guidance is to be accepted, an 'improvement' on Tourneur made either by Symonds or perhaps by his printer nearly three centuries after the play's composition.

F. W. Bateson, *Essays in Criticism* xvii (1967) 389f.

508

What of *Hamlet* or the *Odyssey*? Is the critic's task to be restricted to prim warnings against extending the original area of a poem's usefulness and truth, or is it, as I think, to create and maintain a balance between the 'original' and the 'developed' significances, and by this difficult act to recognize that subtle tension which is the mode of existence of a work of literature?

John Wain, *Essays in Criticism* ii (1952) 111.

509

If a poem can be said to have an eternal, or, as I should prefer to call it, a 'public' meaning, this meaning is not this or that 'interpretation', but the resultant *now* of all plausible interpretations; and, if the scholar's duty is to decide which interpretations are plausible, perhaps the critic's duty is to find their resultant. But the scholar, too, is a reader *now*, and the poem can only fully exist for him, even *qua* scholar, in so far as he is a reader *now*. And he is not, in my sense, a 'reader' until he is, in his reading, interpreting, evaluating, choosing; and, in so far as he is doing so, he is entitled

to *his* say about the poem's 'intention'.

W. W. Robson, *Essays in Criticism* ii (1952) 112f.

510

The total meaning of a work of art ... is extra-historical ... because it is the expression and creation of a human mind and so ultimately irreducible into anything but itself. The mystery of the survival of the significance of works of art brings one face to face with the mystery of the human personality.

Helen Gardner, *The Business of Criticism* (Oxford 1959) 20.

511

It is the essential identity of the literary artifact with Saussure's *parole* that overturns the formalist position. A speech-act is not, except by a perversion of language, a structure.... We must re-introduce into the aesthetic act what Saussure called *le circuit de la parole*. To abstract from this human and temporal process 'the best words in the best order' *after* they have left the author and *before* they reach the auditor, and freeze them into an artificial spatial immobility is to treat *parole* as though it was *langue*. This, indeed, in the final analysis, *is* the Formalist Fallacy. The New Critics have tended to approach poetry, not as the embodiment of human values, but as a museum of emphasis and memorability devices, a kind of syntax.

F. W. Bateson, *English Studies Today* ii (Bern 1961) 75f.

On another view, however, the subconscious, or unconscious is not merely invoked to explain neurotic behaviour, but is thought of as the *discoverable* source of all behaviour, and of all art. A practical consequence of the assumption that it is always discoverable (even in the work of artists about whose lives nothing is known) is that there must be a universally valid set of rules by which the products of conscious action (e.g. works of art) can be related to their origins in the unconscious. A particular pattern, or a particular image, will always be said to have the same meaning in the unconscious, however little the artist may be aware of it. Now if this meaning is *inevitably* present, whether or not the artist was aware of it, and irrespective of anything he may have actively wished to say, then clearly this meaning is in no sense 'intended'. At the same time, such unconscious meanings are public, in the sense that they are accessible to everybody, even though our conscious minds may fail to see them. . . . The real objection to such a hypothesis is not that it is incapable of proof, but that it always carries with it the implication that these unintended public meanings, of which we are not consciously aware, are in some sense the true, the most important, meanings of a work.

T. M. Gang, *Essays in Criticism* vii (1957) 185f.

The import of an art symbol cannot be built up like the meaning of a discourse, but must be seen *in toto* first; that is, the 'understanding' of a work of art begins with an intuition of the whole presented feeling. Contemplation then gradually reveals the complexities of the piece, and of its import. In discourse, meaning is synthetically construed by a succession of intuitions; but in art the complex whole is seen or anticipated first. This creates a real epistemological impasse : artistic import, unlike verbal meaning, can only be exhibited, not demonstrated to any one to whom the art symbol is not lucid. Since there are no semantic units with assigned meanings which, by paraphrase or translation, could be conveyed by equivalent symbols, as words may be defined or translated, there is no way of further identifying the import of a work. The only way to make the feeling-content of a design, a melody, a poem, or any other art symbol public, is to present the expressive form so abstractly and forcibly that anyone with normal sensitivity for the art in question will see this form and its 'emotive quality'.

Susanne K. Langer, *Feeling and Form* (1953) 379f.

Biographical Criticism

514

Real criticism, as I define it, consists in studying each person, that is, each author, each talent, according to the conditions of his nature, in order to make a vivid and pregnant description of him so that he can later be classified and put in his proper place in the hierarchy of art.

C. A. Sainte-Beuve, *Causeries du lundi* (1851-70).

I can enjoy the work itself, but I find it hard to judge in isolation from the man who wrote it.

Idem, Les Nouveaux lundis (1863-70).

515

A biographical method cannot really begin to function until all the facts are in.

S. E. Hyman, *The Armed Vision* (New York 1955) 98.

516

The rage of concentrated attention, the half hallucinations, the anguish and heaving of the heart, the quivering of the limbs stretching involuntarily and blindly for action, all the painful impulses which accompany large desires, exhausted them less; this is why they desired longer, and dared more.... Such feelings we glean still in their portraits, in the straight looks which pierce like a sword; in this strength of back, bent or twisted; in the sensuality, energy, enthusiasm, which breathe from their attitude or look. Such feelings we still discover in their poetry, in Greene, Lodge, Jonson, Spenser, Shakespeare, in Sidney, as in all the rest. ... However far Sidney goes, whatever object he touches, he sees throughout the universe only the name and features of Stella. All ideas bring him back to her. He is drawn ever and invincibly by the same thought; and comparisons which seem far-fetched, only express the unfailing presence and sovereign power of the besetting image. Stella is ill; it seems to Sidney that 'Joy, which is inseparate from those eyes, Stella, now learns (strange case) to weep in thee.' To us, the expression is absurd. Is it for Sidney, who for hours together had dwelt on the expressions of those eyes, seeing in them at last all the beauties of heaven and earth, who compared to them, finds all light dull and all joy stale? Consider that in every extreme passion ordinary laws are reversed, that our logic cannot pass judgment on it, that we find in it affectation, childishness, fancifulness, crudity, folly, and that to us violent conditions of the nervous machine are like an unknown and marvellous land, where common sense and good language cannot penetrate.

Hippolyte Taine, *History of English Literature* (1863); tr. H. van Laun i (Edinburgh 1873) 168f.

517

But truly many of such writings, as come under the banner of unresistible love, if I were a mistress, would never persuade me they were in love: so coldly they apply fiery speeches, as men that had rather read lovers' writings, and so caught up certain swelling phrases, which hang together like a man that once told me the wind was at northwest, and by south, because he would be sure to name winds enough, than that in truth they feel those passions, which easily as I think, may be bewrayed [exposed] by that same forcibleness or Energia, (as the Greeks call it of the writer).

Sir Philip Sidney, The Defence of Poesy (1595); Works, ed. A. Feuillerat iii (Cambridge 1912) 41.

518

Cowley's Mistress has no power of seduction; 'she plays round the head, but comes not at the heart'.... The compositions are such as might have been written for penance by a hermit, or for hire by a philosophical rhymer who had only heard of another sex; for they turn the mind only on the writer, whom, without thinking on a woman but as the subject for his task, we sometimes esteem as learned, and sometimes despise as trifling, always admire as ingenious, and always condemn as unnatural.

Samuel Johnson, Life of Cowley, Lives of the Poets (1781); ed. G. B. Hill i (Oxford 1905) 42.

519

S. Beisly, Shakespeare's Garden (1864)
J. H. Bloom, Shakespeare's Garden (1903)
H. N. Ellacombe, Shakespeare as an Angler (1883)
J. H. Fennell, The Shakespeare Cyclopaedia; or, a ... summary of Shakespeare's Knowledge of the Works and Phenomena of Nature, Pt 1—Zoology—Man (1862)
J. P. Chesney, Shakespeare as a Physician (1884)
H. T., Was Shakespeare a Lawyer? (1871)
M. E. B. Emery, Was Not Shakespeare a Gentleman? (1903)
F. Luetgenau, Shakespeare als Philosoph (1909)
W. L. Rushton, Shakespeare an Archer (1897)
J. A. Heraud, Shakespeare, his Inner Life as Intimated in his Works (1865).

520

Echoing sound, as also reflected light, always interested Shakespeare; he is very quick to notice it, and in the earlier plays he records it often, quite simply and directly, as in the reverberating roll of drums in King John, the smack of Petruchio's kiss resounding

through the church, Juliet's delicate picture of Echo with her
airy tongue repeating 'Romeo'.... He specially loves and describes
repeatedly (in the *Dream, Titus,* and the *Shrew*) the re-echoing
sound of hounds and horn,

> the musical confusion
> Of hounds and echo in conjunction :

its doubling and mocking quality attracts him....

Caroline F. E. Spurgeon (1930); *Shakespeare's Imagery and What it Tells Us*
(Cambridge 1958) 327f.

521

Doubt it not, he had his own sorrows :
those *Sonnets* of his will even testify
expressly in what deep waters he had
waded, and swum struggling for his life;
—as what man like him ever failed to
have to do? It seems to me a heedless
notion, our common one, that he sat
like a bird on the bough; and sang forth,
free and offhand, never knowing the
troubles of other men. Not so; with
no man is it so. How could a man travel
forward from rustic deer-poaching to
such tragedy-writing, and not fall-in
with sorrows by the way? Or, still
better, how could a man delineate a
Hamlet, a Coriolanus, a Macbeth, so
many suffering heroic hearts, if his
own heroic heart had never suffered?

Thomas Carlyle, 'The Hero as Poet', *Heroes and
Hero-worship* (1841); (1897) 108f.

522

I knew then that Shakespeare had loved
his gipsy, Mary Fitton, from the end of
1596 on; and I soon came to see that the
story told in the sonnets was told also
in his plays of that period; and finally
I was forced to realize that 'false Cressid'
and the gipsy Cleopatra were also
portraits of Mary Fitton, whom he loved
for twelve years down to 1608, when she
married and left London for good.

Frank Harris, *My Life and Loves* (1925); (New
York 1963) 263.

523

In the lives of some poets, however simple
or various, the works grow naturally out
of the recorded events, or are in
themselves simple events : the facts
explain the art, and biography is a
synthesis. In the lives of others, the
works of art stand out in severe relief :
no events explain them; they have no
background, no gradations towards
experience, no transitions to events. Then
biography becomes an analysis : we must
seek in the works of art an explanation
of the living force that animated them.

Sir Herbert Read, *Wordsworth* (1949) 19.

524

What horrible crime provoked the remorse of Byron's Manfred? A solution cannot be found on the printed page; therefore it has been sought in the circumstances of the author's banishment from England.

Wayne Shumaker, *Elements of Critical Theory*
    (Berkeley and Los Angeles, Calif. 1964) 42.

525

There is danger of confusing personal and poetic studies; and there is the fault of writing the personal as if it were poetic.

There is a difference between internal and external evidence for the meaning of a poem. And the paradox is only verbal and superficial that what is (1) internal is also public: it is discovered through the semantics and syntax of a poem, through our habitual knowledge of the language, through grammars, dictionaries, and all the literature which is the source of dictionaries, in general through all that makes a language and culture; while what is (2) external is private or idiosyncratic; not a part of the work as a linguistic fact: it consists of revelations (in journals, for example, or letters or reported conversations) about how or why the poet wrote the poem—to what lady, while sitting on what lawn, or at the death of what friend or brother. There is (3) an intermediate kind of evidence about the character of the author or about private or semiprivate meanings attached to words or topics by an author or by a coterie of which he is a member.

W. K. Wimsatt and Monroe C. Beardsley, *The Verbal Icon* (New York 1958) 10.

526

Only a part of an author's imagery comes from his reading. It comes from the whole of his sensitive life since early childhood. 'Why, for all of us, out of all that we have heard, seen, felt, in a lifetime, do certain images recur, charged with emotion, rather than others? The song of one bird, the leap of one fish, at a particular place and time, the scent of one flower, an old woman on a German mountain path, six ruffians seen through an open window playing cards at night at a small French railway junction where there was a water-mill: such memories may have symbolic value, but of what we cannot tell, for they come to represent the depths of feeling into which we cannot peer. We might just as well ask why, when we try to recall visually some period in the past, we find in our memory just the few meagre arbitrarily chosen set of snapshots that we do find there, the faded poor souvenirs of passionate moments.

T. S. Eliot, *The Use of Poetry and the Use of Criticism* (1933) 148.

527

The business of the poet is not to find new emotions, but to use the ordinary ones, and, in working them up into poetry, to express feelings which are not in actual emotions at all. And emotions which he has never experienced will serve his turn as well as those familiar to him. Consequently, we must believe that 'emotion recollected in tranquillity' is an inexact formula. For it is neither emotion, nor recollection, nor, without distortion of meaning, tranquillity. It is a concentration, and a new thing resulting from the concentration, of a very great number of experiences which to the practical and active person would not seem to be experiences at all; it is a concentration which does not happen consciously or of deliberation.... Of course this is not quite the whole story. There is a great deal, in the writing of poetry, which must be conscious and deliberate. In fact, the bad poet is usually unconscious where he ought to be conscious, and conscious where he ought to be unconscious. Both errors tend to make him 'personal'. Poetry is not a turning loose of emotion, but an escape from emotion; it is not the expression of personality, but an escape from personality. But, of course, only those who have personality and emotions know what it means to want to escape from these things.

T. S. Eliot, 'Tradition and the Individual Talent' (1917); *Selected Essays* (1951) 21.

528

To render his mental pattern can be an author's object; he can need to do so; and that need is a sufficient end. (Such a rendering is valuable to many readers because, through it, they have access to important people; an access which, without it, they might be denied. This value may come from an act of sharing— it is stimulating to share something with a distinguished mind. Or the example of what a distinguished mind has made of itself may help the person who has access to it.) Exactly what percentage personality accounts for in those things which poetry is most truly about I do not feel called on to conjecture. All I can say is that personality accounts for only a part, and that it is usually interwoven with other elements.

E. M. W. Tillyard, *The Personal Heresy* (1939) 138.

529

The only two questions to ask about a poem, in the long run, are, firstly, whether it is interesting, enjoyable, attractive, and secondly, whether this enjoyment wears well and helps or hinders you towards all the other things you would like to enjoy, or do, or be.

The value of a poem consisting in what it does to the readers, all questions about the poet's own attitude to his utterance are irrelevant. The question of his 'sincerity' or 'disinterestedness' should be for ever banished from criticism. The dyslogistic terms 'insincere', 'spurious', 'bogus', 'sham', etc., are mere emotive noises, signifying that the speaker is unwilling to keep silence, but has not yet discovered what is wrong with the poem. Unable to answer the real question, 'What, in this series of words, excites a feeling of hostility which prevents enjoyment?' he invents answers to the irrelevant question, 'What was the poet's state of mind when he wrote?'

C. S. Lewis, *The Personal Heresy* (1939) 119f.

530

Despite Winters and others of his view, the fact that a writer is homosexual does not mean that his writing will be dishonest and sterile, or so the example of Shakespeare and Sophocles should argue. All it does mean, as does the information that he is insane, diseased, alcoholic, impotent, or otherwise abnormal, is that this abnormality will be a major factor in determining the form and character of his work.

S. E. Hyman, *The Armed Vision* (New York 1948) 122.

531

There are two exceedingly important notes to be added: the blindness which overtook him in middle life, and the passionate nature which ran to three marriages and continual thought, in the prose and the poetry, on the nature of woman and of the relation between woman and man.

The centres of anguish and struggle which Milton figures in Samson are the blindness and the deliverance to political enemies, on which he had commented jointly in one of the personal passages in *Paradise Lost*, Book vii ... and the vulnerability which comes through a strongly erotic nature. That Samson is Milton in figure is not hard to see; what is more important is that we realize that the operation going on in Samson is hinted at as paralleled in the poet also.

Elizabeth Sewell, *The Human Metaphor* (Notre Dame, Ind. 1964) 147f.

532

And now, with the kaleidoscopic swiftness of a dream, the scene shifts from Abyssinia to Cashmere. But even that surprising shift is not fortuitous. For Abyssinia and Cashmere were linked, for Coleridge, through a circumstance which we have now to see.

I said 'for Coleridge,' since Coleridge's associations of ideas are all that count in Coleridge's dream. And among the sleeping images below the threshold of his consciousness there was one of Cashmere which was definitely associated with the Nile. That will be clear, if we turn back to the reading on which Coleridge was intent at the time when he was jotting down matters of interest in Bartram.

J. L. Lowes, *The Road to Xanadu* (Boston and New York 1927) 379.

533

Perhaps a person who has read Bartram appreciates the poem more than one who has not. Or, by looking up the vocabulary of 'Kubla Khan' in the *Oxford English Dictionary*, or by reading some of the other books there quoted, a person may know the poem better. But it would seem to pertain little to the poem to know that *Coleridge* had read Bartram. There is a gross body of life, of sensory and mental experience, which lies behind and in some sense causes every poem, but can never be and need not be known in the verbal and hence intellectual composition which is the poem. For all the objects of our manifold experience, for every unity, there is an action of the mind which cuts off roots, melts away context—or indeed we should never have objects or ideas or anything to talk about.

W. K. Wimsatt and Monroe C. Beardsley, *The Verbal Icon* (New York 1958) 12.

Probably it was sentence structure which
Johnson had in mind when he once
told Boswell that 'he had formed his
style upon that of Sir William Temple,
and upon Chambers's Proposal for his
Dictionary', or more specifically, 'upon
about twenty lines' of Chambers'
Proposal. Tyers says that Johnson 'set
for his emulation', not Chambers'
Proposal, but the Preface to Chambers'
Cyclopedia, and fixes the beginning of
this emulation, on Johnson's authority,
at the time of the *Plan of a Dictionary*.
Boswell says of both Johnson's
suggestions, 'He certainly was mistaken'
and adds: 'Or if he imagined at first that
he was imitating Temple, he was very
unsuccessful; for nothing can be more
unlike than the simplicity of Temple and
the richness of Johnson.'

W. K. Wimsatt, *The Prose Style of Samuel
Johnson* (1963) 124.

535

The beginning of the discipline of
literary criticism lies in the
recognition of the objective existence of
a work of art.... The writer's personal
history, like the pressure of the age in
which he lived, is a context which can
help us to focus on the work as it is.

Biographical knowledge can sharpen the
sense of the work's objective existence, as
itself, distinct and meaningful in itself.

Helen Gardner, *The Business of Criticism* (Oxford 1959) 16, 22.

536

As [the author] writes, he creates not
simply an ideal, impersonal 'man in
general' but an implied version of
'himself' that is different from the
implied authors we meet in other men's
works. To some novelists it has seemed,
indeed, that they were discovering or
creating themselves as they wrote....
Whether we call this implied author an
'official scribe', or adopt the term
recently revived by Kathleen Tillotson—
the author's 'second self'—it is clear
that the picture the reader gets of this
presence is one of the author's most
important effects. However impersonal he
may try to be, his reader will inevitably
construct a picture of the official scribe
who writes in this manner—and of
course that official scribe will never be
neutral toward all values. Our reactions
to his various commitments, secret or
overt, will help to determine our
response to the work.

Wayne C. Booth, *The Rhetoric of Fiction*
(Chicago 1961) 70f.

Validity of Interpretation

537

Do not interpretations belong to God?

Genesis xl 8.

538

It cannot be doubted that this very task, of finding fitting interpretations and avoiding unnatural ones ... is advantageous in forming the judgments of the young. And rightly trained in these exercises of childhood, they will be more considered in their interpretation of the Church's doctrine, and will not play with inappropriate, tasteless, and absurd allegories, like the Origens and monks, who ... dress every matter without discrimination in all kinds of figures.

Georgius Sabinus, *Fabularum Ovidii interpretatio* (Cambridge 1584) Sig. ¶ 3ᵛ.

539

All meanings, we know, depend on the key of interpretation.

George Eliot, *Daniel Deronda* (1876) ch. vi; ed. B. Hardy (Harmondsworth 1967) 88.

540

O *Felix Culpa!* The Sacramental Meaning of *Winnie-the-Pooh* by C. J. L. Culpepper, D.Litt., Oxon.
A. S. Milne's Honey-Balloon-Pit-Gun-Tail Bathtubcomplex by Karl Anschauung, M.D.

Chapter heads in Frederick C. Crews, *The Pooh Perplex, In Which It is Discovered that the True Meaning of the Pooh Stories is Not as Simple as is Usually Believed ... But for Proper Elucidation Requires the Combined Efforts of Several Academicians of Varying Critical Persuasions* (New York 1963).

541

Once the author had been ruthlessly banished as the determiner of his text's meaning, it very gradually appeared that no adequate principle existed for judging the validity of an interpretation. By an inner necessity the study of 'what a text says' became the study of what it says to an individual critic. It became fashionable to talk about a critic's 'reading' of a text, and this word began to appear in the titles of scholarly works.

E. D. Hirsch, *Validity in Interpretation* (New Haven and London 1967) 3.

542

There is no true meaning for a text. No author's authority. Whatever he may have *wanted to say*, he has written what he has written. Once it is published, a text is like a machine which each person can use as he pleases, and according to his own resources: it's not certain that the constructor will use it any better than anyone else.

Paul Valéry, 'Concerning the *Cimetière Marin*' (1933); *Oeuvres complètes* ed. J. Hytier i (Paris 1957) 1507.

injustice to argue that the times necessitated their manner of understanding, or even that their positions could not be reversed. Both of them would have agreed that at least one of them must be wrong.

E. D. Hirsch, *Validity in Interpretation* (New Haven and London 1967) 137.

543

Each different sort of audience requires a different strategy of interpretation, as all teachers and lecturers are aware. The historicity of all interpretations is an undoubted fact, because the historical givens with which an interpreter must reckon—the language and concerns of his audience—vary from age to age. However, this by no means implies that the meaning of the text varies from age to age, or that anybody, who has done whatever is required to understand that meaning, understands a different meaning from his predecessors of an earlier age. No doubt Coleridge understood *Hamlet* rather differently from Professor Kittredge. The fact is reflected in their disparate interpretations, but it would be quite wrong to conclude that this disparity was caused merely by the fact that they lived in different periods. It would do both Coleridge and Kittredge an

544

All works of art, whatever else they may be, are historical objects, and to approach them as such is, I believe, a fundamental necessity if they are to realize their power fully over us. 'All good art is contemporary' is a well-known critical maxim. It needs to be balanced by the statement that 'All art, including contemporary art, is historical'. One of the main difficulties we have in coming to terms with contemporary art is the difficulty we have in thinking of ourselves and of our own age as historical. We know both too much and too little of our own context to see the work in perspective.

Helen Gardner, *The Business of Criticism* (Oxford 1959) 17.

545

There was a time when Milton walked the street,
And Shakespeare singing in a tavern dark

Would not have much impressed Sir Edward Clarke.
To be alive—ay ! there's the damning thing,
For who will buy a bird that's on the wing?
Catch, kill and stuff the creature, once for all,
And he may yet adorn Sir Edward's hall;
But while he's free to go his own wild way
He's not so safe as birds of yesterday.

Sir Henry Newbolt, 'Le Byron de Nos Jours'; *Poems New and Old*
(1912) 228.

546

Interpretation is the revenge of the
intellect upon art.... The temptation to
interpret *Marienbad* should be resisted.
What matters in *Marienbad* is the pure,
untranslateable, sensuous immediacy of
some of its images, and its vigorous if
narrow solution to certain problems of
cinematic form.... In place of a
hermeneutics we need an erotics of art.

Susan Sontag, *Against Interpretation* (1967) 7,
9, 14.

547

Enjoyment that proceeds from understanding is called appreciation....
Appreciation, unlike enjoyment, can be
partly taught.... What constitutes my
appreciation as such is not that my
enjoyment was caused by a certain set
of phenomena, but that I have brought
to bear on them a certain abstractive and
appreciative skill.

F. E. Sparshott, *The Concept of Criticism* (Oxford 1967) 112f.

548

Read Aristotle's *Poetics*, not as a philosophical exercise in definition, but as
instruction in one way to read tragic
poetry, and it takes on a new life. Many
of the other dicta of the aestheticians
can also be examined in this light.

W. E. Kennick, in *Collected Papers in Aesthetics*, ed. C. Barrett (Oxford 1965) 10.

549

Sometimes an interpretation merely
'deepens' ... understanding, but
sometimes it may genuinely 'alter' ...
understanding.... When a commentary
deepens our understanding of a text, we
do not experience any sense of conflict
with our previous ideas. The new
commentary does indeed lay out
implications we had not thought of
explicitly, but it does not alter our
controlling conception of the text's
meaning.... On the other hand, when
we read a commentary that alters our
understanding, we are convinced by an
argument (covert or open) that shows

our original construction to be wrong in some respect.

E. D. Hirsch, *Validity in Interpretation* (New Haven and London 1967) 130.

550

Where they cannot contest the truth of the common interpretation, they get themselves room for dissertation by imaginary amphibologies [Empsonian ambiguities], which they will have to be designed by the author. This disposition of finding out different significations in one thing, may be the effect of either too much, or too little wit : for men of a right understanding generally see at once all that an author can reasonably mean, but others are apt to fancy two meanings for a want of knowing one. Not to add, that there is a vast deal of difference between the learning of a critic, and the puzzling of a grammarian.

Alexander Pope, Preliminary note to *The Iliad of Homer* (1715) i; ed. M. Mack i (1967) 82.

551

... a feeling we have all had : that the study of mediocre works of art remains a random and peripheral form of critical experience, whereas the profound masterpiece draws us to a point at which we seem to see an enormous number of converging patterns of significance.

Northrop Frye, *Anatomy of Criticism* (Princeton, N.J. 1957) 17.

552

In the symbol or work of depth there are as many meanings as critics can find levels or vocabularies with which to explore; name it, in other words, and you can have it.

S. E. Hyman, *The Armed Vision* (New York 1955) 401.

553

Listen to some of the ways in which the ideal and fully rounded critic would proceed in examining a poem. He would explain 'what the poem is about'; in other words, he would paraphrase it, perhaps in several ways successively in order to bring out all the layers of simultaneous meaning. He would relate the poem to earlier sources and analogues, assign it to a relevant tradition, and compare it in detail with other works, both older and contemporary, inside and outside the tradition.... He would interpret the poem psychoanalytically as motivated by deep wishes and fears.... He would examine its structure in terms of image clusters organised by acts of unconscious association.... He would read the poem as a social document shaped by pressures exerted by the poet's social class.... He would discuss social and political attitudes recommended by the poem, whether explicitly or by implication.

Wayne Shumaker, *Elements of Critical Theory* (Berkeley & Los Angeles, Calif. 1964) 16f.

554

Innumerable Ph.D. candidates yet unborn have their thesis subjects waiting for them—an Old Norse word count of *Finnegans Wake*, II, iii; the identity of Magrath; the prosodic system of *Ulysses*; Joyce as Marxian allegorist; the misuse of stretto in the 'Sirens' episode; HCE and the schizophrenic syndrome—Joyce might as well, in his last great dense book, have left us twenty pages of possible titles (perhaps he did; I must look again). Twin heavens for the scholars, *Ulysses* and *Finnegans Wake* are, because of the amount of research that already fences them round, being more and more regarded as mystical codices and less and less as masterly novels intended to entertain.

Anthony Burgess, *Here Comes Everybody* (1965) 11.

555

One can prove that *Ulysses* does not take place in Liverpool, but it is doubtful whether one could prove that it was not a solar myth. One of the things that make paranoia possible is that interpretations can seldom be disproved, even if they are such as no person in his sane sense would accept.

F. E. Sparshott, *The Concept of Criticism* (Oxford 1967) 58.

556

The distinction between what we can intersubjectively agree upon as a given poem and alternative interpretations of it cannot be absolute, since there is mutual modification between organizing view-point and determination of the constituents of a poem. Thus, whether a given phrase is ironic, whether all the various meanings of an ambiguous word are relevant to a poem, will depend on how we view the whole; but our view of the whole is not created out of nothing. Our view of the whole must be based on our accurate apprehension of certain written or spoken words and their meanings—otherwise our interpretation will not be of the entire poem in question.

Isabel C. Hungerland, 'The Interpretation of Poetry' *Aesthetic Inquiry* ed. Monroe C. Beardsley (Belmont, Calif. 1967) 120f.

557

A metaphor is a miniature poem, and the explication of a metaphor is a model of all explication. The problem of construing the metaphor is that of deciding which of the modifier's connotations can *fit* the subject, and the metaphor means *all* the connotations that can fit—except those that are further eliminated by, because they do not fit, the larger context.... We have employed two principles ... the Principle of Congruence ... in assembling, or feeling out, the admissible connotations of words in a poem, we are guided by logical and physical possibilities. But second, there is the Principle of Plenitude. All the connotations that can be found to fit are to be attributed to the poem: it means all it *can* mean, so to speak....

Where a poem is as a whole ambiguous,

in the strict sense, it has no single correct explication, though it has a limited number of equally correct ones....

If the value of a poem depends in part on its coherence and complexity, then in the long run adopting the two principles will maximize poetic value.

Monroe C. Beardsley, *Aesthetics* (New York 1958) 145ff.

558

The interpretation and evaluation of a poem are rarely separable steps in criticism. We do not *first* interpret it and then evaluate it, taking each step with finality. Rather, we test a tentative interpretation by considering the tentative evaluation of the poem to which it leads, progressively altering each in the light of the other.

C. L. Stevenson, 'On the reasons that can be given for the interpretation of a poem', *Philosophy Looks at the Arts*, ed. J. Margolis (New York 1962) 123f.

559

Most obvious are the stringencies of subject matter or, as we may call them, *standards of correspondence*. T. S. Eliot's reference to Agamemnon in the poem *(Sweeney Among the Nightingales)* ... provides warrant for certain interpretations on the basis of knowledge about the myth in question.... Another set of stringencies have reference to the genesis of the art work, and so may be called genetic standards or *standards of intent*. Here knowledge about the artist— whether directly in the form of biographical material or indirectly in terms of his society—serves as a test of adequacy of interpretation.... A third set of stringencies has reference to the interrelations of the elements of the interpretations. We may refer to these as *standards of coherence* : an interpretation of a particular work is tested by the coherence with the rest of the work it gives to this part.

Abraham Kaplan and Ernst Kris 'Aesthetic Ambiguity', *Philosophy and Phenomenological Research* viii (1948) 431f.

560

Then, as the earth's inward narrow crooked lanes
Do purge sea water's fretful salt away,
I thought, if I could draw my pains,
Through rhyme's vexation, I should them allay,
Grief brought to numbers cannot be so fierce,
For, he tames it, that fetters it in verse.

John Donne, 'The Triple Fool'; *The Elegies and the Songs
and Sonnets*, ed. H. Gardner (Oxford 1965) 52.

561

[According to Freud, art] has a therapeutic effect in releasing mental tension; it serves the cultural purpose of acting as a 'substitute gratification' to reconcile men to the sacrifices they have made for culture's sake; it promotes the social sharing of highly valued emotional experiences; and it recalls men to their cultural ideals. This is not everything that some of us would find that art does, yet even this is a good deal for a 'narcotic' to do.

Lionel Trilling, *The Liberal Imagination* (1951) 46.

562

A particularly rich and complex set of fantasies stems from the child's thoughts about what adults do when they are alone, particularly what they do with the organ which has become so important to him, and by his own curiosity about where he came from. He has what the psychoanalysts call 'primal scene fantasies', which form the basis for a later interest in watching drama and other performances.

N. H. Holland, *The Dynamics of Literary Response* (New York 1968) 45.

563

One of Freud's ideas, perhaps the central one, is that the artist refuses to remain in that hallucinated condition to which the neurotic regresses, where the wish and the fulfilment of the wish are one. For the artist, unlike the neurotic, the fantasy is a starting point, not the culmination, of his activity. The energies which have initially driven him away from reality, he manages to harness to the process of making, out of the material of his wishes, an object that can then become a source of shared pleasure and consolation. For it is distinctive of the work of art, in contrast, that is, to the daydream, that it is free of the excessively personal or the utterly alien elements that at once disfigure and impoverish the life of fantasy.

R. Wollheim, *Art and its Objects* (1968) 100f.

564

The truth is that life is a mingling of the individual elements and the formal stock-in-trade; a mingling in which the individual, as it were, only lifts his head above the formal and impersonal elements. Much that is extra-personal, much unconscious identification, much that is conventional and schematic, is none the less decisive for the experience not only of the artist but of the human being in general.

Thomas Mann, 'Freud and the Future', *Essays*, tr. H. T. Lowe-Porter (New York 1957) 316.

565

Fantasies ... occupy a special prior and primitive place in our mental life, and, therefore, a psychoanalytic reading of a literary work in terms of fantasy has also a special status. It is not simply a reading parallel to other readings from ideologies, Marxist, Swedenborgian, Christian humanist, or whatever; it is the material from which other such readings are made.

N. H. Holland, *The Dynamics of Literary Response* (New York 1968) 31.

566

The call of duty to kill his stepfather cannot be obeyed because it unites itself with the unconscious call of his nature to kill his mother's husband, whether this is the first or the second; the absolute 'repression' of the former impulse involves the inner prohibition of the latter also.

Ernest Jones, *Hamlet and Oedipus* (New York 1949) 90.

567

The well-known stubbornness, conscientiousness, and idealism of the compulsive neurotic come through in fictional worlds as the undeviating, wholly committed, absolutist ethics of characters like the creative thinkers in Hawthorne, the Christians of Bunyan, the Knights and Ladies of Spenser, the eternally fixed immortal souls of *The Divine Comedy*. The perfect instance of a compulsive character working in the pursuit of high cultural aims, and therefore transcending the bounds of neurosis, while still retaining the formative character type implied by the neurosis, would be Aeneas. Virgil's hero does not deviate from the destined path, and it is only natural that during the middle ages the *Aeneid* be given an allegorical reading. Aeneas is the original 'Displaced person', as Eliot has said, implying his alienation from a home toward which he always gravitates, and for which he is compelled to create a substitute.

Angus Fletcher, *Allegory: The Theory of a Symbolic Mode* (Ithaca, N.Y. 196) 288.

An hypothesis was proposed for investigation, formulated in terms suggested by Dr Jung, that archetypal patterns, or images, are present within the experience communicated through poetry, and may be discovered there through reflective analysis. These patterns were likened ... to the culture patterns studied by anthropologists. As corresponding to certain ancient and recurring themes of poetry—such as that of an usurping monarch overthrown by the heir of the king he has displaced,— the patterns, viewed psychologically, may be described as organizations of emotional tendencies, determined partly through the distinctive experience of the race or community within whose history the theme has arisen.... The patterns we have called the Rebirth and Paradise-Hades archetypes, while finding expression in myths and legends of particular communities, could also be felt as characterizing the flow, or texture, of universal experience. Similarly, the images studied of man, woman, god, devil, in any particular instance of their occurrence in poetry can be considered either as related to the sensibility of a certain poet, and a certain age and country, or as a mode of expressing something potentially realizable in human experience in any time or place.

Maud Bodkin, *Archetypal Patterns in Poetry* (Oxford 1963) 314f.

569

The obvious limitation of traditional Freudian literary analysis is that only one study can be written, since every additional one would turn out to say the same thing. Ernest Jones could do a beautiful job finding the underlying Oedipus complex in *Hamlet*, but had he gone on to analyse *Lear* or *A Midsummer Night's Dream* or the *Sonnets* he would have found to his surprise that they reflected Shakespeare's Oedipus complex too, and, in fact, granting his theories, he would have made the same discovery about any other work of art....

Here Maud Bodkin's *Archetypal Patterns in Poetry* is the hope. By focussing, not on the neurosis of the artist, not on the complexes concealed beneath the work, not on the art as a disguised fulfilment of repressed wishes, but on how a work of art is emotionally satisfying, what relationship its formal structure bears to the basic patterns and symbols of our psyches, she has furnished psychological criticism with endless vistas.

S. E. Hyman, *The Armed Vision* (New York 1955) 159f.

570

Two consequences should follow from the truth of the Freudian theory : types of art should vary significantly from culture to culture according to the predominating stresses, and hence types of neurosis, imposed by the culture; and the most neurotic cultures should produce the most art and value it most highly, while cultures relatively free from neurosis should be more nearly devoid of art. If there is any evidence to support either of these propositions, it has escaped my notice. The vulnerability of the Freudian theory of dreams is yet more of a threat than this apparent failure of verification: if different theories of the meaning of dream symbolism can be applied with equal success, no one system of interpretation can be made basic to a theory of art. Yet one cannot dismiss the theory as a curiosity ... for ... even those who explicitly reject piecemeal all that Freud and his followers have said about art can scarcely help thinking about art, as about all human life, in terms derived from his work.

F. E. Sparshott, *The Structure of Aesthetics* (1963) 249.

571

Is there a legitimate distinction between a well written case-report and a thoroughgoing psychological novel?

Leo A. Spiegel, 'The New Jargon: Psychology in Literature', *Sewanee Review* xl (1932) 476.

572

Shakespeare's romantic tragedy, like all other great popular tragedy, presents human nature, not a doctrine of human nature; heroes, not weaklings, or psychopathic cases; and, above all, men as we know them, not curiosities of the contemporary or even the Elizabethan psychology or physiology. In himself Hamlet is not more a prey to melancholy than he is (as thought by other recent scholars) to the deadly sin of sloth....

Audiences at a tragedy ... were not ... expecting to sit in at a clinic.

Elmer Stoll, *Hamlet the Man* (1935) 10.

573

It is tempting to draw parallels between our experience of life and of fictional characters. Thus it is ridiculous to isolate characters from a novel and discuss them as totally autonomous entities; the novel itself is nothing but a complicated structure of artificially formed contexts parallel to those within which we experience real people. But can we go further than this? Can we say that the author, however he may disguise himself, is to his characters what we are to other people—the one context that must exist if we are to experience anything at all? The answer here must be no; in this case the analogy is false. For the author is not to his characters as we are to other people; his relationship to them is not human but god-like. However invisible he may make himself, whatever narrative techniques he may use to conceal his exit from fiction, the novelist is and must be both omnipotent and omniscient. The last word is, both literally and metaphorically, his alone.

This being so, the novelist may confer on us his god-like power and privilege; we, too, can see the fictional character in his private self, secret, entirely solitary.

W. J. Harvey, *Character and the Novel* (1965) 31f.

The novel, which presents a whole and rounded character, follows his development over an extended stretch of time, from one phase of life to another, shows him in the act of making choices and then shows the consequences of the choices.... It lasts long enough, piles up enough confirmatory detail, to absorb us completely into its world. At the end we say to ourselves, yes, life is like that. The novel does not present a single moment of insight, it presents a web of circumstance very like that in which we find ourselves actually entangled. We can make moral judgments about its characters and their situations very much as we can make moral judgments about our own lives.

Graham Hough, *The Dream and the Task* (1963) 42.

From the beginnings of romantic poetry the artist has been, as M. Beguin says of Lichtenberg, 'malade de son différence avec son temps'. The great poet of the modern city, Baudelaire, was a self-confessed 'seer'. The *frisson nouveau* upon which Hugo congratulated him proceeded from the study of a fallen humanity in the new context; his mythology is of the perversion, the *ennui*, the metaphysical despair of men and women subjected to what Dickens (in this respect Baudelaire's English equivalent—compare *Le crépuscule du matin* with certain passages in *Little Dorrit*) called 'the shame, desertion, wretchedness and exposure of the great capital....' Yet Baudelaire, so sensitive to the horror of the modern city, remains true to the romantic tradition in abstaining from any attempt to alter the social order, and despises the 'puerile Utopias' of some other romantic poets. And his answer, to the question, what has the movement, whose poets find themselves in this dreadful situation, done for us, is striking: it has 'recalled us to the truth of the image'.... The Image, for all its concretion, precision, and oneness, is desperately difficult to communicate, and has for that reason alone as much to do with the alienation of the seer as the necessity of his existing in the midst of a hostile society.

Frank Kermode, *Romantic Image* (1961) 4f.

That the artist is not as a rule consciously concerned with communication, but with getting the work, the poem or play or statue or painting or whatever it is, 'right', apparently regardless of its communicative efficacy, is easily explained.... The dissipation of attention which would be involved if he considered the communicative side as a separate issue would be fatal in most serious work.

I. A. Richards, *Principles of Literary Criticism* (1924); (1967) 18.

To discover the fundamental problem common to all mankind, I must ask myself what my fundamental problem is, what my most ineradicable fear is. I am

certain then to find the problems and
fears of literally everyone. That is the
true road into my own darkness, which
I try to bring to the light of day.... A
work of art is the expression of an
incommunicable reality that one tries to
communicate—and which sometimes can
be communicated. That is its paradox
and its truth.

Eugene Ionesco, 'The Playwright's Role' (1958);
Notes and Counter-notes (1964) 95f.

578

I, long before the blissful hour arrives,
Would chant, in lonely peace, the spousal verse
Of this great consummation:—and, by words
Which speak of nothing more than what we are,
Would I arouse the sensual from their sleep
Of death, and win the vacant and the vain
To noble raptures; while my voice proclaims
How exquisitely the individual mind
(And the progressive powers perhaps no less
Of the whole species) to the external world
Is fitted;—and how exquisitely, too—
Theme this but little heard of among men—
The external world is fitted to the mind;
And the creation (by no lower name
Can it be called) which they with blended might
Accomplish:—this is our high argument.

William Wordsworth, Preface to The Excursion (1814)
ll. 56-71.

579

The cultivation of those sciences which
have enlarged the limits of the empire of
man over the external world, has, for
want of the poetical faculty, propor-
tionately circumscribed those of the
internal world; and man, having enslaved
the elements, remains himself a slave....
The cultivation of poetry is never more
to be desired than at periods when,
from an excess of the selfish and
calculating principle, the accumulation
of the materials of external life exceed
the quantity of the power of
assimilating them to the internal laws
of human nature.

P. B. Shelley, A Defence of Poetry (1821); Works
ed. R. Ingpen and W. E. Peck vii (1930) 134f.

580

A socialist biased novel fully achieves
its purpose, in my view, if by

conscientiously describing the real mutual relations, breaking down conventional illusions about them, it shatters the optimism of the bourgeois world, instils doubt as to the eternal character of the existing order, although the author does not offer any definite solution or does not even line up openly on any particular side.

Friedrich Engels, Letter to Minna Kautsky, 26 November 1885.

581

This policy of letting a hundred flowers blossom and a hundred schools of thought contend is designed to promote the flourishing of the arts and the progress of science; it is designed to enable a socialist culture to thrive in our land. Different forms and styles in art can develop freely.... We think that it is harmful to the growth of art and science if administrative measures are used to impose one particular style of art or school of thought and to ban another. Questions of right and wrong in the arts and sciences should be settled through free discussion in artistic and scientific circles and in the course of practical work in the arts and sciences. They should not be settled in summary fashion.

Mao Tse-Tung, *On the Correct Handling of Contradictions Among the People* (Peking 1957) 48f.

582

[I] have learned more [from Balzac about French society] than from all the professional historians, economists, and statisticians of the period put together.

Friedrich Engels, Letter to Margaret Harkness, April 1888.

583

Great Expectations is the perfect expression of a phase of English society: it is a statement, to be taken as it stands, of what money can do, good and bad; of how it can change and make distinctions of class; how it can pervert virtue, sweeten manners, open up new fields of enjoyment and suspicion. The mood of the book ... the unquestioned assumption that Pip can be transformed by money ... were only possible in a country secure in its eternal economy, the expanding markets abroad.... Pip's acquired 'culture' was an entirely bourgeois thing: it came to little more than accent, table manners and clothes.

Humphry House, *The Dickens World* (Oxford 1942) 159.

584

The most valuable works of art so often have a political implication which can be pounced on and called bourgeois. They carry an implication about the society they were written for; the question is whether the same must not be true of any human society, even if it is much better than theirs. My own difficulty about proletarian literature is that when it comes off I find I am taking it as pastoral literature; I read into it, or find that the author has secretly put into it, these more subtle, more far-reaching, and I think more permanent, ideas.

William Empson, *Some Versions of Pastoral* (1935) 20f.

585

The concept of 'socialist realism', perfectly valid in itself, has frequently been abused and misapplied to academic historical and genre paintings and to novels and plays in fact based on propagandist idealizations. For this reason, as well as for certain others, the term 'socialist art' seems to me to be better. It clearly refers to an attitude—not a style—and emphasizes the socialist outlook, not the realist method. 'Critical realism' and, even more widely, bourgeois literature and art as a whole (that is to say, all great bourgeois literature and art) imply criticism of the surrounding social reality. 'Socialist realism' and, even more widely, socialist art and literature as a whole imply the artist's or writer's fundamental agreement with the aims of the working class and the emerging socialist world.

Ernst Fischer, *The Necessity of Art* (Harmondsworth 1963) 107f.

586

There was a time when literature assumed that the best ideals of politics were naturally in accord with its own essence, when poetry celebrated the qualities of social life which had their paradigmatic existence in poetry itself. Keats's *Poems* of 1817 takes for its epigraph two lines from Spenser which are intended to point up the political overtone of the volume: 'What more felicity can fall to creature/Than to enjoy delight with liberty'.... But the old connection between literature and politics has been dissolved. For the typical modern literary personality, political life is likely to exist only as it makes occasion for the disgust and rage which are essential to the state of modern spirituality, as one particular instance of the irrational violent and obscene fantasy which life in general is, as licensing the counter fantasy of the poet.

Lionel Trilling, *Beyond Culture* (Harmondsworth 1967) 82f.

587

If [Hamlet] could ask the players to hold the mirror up to nature, it was because the Elizabethan theatre was itself a mirror which had been formed at the centre of the culture of its time, and at the centre of the life and awareness of the community. We know now that such a mirror is rarely formed.... Thus the very *idea* of a theatre, as Hamlet assumed it, gets lost; and the art of drama, having no place of its own in contemporary life, is confused with lyric poetry or pure music on one side, or with editorializing and gossip on the other.... The dramatic art of Shakespeare and the dramatic art of Sophocles ... were developed in theatres which focussed, at the centre of the life of the community, the complementary insights of the whole culture.... The theatres of Racine and Wagner are, by comparison, arbitrary inventions, and the images they reflect— images of reason or passion—are artificially limited, and thus in a sense even false.

Francis Fergusson, *The Idea of a Theatre* (Princeton, N.J. 1949) 14ff.

artists. The renewed emphasis on communication is a valuable sign of our recovery of community.

Raymond Williams, *Culture and Society* (Harmondsworth 1963) 244.

588

Nearly all theoretical discussions of art since the Industrial Revolution have been crippled by the assumed opposition between art and the actual organization of society, which is important as the historical phenomenon that has been traced [by Williams] but which can hardly be taken as absolute. Individual psychology has been similarly limited by an assumption of opposition between individual and society which is in fact only a symptom of society's transitional disorganization. Until we have lived through this, we are not likely to achieve more than a limited theory of art, but we can be glad meanwhile that the starting point which has for so long misled us—the artist's necessary abnormality— is being gradually rejected in theory, and almost wholly rejected, in terms of practical feeling, among a majority of

589

After three thousand years of explosion, by means of fragmentary and mechanical technologies, the Western world is imploding. During the mechanical ages we had extended our bodies in space. Today, after more than a century of electric technology, we have extended our central nervous system itself in a global embrace, abolishing both space and time as far as our planet is concerned. Rapidly, we approach the final phase of the extensions of man—the technological simulation of consciousness, when the creative process of knowing will be collectively and corporately extended to the whole of human society, much as we have already extended our senses and our nerves by the various media.

Marshall McLuhan, *Understanding Media* (1967) 11.

Moral Influence

590

I believe, to be sure, that ethical interest is the only poetic interest, for the reason that all poetry deals with one kind or another of human experience and is valuable in proportion to the justice with which it evaluates that experience.

Yvor Winters, *In Defence of Reason* (1960) 505.

591

The moral life of man forms part of the subject matter of the artist, but the morality of art consists in the perfect use of an imperfect medium. No artist desires to prove anything. Even things that are true can be proved.

No artist has ethical sympathies. An ethical sympathy in an artist is an unpardonable mannerism of style.

Oscar Wilde, Preface to *The Picture of Dorian Gray* (1891); *Works* (1966) 17.

592

You are right in demanding that an artist should take a conscious attitude to his work, but you confuse the two conceptions: *the solution of a question and the correct setting of a question*. The latter alone is obligatory for the artist. In *Anna Karenina* and in *Onegin* not a single problem is solved, but they satisfy completely because all the problems are set correctly. It is for the judge to put the questions correctly; and the young men must decide, each according to his taste.

Anton Chekhov, Letter to A. S. Suvorin, 27 October 1888: *Selected Letters* tr. S. Lederer, ed. L. Hellman (1955) 57.

593

Besides, men who read from religious or moral inclinations, even when the subject is of a kind of which they approve, are beset with misconceptions and mistakes peculiar to themselves. Attaching so much importance to the truths which interest them, they are prone to overrate the authors by whom these truths are expressed and enforced. They come prepared to impart so much passion to the poet's language, that they remain unconscious, how little, in fact, they receive from it.

William Wordsworth, Essay Supplementary to the Preface, *Lyrical Ballads* (1815); *Works* edn. E. de Selincourt ii (Oxford 1952) 411f.

594

The didactic novel is so generally devoid of vraisemblance as to teach nothing but the impossibility of tampering with natural truth to advance dogmatic opinions. Those, on the other hand, which impress the reader with the inevitableness of character and environment in working out destiny, whether that destiny be just or unjust, amiable or cruel, must have a sound effect, if not what is called a good effect, upon a healthy mind.

Thomas Hardy, 'The Profitable Reading of Fiction' (1888); *Thomas Hardy's Personal Writings* ed. H. Orel (1967) 118.

595

He seems to write without any moral purpose.... He makes no just distribution of good or evil, nor is always careful to shew in the virtuous a disapprobation of the wicked.... It is always a writer's duty to make the world better, and justice is a virtue independent on time or place.

Samuel Johnson, *Preface to Shakespeare* (1765); *Works*, Yale edn. vii (New Haven and London 1968) 71.

596

Since wickedness often prospers in real life, the poet is certainly at liberty to give it prosperity on the stage. For if poetry is an imitation of reality, how are its laws broken by imitating the world in its true form? The stage may sometimes gratify our wishes, but if it be truly the mirror of life, it ought to show us sometimes what we are to expect.

Samuel Johnson, Life of Addison, *Lives of the Poets* (1781); ed. G. B. Hill iii (Oxford 1905) 135.

597

But man or woman who publishes writings inevitably assumes the office of teacher or influencer of the public mind.... He can no more escape influencing the moral taste and with it the action of the intelligence, than a setter of fashion in furniture and dress can fill the shops with his designs and leave the garniture of houses and persons unaffected by his industry.

George Eliot, 'Leaves From a Notebook: Authorship' (1897): *Works*, Copyright edn. (1908-11) 291.

598

The great design of arts is to restore the decays that happened to human nature by the fall, by restoring order.... If the end of poetry be to instruct and reform the world, that is, to bring mankind from irregularity, extravagance, and confusion, to rule and order, how this should be done by a thing that is in itself irregular and extravagant, is difficult to be conceived.

John Dennis, *The Grounds of Criticism in Poetry* (1704) ch. ii; *Critical Works* ed. E. N. Hooker i (Baltimore, Md. 1939) 335.

599

And in the latter end of the Fourth Canto she talks like an
errant suburbian :

> Oh, hadst thou, cruel, been content to seize
> Hairs less in sight, or any hairs but these.

Thus, sir, has this author given his fine lady beauty
and good breeding, modesty and virtue in words, but has in
reality and in fact made her an artificial daubing jilt,
a tomrig and a lady of the lake

John Dennis, 'Remarks on Mr Pope's *Rape of the Lock*', *Several
letters to a friend* (1728); *ibid*. ii 335.

600

> Immodest words admit of no defence,
> For want of decency is want of sense.

Wentworth Dillon, Earl of Roscommon, 'An
Essay on Translated Verse' (1684) 113f.

601

Let those read who will and let those who
will abstain from reading. No man wishes
to force men's food down the throats of
babes and sucklings. The verses analysed
[Swinburne's own *Poems and Ballads*]
were written with no moral or immoral
intent, but the upshot seems to me to be
moral rather than immoral, if it needs to
be one or the other. Purity and prudery
cannot keep house together. And if
literature is not to deal with the full life
of man, and the whole nature of things,
let it be cast aside with the rods and
rattles of childhood.

A. C. Swinburne, 'Notes on Poems and Reviews'
(1866); *Complete Works* ed. Sir E. Gosse and T.
J. Wise xvi (1926) 363f.

602

Pornography is of course, in a formal
sense, literature. Furthermore, it is
impossible to object theoretically to its
purposes. There is, on the face of it,
nothing illegitimate about a work whose
purpose or intention is to arouse its
readers sexually. If it is permissible for
works of literature to move us to tears,
to arouse our passions against injustice,
to make us cringe with horror, and to
purge us through pity and terror, then
it is equally permissible—it lies within
the orbit of literature's functions—for
works of literature to arouse us sexually.
Two major works of literature may be
adduced which undertake this project....
Madame Bovary and the final section of

Ulysses. I will go one step further and assert that anyone who is not sexually moved or aroused by Emma Bovary or Molly Bloom is not responding properly to literature, is not reading with the fullness and openness and attentiveness that literature demands.

Literature possesses, however, a multitude of intentions, but pornography possesses only one.

Stephen Marcus, *The Other Victorians* (1966) 277f.

603

A man, to be greatly good, must imagine intensely and comprehensively; he must put himself in the place of another and of many others; the pains and pleasures of his species must become his own. The great instrument of moral good is the imagination; and poetry administers to the effect by acting on the cause.

P. B. Shelley, A *Defence of Poetry* (1821); *Works* ed. R. Ingpen and W. E. Peck vii (1930) 118.

604

The experience of tragic drama both gives in the figure of the hero an objective form to the self of imaginative aspiration, or to the power-craving, and also, through the hero's death, satisfies the counter-movement of feeling toward the surrender of personal claims and the merging of the ego within a greater power—the 'community consciousness'.

Maud Bodkin, *Archetypal Patterns in Poetry* (Oxford 1963) 23.

605

The character, whose fortune we have been called in to see, or the personality of the writer, must keep our sympathy, and whether it be farce or tragedy, we must laugh and weep with him and call down blessings on his head. The character who delights us may commit murder like Macbeth, or fly the battle for his sweetheart as did Antony, or betray his country like Coriolanus, and yet we will rejoice in every happiness that counts to him and sorrow at his death as if it were our own. It is no use telling us that the murderer and the betrayer do not deserve our sympathy.... We understand the verdict and not the law; and yet there is some law, some code, some judgment. If the poet's hand had slipped, if Antony had railed at Cleopatra in the tower, if Coriolanus had abated that high pride of his in the presence of death, we might have gone away muttering the Ten Commandments.

W. B. Yeats, *Plays and Controversies* (1923) 103f.

606

It is dangerous to generalize too precisely about the spirit of tragedy; but we can say that there the problem of evil and suffering is set before us; often it is not answered, but always there is something that makes it endurable.

F. L. Lucas, *Tragedy* (1927) 56f.

607

We have then, I suggest, in the tragic experience the perception of an order, imposed by the dramatist upon an experience which is bounded in time and space as an action, and as action involves the ambivalent attitudes of recognition, participation in, and conscious rejection of major moral values, but which is unlimited in time and space by reason of its ritual values, its ability to imply the existence of *orders* of various kinds, its power, through its imagery in general and through the archetypes in particular, to convert subliminal forces into active agents for the integration of personality.

T. R. Henn, *The Harvest of Tragedy* (1966) 91.

608

More and more mankind will discover that we have to turn to poetry to interpret life for us, to console us, to sustain us. Without poetry, our science will appear incomplete; and most of what now passes with us for religion and philosophy will be replaced by poetry.

Matthew Arnold, 'The Study of Poetry' (1880); *Essays in Criticism: Second Series* ed. S. R. Littlewood (1938) 2.

609

Though no religion can escape the binding weeds of dogma, there is one that throws them off more easily and more light-heartedly than any other. That religion is art; for art is a religion. It is an expression of a means to states of mind as holy as any that men are capable of experiencing; and it is towards art that modern minds turn, not only for the most perfect expression of transcendent emotion, but for an inspiration by which to live.

Clive Bell, *Art* (1914) 227.

610

Aesthetic and religious raptures seem to be, subjectively, very similar. They are not the same, because they plainly relate to different objects: aesthetic rapture distracts from religious duties, religious rapture aids them. But some have inferred from the similarity that God is a hypostatized correlate for an aesthetic rapture, or that art affords an intimation of divinity. Both kinds of rapture lend themselves to explanation as sublimations of sexual ecstacy: it is notorious that mystical writers often use the metaphor of sexual passion, and Plato in his *Symposium* joins the sexual and the aesthetic in an erotic continuum.

The tangled problems of aesthetics, no doubt, are hardly likely to be cleared up by interlocking them with the equally tangled problems of the philosophy and psychology of religion. But, despite the inconvenience, it may be unrealistic to keep them separate.

F. E. Sparshott, *The Structure of Aesthetics* (1963) 296.

611

Art in the service of religion, all sanctimonious talk to the contrary notwithstanding, is no more likely to be successful as art than art in the service of capitalism or communism.

D. W. Prall, *Aesthetic Analysis* (New York 1936) 158.

Index

Index